Jon Smith is the United Kingdom's pre-eminent super-agent, whose reach extends far beyond football and the Premier League he helped to create. He has worked with an eclectic range of public figures from Diego Maradona to Mikhail Gorbachev, and was the promoter of some of the biggest US sports in the UK. He is now a leading multi-platform commentator.

James Olley is a journalist, biographer and opinion-former with a decade's experience reporting on the biggest events in football for the *London Evening Standard*. He is a regular contributor for the BBC, Sky Sports and talkSPORT and currently holds the prestigious Sports Journalists' Association title of 'Regional Journalist of the Year'.

D0112753

THE DEAL

JON SMITH

WITH JAMES OLLEY

CONSTABLE • LONDON

CONSTABLE

First published in Great Britain in 2016 by Constable
This paperback edition published in 2017

1 3 5 7 9 10 8 6 4 2

Copyright © Jon Smith, 2016, 2017

The moral right of the author has been asserted.

A CIP catalogue record for this book
is available from the British Library.

ISBN: 978-1-47212-303-9

Typeset in Bembo by SX Composing DTP, Rayleigh, Essex
Printed and bound in Great Britain by Clays Ltd, St Ives plc

Papers used by Constable are from well-managed forests
and other responsible sources.

Constable
An imprint of
Little, Brown Book Group
Carmelite House
50 Victoria Embankment
London EC4Y 0DZ

An Hachette UK Company
www.hachette.co.uk

www.littlebrown.co.uk

To Janine, Ross, Scott and Lee:
without you the journey would have had no purpose
x

Contents

Prologue

Ukraine, 2014

Sleeping is difficult in the safe house. The tired and dilapidated décor is uncomfortably juxtaposed with a tension heightened by the intermittent sound of nearby gunfire in Odessa's city centre.

The best I can do is doze. Thoughts are racing through my head about whether the deal would actually be completed, whether I would stay alive. Not necessarily in that order.

Daylight begins to break through the tattered curtains. Suddenly, a monstrously imposing man bursts into my room, bristling with aggression.

'He's dead because of you!' he cries. 'Give me your fucking phone, get dressed and get outside. Now!'

I have been accused of many things during my career, but never before of colluding to murder the associate of a potential business partner. But this was where my work had taken me – the middle of a battlefield in Odessa, a port city unable to escape the violence and bloodshed endemic throughout Ukraine amid escalating hostility with Russia.

Except, on a battlefield, you know where the enemy is. This was a city alien to me, with anyone we encountered a potential friend or foe. A person we did business with could be a mediator or a murderer. I had come as the former but been labelled the latter.

This is a covert war fought with a randomness of target and location that puts everybody permanently on edge. Eyes dart in all directions when you enter a room, analysing the threat level before them. Suspicion abounds.

It was a terrifying backdrop against which to do business. Trust felt like an expired, almost naïve concept. Two days earlier, we had barely been in the country an hour before two people were killed within earshot. Part of me felt we should never have got involved or perhaps should have undertaken more research on the prospective clients beforehand, but reliable information is often scarce in a region like this.

An ownership group in Odessa had approached Italian agent Roberto De Fanti – who had until January of that year been Director of Football at Sunderland – to express an interest in buying Sheffield Wednesday. Roberto had become a respected acquaintance of ours through previous dealings and we had strong links to Wednesday's then owner Milan Mandaric through my friend and associate Peter Storrie. Milan and Peter worked together at Portsmouth. The financial implosion of that club and a separate court case, in which both stood trial on two counts of tax evasion, meant their futures in the game were uncertain until their acquittals in 2012.

I had taken Peter on as a consultant because I respected his experience, contacts and numerical ability. He remained close with Milan, who had bought Wednesday in 2010 but was keen to sell four years later because he felt the club had reached a natural point in its evolution where a new, younger owner would be better suited.

My personal interest in making this deal happen deepened due to a longstanding friendship with Lord Sebastian Coe, who grew up in Sheffield and has an affinity with Wednesday despite his widely known allegiance to Chelsea. He often joked to me that if I ever helped sell the club, he would perhaps consider becoming chairman. Seb even offered to speak to José Mourinho to see if he might be interested. At the time, that was not as fanciful as it may sound because José was without a club and open to suggestion.

Roberto told me this investment group had owned teams in Ukraine but were keen to buy an English club. The concern was that they actually wanted to get some of their cash – wherever it had come from – out of Ukraine and thought a football club in the UK would be a good, safe home for it. As they had experience in owning clubs, they wanted to find a team with a potential real-estate play and they saw Sheffield Wednesday as having that capacity.

Calls were going backwards and forwards and I had to decide whether it was worth the risk to travel. They would not come to the United Kingdom; we had to go to them.

Thirty years of completing transactions all over the world has enabled me to build up a network of protection I can call on if required, but I didn't really know anyone in Ukraine. The country was burning at the time and, if trouble broke out within the deal or around us, I had no idea where the exits were; any agent will tell you to determine your exit strategy before entering any negotiation.

I had spoken to Richard Creitzman, who was working on Roman Abramovich's team when they bought Chelsea. Richard had been one of the passengers on the notorious helicopter flight over London in 2003, in which – so the story goes – the Abramovich team was about to complete the purchase of Chelsea, when they flew past Fulham's Craven Cottage. The ground was being redeveloped at the time with Fulham playing at Loftus Road. The grass had grown out to a foot high in places and, in tandem with the beginnings of stadium renovation work, Fulham's charming home looked unusually ramshackle.

Richard pointed towards the shabby sight before them. 'That's Chelsea down there,' he said.

Roman's eyes widened in disbelief.

'Only joking – that's really Fulham,' Richard said.

'Don't joke,' Roman said in that steely manner of his.

Richard was established as one of the working directors at Chelsea and so he and I became quite friendly over the years. He ultimately left Roman and went back to Moscow but remained my only link to the region. I called him to ask what would happen if it all went horribly wrong out there.

He said, 'It's OK. Odessa is a major port with a unique population and "style" all of its own. It is famous across the former Soviet Union as a city where the laws are liberally interpreted and a lot of criminal activity allegedly occurs. A number of local and Russian businessmen work and operate there so, if you go, be careful. I'd be happy to organise some security if required.'

It was a risk but one I felt was worth taking. A few months earlier, I had negotiated the sale of Leyton Orient from Barry Hearn to Francesco Becchetti. Selling football clubs seemed like a good line of work so the chance to pull together a deal for Wednesday felt too good to pass up.

Another incident hinted at the Odessa group's credibility. A consultant of mine had spoken to them three weeks before about facilitating a deal to take a well-known player from a Premier League club into a prominent Ukrainian club. The fee was to be in the region of six million euros with a net wage of four million euros a year. Three million would be paid up front and a further one million six months later. The structure of those payments was strange but, during the course of negotiations, my consultant spoke of their range of connections which included several leading figures in the world of football. The deal eventually fell through because the Odessa group dragged their heels and the player lost interest but, on balance, there had been enough to suggest that a meeting over Sheffield Wednesday was worthwhile.

In the weeks before we arrived, violence had flared up badly in Ukraine. Malaysia Airlines flight MH17 from Amsterdam had been shot down in rebel-held territory close to the border with Russia. All 298 people on board had died, with Russia and Ukraine each blaming the other. Fighting continued with Russian military incursions into Ukraine growing ever greater.

Odessa was not incident-free but had been relatively calm by comparison, so we made the judgement call to proceed. Peter, Roberto and I embarked upon the 1,424-mile trip east from London on the morning of Monday 25 August.

It is at this point in the story that I need to make a confession. The names of our contacts in Odessa have been changed for my ongoing safety and that of my associates. They are not individuals I am comfortable naming publicly, even now.

The guy who met us at the airport – let's call him Fabian – was like a family man on acid. He claimed to have strong legal links to one of the bigger clubs in Spain, and spoke in a high-paced stream of consciousness with no filter. Most of it was utter nonsense but the relentless rambling still acted as an unnerving soundtrack to our journey.

We were whisked in the back of a people-mover with Fabian, a driver and a bodyguard to the stadium and it was nothing short of majestic. The dressing rooms were akin to the opulence of a five-star hotel. No expense had been spared. After a guided tour, we were taken to our hotel. The people-mover stopped two hundred yards away with traffic gridlocked in front of us. There was a commotion up ahead. People began scattering.

Fabian and the bodyguard got out, walked down the road and tried to find out what was happening. I got out to stretch my legs but, as I did so, Fabian came running back towards the car shouting that two people had been shot dead in the lobby of our hotel. The bodyguard reached across and grabbed me with such force that I felt momentarily winded. He propelled me back into the car. People were running past the windows with terrified looks on their faces. Cars were mounting the pavement to escape the mayhem.

'We have to go – you can't stay here,' said the bodyguard. 'We are going to take you to a safe house.'

My mind was a blur. Did that really just happen? Fortunately, we had pulled up by an alleyway leading away from the tumult ahead. The driver quickly manoeuvred the car down this tight, single-lane road with barely an inch to spare on either side of the vehicle. I remember thinking he seemed to be a rather adept getaway driver, which was useful now, but the origin of his talent didn't bear thinking about.

The car hurtled from one road to the next along the backstreets of Odessa. Fabian was jabbering away a mile a minute about how 'this is just what happens here' and 'everything is fine – you have the IRA, don't you? That's the same . . . ' Not quite.

The world felt like it was closing in on us. My clothes stuck to me as the car's air conditioning failed, enhancing the claustrophobia. Our bodyguard turned his head to face us in the back. 'Phones. Now!' he growled.

By now we start to think we're being kidnapped. We feel confused and scared.

'People track us,' he continued. 'We don't want people to know where we are because of your phones.'

In all the years I have completed deals everywhere from Swaziland to several countries that were once behind the Iron Curtain, nothing like this had ever happened to me. Fabian told us this was protocol and my consultant, who had spoken to them about us previously, told us he had had to surrender his mobile, too, so there was some comfort in that consistency, but still it felt like naïvely acquiescing to anonymity.

We eventually arrived at what they described as a safe house, at the end of a cul-de-sac. At the top of the short lane, they parked the people-mover across the road with two men either side, standing guard. It was an open prison; we were trapped. I didn't know if that was a good or bad thing.

The house was barren. My bed had springs sticking out of it. There was no food, not even a glass of water. I did have a balcony but I wasn't overly keen to go outside.

After a while, temptation got the better of me and I stepped out on to the ledge. I peered down to the end of the road and a guard shot a look straight up at me with eyes that seemed to question the temerity of my decision to breathe the same air. Back inside I went.

Roberto, Peter and I kept ourselves calm by rationalising the situation as best we could. People back in England knew we were here. What could they get for injuring us? Was it a crime syndicate in the Ukraine planning to ask our families for money?

A long hour passed. They told us there would be a delay in meeting the investment group's chief – Dimitri seems an appropriate name to take from Ukraine's past – because eight people had been killed during a nearby march in the city. I closed the curtains, as if that would make us more secure.

Another couple of hours went by and eventually we were bundled back into the people-mover and taken on a circuitous route out of the city to a meeting point where Dimitri was waiting. We were not allowed to take our bags. That journey was tortuous as it was impossible to keep track of our bearings. We had no phones, no belongings, but at least there was no ransom demand. Not yet, anyway.

We arrived at a disused, broken-down factory, a place that had fallen into a derelict state after years of neglect. I could feel my heart racing. Around the back of the factory was a corridor leading to another out-building, behind which was a door. We were shown in and suddenly the surroundings were rather more grandiose. Carpets! I remembered those. There were golden statues, opulent light-fittings . . . it felt like a scene from Alice in Wonderland *compared to what we'd experienced before.*

There were no windows. A man, Dimitri, was sitting on what could have passed for a throne. He was in his thirties, about 5ft 9in tall and fit as a butcher's dog. He was on his mobile, deep in conversation, while next to him sat a very attractive, voluptuous woman in her early thirties, clearly not afraid to display her assets. We were sitting in silence on the other side of a desk barely four feet away.

He finished his call and, at the end of an exasperating pause, he turned his stony face towards me and simply said, 'Hello.'

I thought I might as well take the lead. 'Hi, I'm Jon. This is Peter and Roberto,' I said tentatively, gesturing towards each in turn.

'I know you are Jon,' replied Dimitri, with no warmth at all. 'I also know about the consultant you sent here three weeks ago. He was bad.' Dimitri accused him of lying throughout the deal and bad-mouthing his family. This was the first I had heard of any of it — I didn't believe a word.

The atmosphere in the room was nasty. Normally there is chit-chat at the start of a deal — it is convivial because everybody wants to do business and make some money. It is fluffy, light. This was anything but.

He was sitting directly opposite me and talked about my colleague in the most disparaging terms. I told him I was not aware of those accusations until now, but I had to hold my ground because I needed to elicit some respect from him. I had to defend my position while admitting that what had happened here in Odessa was not under my control. I was quickly realising just how apposite that statement was.

I tried to make light of the situation, maintaining eye contact so as not to appear intimidated, and act in a conciliatory manner, accompanying my words with a smile at regular intervals.

Dimitri shuffled some papers in front of him. I had to double-take at the rearranged pile. There was now a revolver visible on the desk, pointing directly at me. Roberto breathed in sharply, involuntarily yet audible to everyone in the room.

Peter leant into my ear and whispered, 'I'm pleased I didn't sit in that seat.'

I said to Dimitri, 'Is it possible you could point that the other way?'

Dimitri smiled. It was the first time he had done so and it felt like a minor breakthrough.

I continued to explain that my company, First Artist, had a longstanding reputation for being a professional enterprise that pioneered football agency work in the UK and that we had come here to help facilitate their intention to buy a football club. He probably knew all that anyway but I had to establish some semblance of authority. The gun was still lying on the desk, but the conversations we had come all this way to have had, at least, now finally started.

My idea for Sheffield Wednesday was partly born from discussions with Seb Coe, who had agreed with me that the authorities could potentially respond favourably to relocating the club away from Hillsborough. He even indicated that he would speak to local MP Richard Caborn, former Minister for Sport and Labour MP for Sheffield Central, to test the validity of that theory. Given the tragedy that occurred there in 1989, a prospective owner could instigate a move without many of the tribal problems that exist whenever a football club leaves its spiritual home. There is usually a powerful and positive emotional legacy left behind, but I didn't think that that would be the case with Hillsborough because so many people had died there in such awful circumstances.

The city would potentially help offset the cost, too. The Don Valley Stadium was built for the 1991 World Student Games, but thereafter cost the council millions of pounds while falling into a state of disrepair. A potential new owner, then, could take this wonderful brand and move it to a new state-of-the-art venue, while simultaneously turning Hillsborough into a property development to help fund the overall project.

But, importantly, at the core of this transaction must be a tasteful memorial to the 96 football fans who lost their lives in 1989 and, if we managed to convince the council that the whole development would be big enough, then there should be the means to give an apartment to every bereaved family. As long as it was marked with respect, I didn't think supporters would have an insurmountable sadness at leaving Hillsborough, a view shared by Seb under those circumstances.

Dimitri nodded in approval as I laid out the proposal. The relationship was warming now, even to the extent that he decided to move the gun. It disappeared under the table, perhaps still pointing at me for all I knew, but I was willing to interpret that as progress.

Milan was due to arrive at this point and, just as I was about to ask Peter discreetly where he was, right on cue he walked in. Conversations progressed well, opening out into general football chat, which was completely meaningless but it had the welcome effect of defusing the tension.

Soon, it was approaching 11.30 p.m. We hadn't eaten anything since the plane and now Dimitri decided it was dinner time. We all headed back into the city and arrived at a deserted hotel restaurant. We were frisked upon entering – which was disconcerting in itself – but the issue of security afforded us an opportunity to ask for our phones back. I immediately phoned my wife Janine. Normally we would speak a few times a day when I'm abroad, so I was at least able to make contact and allay the worst of her fears.

A lengthy dinner ensued and talk turned to politics. I mentioned Ukraine president Petro Poroshenko, who took office a couple of months earlier in June. The mere use of his name launched a 90-minute diatribe about how Poroshenko was the most abhorrent politician ever to walk the Earth. It was a litany of name-calling and hopeful prophecies of his imminent assassination. The vitriol was unrelenting but at least the death threats were aimed at someone other than us. The Ukrainians clearly worked closely with the

Russians in some capacity — I wasn't sure I wanted to know how — and heralded Vladimir Putin as an exemplary leader.

Dinner ended on good terms, although with a strict requirement for us to be up and ready at 7 a.m. that morning to continue discussions.

At around 2.30 a.m., we arrived back at the safe house. Roberto, Peter and I threw our aching limbs on the mercy of a couple of rickety pieces of furniture, which looked every bit as world-weary as I felt.

'What do we think then — is this for real?' I asked.

Roberto was upbeat despite our qualms as to why this syndicate seemed so concerned by gangsters in the city. But, they had a lot of cash to make a deal of this size happen. I had my doubts as to whether they would pass the Football League's 'fit and proper person's test' for new owners, so some checks would need to be done here.

Despite the trauma of the day, it felt as though something positive could yet come out of all this. Of course, the security detail kept us under constant watch, but my head hit the synthetic pillow containing more optimistic thoughts than seemed possible earlier in the day.

* * *

The burly bodyguards duly arrived at 7 a.m., thudding on the door in uncompromising fashion. Bleary-eyed, the three of us stumbled into a gloriously bright morning and then the people-mover. We arrived at a luxurious country club to continue talks in a picturesque location under a large parasol sheltering us from the heat and now, believe it or not, a deal started to be done.

Milan's price and payment structure was received promisingly enough. The total figure was thirty million pounds with 50 per cent paid on completion and then the rest in two further instalments over the subsequent twelve months, which made sense.

It was a productive day, certainly compared with the previous one.

At 2 p.m., we asked to be allowed to phone home. Our requests were granted, and I rang Janine again just to touch base, but I felt it would be easier on her not to know the full extent of the uncertainty that still engulfed us.

Peter took longer than the five minutes agreed and suddenly the atmosphere turned fraught once again. The bodyguard began shouting, 'Give me the fucking phone, now!' evidently ready to take Peter's wrist along with his Blackberry should he not have complied.

They took us to see the training facilities of a team they claimed to co-own. Again, I'd rather not name which one. We met the coach and several of the backroom staff. The façade of each building was dated and unloved but, once inside, the rooms were beautifully finished to a very high specification; this display of largesse was clearly for Milan's benefit, to exemplify the investment they would make in Sheffield Wednesday's infrastructure.

It went on for hours and hours. Eventually, Dimitri broke the monotony. 'Tonight, we are going to have a party!' he declared. None of us felt in a particularly celebratory mood given the endless tension that surrounded the entire trip. Having said that, at least nobody had died that day. Via a short trip to what they described as their headquarters – a dank, small office in the city centre – for some minor paperwork, we were driven again to another apparently disused building, but the bleak first impression again gave way to what was nothing short of a fantasy land.

A sprawling swimming pool benefited from the addition of spiralling slides and a zip wire suspended across the water. Beautiful women were liberally scattered around all sides of the pool, while indoors the palatial corridors led to a variety of grandiose rooms containing anything from sumptuous restaurants to handcrafted Russian snooker tables.

We were told to get changed into robes for 'health and safety reasons'. I had no idea why, but it became clear later when Peter had his wallet pinched, including about £300 in cash, presumably by one of the girls.

'These girls are here for your pleasure,' said Dimitri.

Cavorting with crazy Ukrainian hookers was the last thing we needed, primarily because we were all happily married, but also because I had a strong suspicion that everything we were doing was being recorded on camera somewhere. Even the slightest 'interaction' with the girls – which none of us pursued or were remotely interested in – could be used against us in this deal.

Dimitri was adamant, though. 'Which one do you want?' he asked, as a parade of tired-looking prostitutes sashayed their way past us in a Generation Game-style conveyor belt. One of them passed me wearing only mink. I felt like shouting, 'Cuddly toy!' but it would have been lost in translation. Not that any of them looked particularly cuddly either. And in any case, we would have risked insulting his hospitality given that we had politely declined.

'Fine! You girls, fuck off,' said Dimitri. 'Bring in some more.'

I almost lied to Dimitri and told him I was gay but, given the region's dubious track record on equal rights, there are some out there who would consider being gay or black as the only thing worse than a football agent.

Dimitri showed us his battle scars. There were bullet wounds and stab scars on his torso, some the consequence of what he described as 'business deals gone wrong'. Fabian had a tattoo of a dagger on his neck. Meanwhile, Milan was trying to bring negotiations to a head and all this felt an uncomfortable distraction from the fact that a deal was yet to be agreed. As the clock ticked past 2.30 a.m., he forced the issue. 'We have to go tomorrow so we need to know if we have a deal,' he said, instigating a marked tempo change. 'I am a Serbian and you are a Ukrainian. We have the same values. If you shake my hand now, we have a deal.'

The conversation continued as if nothing had been said. All Dimitri had to do was shake hands . . . and he wasn't doing it.

An hour later, Milan tried again. 'Shake my hand,' he said, with more conviction than before. Finally, they did. It was a poignant moment because, at last, we crossed the Rubicon.

Peter made detailed notes of the specifics. There was something comical in the sight of a middle-aged man wearing a kimono dressing gown, balancing a waitress's notebook on his knees and trying to put together the finer points of a multi-million pound deal. It was a far cry from the Fratton Park boardroom.

Our commission was to be three million pounds. It had been a hard three days but, as we returned to the safe house with eyelids weighing heavy, the three of us were relatively happy given the proposed remuneration. Roberto brought the Ukrainians to the table, Peter had Milan, and it came together through my organisation, so we would each take one million pounds. The split was easy.

I don't consider myself to be blessed with great talent but being an agent is about more than just representing somebody. Where I feel arguably most adept is facilitating meetings at which each party can further their interests.

Our phones had been returned to us briefly so I sent a text to Janine telling her I was OK. The relief of our impending flight home washed over me, cushioning the sharpness of the springs as I climbed into bed back at the safe house. I reached into my bag and found my iPad displaying an Internet signal. An unsecured connection nearby allowed me to access my emails for the first time. For a moment, I felt reconnected with reality.

I responded to a few, enthused by the knowledge that, in twelve hours, we would return to normality with another deal done and a healthy financial return to show for it.

* * *

I can't sleep. Something doesn't feel right. The best I can do is doze. Thoughts are racing through my head about whether the deal would actually be completed, whether I would stay alive. Not necessarily in that order.

Suddenly, a monstrously imposing man bursts into my room, bristling with aggression.

'He's dead because of you!' he cries. 'Give me your fucking phone, get dressed and get outside. Now!'

It felt like a dawn raid. Is there a final twist?

'Hold on . . . I am just waking up,' I say.

'Give me your fucking phone!' he repeats, with even more hostility than before.

'I gave you it last night,' I reply, gathering myself.

'What else have you got?' he says.

'An iPad.'

'Give me the fucking iPad!' he says as he pulls a phone from his pocket and I realise he is in the middle of a call. It is Dimitri at the other end. The bodyguard hands me the phone.

Dimitri is apoplectic. 'Give him all your fucking devices. My guy has been killed. They have been tracing your devices. Do what you are fucking told or we'll fucking sort you out. I want to see you now. Now!'

A sense of helplessness has returned. I rack my brains. It must be me – I used the iPad on an unsecured network. Any of these guards could break me in two by looking at me and it seemed I had facilitated the death of one of their associates.

He lets me clean my teeth. I brush while nervously glancing at the bodyguard behind me in the mirror. Having my back to him for so long feels like asking for trouble.

Fabian re-emerges. He is blaming me. Now, more than ever, I think we are being kidnapped. We appeared to have struck a deal last night and now our lives are threatened.

We are taken to Dimitri's office in central Odessa. I explain I emailed a couple of people back in the UK because my iPad had Internet access.

'You could have got the guy killed,' he says. For the first time, there is an element of doubt over my culpability. This isn't the behaviour of somebody who is about to buy a big football club in England. So what's going on? Is it a farce? Are we being kidnapped? Is it all an elaborate act and, if so, to what end?

We are told we have to pay the Army to get us out of the country. It costs about 40,000 Ukrainian hryvnia, which equates to 2,300 euros each. 'Give us your credit card now because we have to organise it,' says Dimitri. By this point, Roberto, Peter and I just want to get out by whatever means necessary. And here was an escape route, even if it seemed trap-laden.

We all hand our plastic over, simultaneously making a mental note to cancel our cards at the earliest opportunity to prevent any unauthorised activity. There is tension in the room but it is not quite as frightening as before. Nobody has pointed a gun at me; nobody has told us we can't go home, but we are getting close to our flight time. We're going to miss our plane. The more I say that, the more Fabian starts talking nonsense. He starts talking about the Beatles.

'What do you think A Hard Day's Night actually meant?' he says.

I don't fucking care . . . Can we go now, please? I think to myself. He doesn't want an answer anyway because he never pauses long enough.

They don't want us to make our plane. Eventually, the conversation peters out. There is nothing left to talk about. Our flight has gone. A bog-standard car resembling a taxi arrives, our phones are returned to us and we are told to leave.

'We will meet you in Trafalgar Square next week,' says Dimitri, suggesting the deal is still on. They claim to have an office there. 'I'll let you know which day I am coming over . . . we'll look at the stadium and begin due diligence in the coming days.'

For the first time, no security travels with us. The traffic is terrible but we get to the airport to find there is no military assistance whatsoever. I don't feel safe. We are told there are no flights to London or Milan, where Roberto *is heading. The only flight out was to Kiev. It was still Ukraine – and in an area where trouble was flaring – but just escaping Odessa constituted progress under the circumstances.*

Expecting to be fast-tracked, we mentioned Dimitri's name to the military. They had never heard of him. We muddled through Departures and as we took off, we began to relax and thoughts once more turned to whether this deal was genuine.

Kiev airport is huge, modern and they sell sandwiches. It felt decidedly well-appointed. We flew back to London and I got home at 11 p.m. Janine was greatly relieved. We talked for two hours across the kitchen table about the whole experience but I couldn't speak with conviction about whether we would eventually have anything to show for it. I slept very, very well.

* * *

The first few days afterwards are quite positive. There is regular email contact and things seem to be edging forward. But then communications go deathly quiet for about ten days. Roberto fills that silence by phoning a good contact he had at a reputable, high-ranking European club. He says, 'These Ukrainian guys have got more money than God. Don't worry about it, it'll be fine. They just have some issues back there at the moment.'

After another few days, the silence is deafening. I phone Dimitri. 'It's fine,' he growls. 'I'll call you tomorrow. My father has had some problems.'

A couple of emails trickle out from him the next day. One is an apology, the other nothing of any consequence and there are no more requests for due diligence, no timetable for coming to the UK.

I fear the worst. You don't leave a deal like this hanging for two weeks. Milan kept faith because, as a Serbian, he felt some kind of empathy with the Ukrainians. He knew their mind-set better than us but, to me, it still felt all wrong.

Finally, a colleague sent me an article from a Swiss newspaper that exposed a scam in the Ukraine where football agents were brought over ostensibly to negotiate the purchase of a club and then mistreated. One agent had been killed; others had been kidnapped. Money had changed hands. We found out Dimitri's father, who was always very influential in the background, had seemingly disappeared without trace. There were even unsubstantiated rumours that he had ended up in jail. It was all an elaborate fallacy. That was the end of that.

Looking back on it now, it remains a puzzle. I still can't figure out the real story. They can't have been who they claimed, yet we only parted with 2,300 euros plus a contribution towards the party before they threw in the food, drink and, er, other 'entertainment'.

To make an extortion racket viable, surely they would need to bring agents over all the time, but we never saw anyone else there and nobody I know aside from my consultant had been there. We should have researched these people better beforehand but in fact our preliminary checks had somehow all come back positive.

I now know there was no Marble Arch office. I also found out that Odessa's supposed contact was said to have links to the mafia — whoever they may be. That would have set alarm bells ringing from the outset and you might ask why anyone would ever countenance dealing with such unsavoury characters. But people are naïve in the extreme if they think football transactions are only conducted between upstanding businessmen with legitimate funding.

It is often a murky world . . . but not always in the way you might think.

1

Deadline Day

Football is a game of fine margins. The difference between winning and losing a match can be a determined by a moment of brilliance or an individual mistake. Timing is everything.

Football is also no longer solely a sport. It is now inextricably a business and the same tight parameters exist in the boardroom; chairmen and chief executives are all defined as successes or failures depending upon brief moments in time: a risk taken, a decision made.

Everybody is looking for an angle. They'll even go to war-torn regions to find one. People in football regularly take chances just like our Ukraine trip because the power of money is absolute: the right deal can make or break a club.

Player transfers are big business. Few managers now control a club's transfer policy alone; the emergence of Sporting Directors, transfer committees and recruitment departments in recent years is evidence of the pivotal importance identifying and acquiring the right players has in the workings of a modern-day, top-level club. Agents therefore facilitate the most crucial element of a club's strategy. The implementation of transfer windows for the 2002–03 season suddenly introduced a biannual finite timeframe; it instantly became a scramble to sign the best players for an appropriate price at the right time.

Sky Sports transformed this business of football into a televisual event, making a personality out of presenter Jim White and illustrated by a sea of yellow tickers, ties and ticking clocks. All the negotiation, posturing and positioning of a transfer window is distilled down into one or two days of acute pressure which often does not reflect well on anyone in football.

Deadline day itself is unnecessarily emotional. For the small agents – the ones who are waiting to pay their fuel bill for the rest of the year in one working day – God help them, because it is as unpredictable as the weather. Some agents start the day with about a dozen or so possible transactions, many of them interlinked: if one club sells a player, that same club will go for another who could then in turn release a position for a third transfer and so on. There are a variety of options when you start at 6 a.m. and they fall away one by one throughout the day. For the ones that do get traction, you have to scurry around to get the paperwork done. If you badly need a deal to go through, it is a countdown fraught with stress, tension and panic.

The following day is very depressing if things went awry because there is nothing you can do to rectify the situation. It is like taking a morning stroll into a nightclub where you made a fool of yourself the night before: you are surrounded by reminders of the mistakes you made with no recourse available. Everyone has left the party. The hangover is terrible if you have not made the one deal that could make or break your year; January is almost never as big so you might have to wait a year to atone the error, especially as it often takes the full length of a contract to get paid.

I can understand why, from the outside, people look at clubs panicking to act on deadline day and think the whole picture utterly embarrassing and avoidable. Some of those clubs will have pursued targets that haven't come off; others hamstrung by decreasing flexibility from their banks are reliant on a chain of deals happening before the one they want to complete can go ahead. That possibility doesn't open up until late in the window because everyone is playing chess.

An agent's job is to make that breakthrough but sometimes neither side is willing to move while there is time to stand still; two weeks from the window closing gives everyone plenty of space to assess their options, and completing a deal early is sometimes seen as sticking on 16 when you could take another card that gets you to 21.

The summer window is complicated by the fact that a manager's ideas are often formulated during pre-season and then the first few games dictate their actions towards the end of the window. It surprises many people outside the game but snap decisions are often taken with the season just a few games old, prior to the summer window closing. Managers are under immediate pressure and the temptation to act – knowing otherwise nothing can be done until January – is often too great.

January isn't usually a big trading window. It is more often a tidy-up of deals that were incomplete, mismanaged or simply not possible during the summer. January can be the time when a chain of deals is finally completed – perhaps a club replaces a player sold on deadline day that left them short. Nobody wants to be left with an incomplete squad and, when a club is caught between two possible options, it has ramifications for all involved.

In 2012, Anton Ferdinand was going to QPR from West Ham. The deal broke down because the two clubs couldn't agree a fee. Those conversations were nothing to do with us but we then got a call from QPR about Sebastien Bassong, who was surplus to requirements at Tottenham. We went in and did the deal quickly. Bassong says goodbye to his team-mates and leaves the Chigwell training ground for what he thinks is the last time.

QPR manager Harry Redknapp was one of our clients at the time but, unbelievably, he hadn't been available for us to talk to him during that day. To compound the miscommunication, Harry tells the QPR board, unbeknown to us, he doesn't want Bassong after all; he still wants Anton Ferdinand. But by this time, Anton is in his car driving up north. He has got as far as Northampton. QPR phone him and say, 'Look, Harry loves you. You have one last chance to sort out a move because your replacement is on his way down here. Let's agree some terms that work for us both.'

It is mid-afternoon, so he has time to turn the car around before the 11 p.m. deadline. QPR stall Bassong in the meantime. We should be in the loop between Harry and QPR but, to our own detriment, we aren't. It was our own slack management – maybe we presumed that Harry would take it upon himself to keep us posted. You have to square the circle of intelligence, but we left a huge hole in the middle.

So we are in the dark and the delay on Bassong is an ominous sign. Time ticks away. The player begins to get edgy. Eventually, we get hold of Harry. He tells us he really doesn't want Bassong. Apparently, he's not a bad player but just the wrong fit. Almost in the same breath, Anton arrives back at Loftus Road and they complete the deal, leaving Bassong to trudge back to Spurs and say,

'Hi. I'm not going anywhere after all.' It was difficult for him as he had mentally moved on from Tottenham.

It raises an interesting point about the collateral damage of deadline day; the manager has to make a judgement call but Bassong had to rebuild his career on the whim of one man's opinion. And now that Spurs didn't want him, he had to face up to the prospect of at least four months as a bit-part player, earning the bare minimum his contract dictated while finding the motivation to continue for a manager who had such a low opinion of him that he tried to ship him out.

As an agent, you do your best to console a player and it is another side of our industry that people don't see. Footballers are often painted as mercenaries and, while they have far greater power over their own destiny than ever before, that doesn't prevent occasions when clubs can toy with their emotions. Italian clubs are very good at trying to wreck someone else's deal and then nick the player on the cheap.

Take Fabio Borini's move from Liverpool to Sunderland in 2015. A Serie A club get involved and say, 'We really love you and want you here. What's the price . . . ten million? No, we can't do that. We'll do six million.' So they have turned the player's head but made an uncompetitive offer. As nice as Wearside is, there are obvious attractions to living your life on the Continent and so the player hangs around thinking they may go to eight million, a figure Liverpool might take. But the Serie A club never do. They go to six-and-a-half million and hope for the best. The Italians do it time and time again. But, in the end, Sunderland offered eight million plus two million in add-ons, which was enough to render the Italians an irrelevance because they didn't look serious by comparison.

Borini was quite happy to go to Sunderland but the Serie A club made that deal far more complicated than it needed to be. His view of life was that he didn't want to get into the last year of his contract not playing first-team football for Liverpool and have his stock fall so far that no Premier League or major European team would consider him worth taking. He could have become a forgotten man. That is the risk, not so much at the very top, but even for a squad player at a top-six club.

Never are the stakes higher than on deadline day and we were involved in what to this day stands as the quintessential example of the dynamics involved: Andrey Arshavin's transfer from Zenit St Petersburg to Arsenal in February 2009.

My brother Phil and Arsène Wenger had been working on this for some time but without any joy. He had an agent called Dennis Lachter. Funnily enough, Phil was playing in a local Maccabi League football team in north London with Dennis's cousin, Joe. Through Joe, we got to Dennis and, through Dennis, we started talking with Andrey. A dialogue began in November which went on through December and into the January transfer window. Initially, the two clubs were a long way apart in their valuation. Arsenal originally offered eight million with Zenit demanding fifteen million. Zenit enquired about a player-plus-cash exchange but that discussion never got off the ground. It was about the only concession they would even hint at.

Arsenal moved a little and offered ten million. We got to mid-January and the deal had completely stalled. The problem was that Zenit is actually Vladimir Putin's club – the Russian president supported them as a boy. Zenit's Director General was a guy called Maxim Mitrofanov, above him was another board member and above him was the president of Gazprom, Alexey Miller. Above Miller was Putin.

We tried to move all sorts of ways around it – payment structures where money was loaded at the front end, for example. Arsenal kept trying. They went up to twelve million at the start of the last week of the window. Suddenly, the Russians claimed they required an additional payment to clear a debt Andrey had accrued from not fulfilling a contractual obligation somewhere along the line. That added a sizeable six-figure sum to the final figure but, eventually, Arsenal indicated they would absorb that payment in his image rights terms as part of any deal.

Still, the Gazprom chief dug his heels in. Everyone was stretching again and Arsenal were losing faith. I told them to keep going because the end of the window always focuses people's minds and, at that moment, Andrey really wanted to move to London. Andrey was potentially damaged goods for Zenit, mentally, because although he loved the club, his head was now with Arsenal.

Arsène was involved at every step. Every conversation with Arsenal was based around how Arsène was feeling and things he thought they could do to bridge the gap. He offered them a game at the Emirates Cup – that's probably worth about half a million in revenue – and Arsène was completely in control of that environment. At the time, Ivan Gazidis had just come in as chief executive and was learning the ropes. It was his first month and so I was dealing with the then Managing Director, Ken Friar, whom I love dearly and have known forever. He is a fine, upstanding gentleman and completely what you want from your favourite uncle. But he is quite old school; he would settle upon a price and not budge from it.

I made a phone call. 'Hi, Arsène,' I said. 'We appear to be stuck.'

'Yes, it is stuck. We need to try and find a way forward. Let me speak with Ken Friar,' he said.

Of course, there was also the additional information I could provide having spoken with Andrey's agent Dennis Lachter, which Zenit were already aware was happening.

Technically we might not have been given permission but that's my job for a club or a player at any given time. I am the bridge the club can't cross. In most cases of employment exchanges in any walk of life, the potential employee and prospective employer have had some sort of prior connection. If you are going to leave a place of work for another job, you either apply for a publicly advertised role or you are headhunted. There are agencies set up to conduct the latter as an intermediary and that is widely acknowledged. There has to be a person ready to break the conventional ethical boundaries of not pinching other people's staff and actually make contact. So we sometimes facilitate that in football.

Disputes between players, agents or clubs are dealt with under the arbitration clause in the FA's laws of the game, known as Rule K. I used to call it Rule K9 because it is a dog of a regulation.

What should happen is that Zenit talks to Arsenal directly and vice versa. Zenit will say if the player is for sale or not. If Arsenal then ask to speak to the player, Zenit should say, 'No, you can't, until you have done a deal with us.' That's what was going on but our view was that we had to talk to the player because only by doing that would he put pressure on the club to close the gap in terms of price. If it is close, there are ways we can do it without him. But when it is this large, it is basically impossible without involving the player.

This happens all the time, but everyone in football has to

subscribe officially to the laws of the game, including Rule K, even though it is impossible to enforce and invalid in reality. Gary Lineker once said tapping up was like speeding – we've all done it even though we shouldn't. Except, as Lineker points out, speeding is illegal under the laws of the land, tapping up is not and only an offence within the rules of football. And what an absurd rule it is.

Arsène and Arsenal played it by the book. He told me, 'If you want to talk to the player, that is up to you.'

There was no direct contact prior to a fee being agreed. Sometimes I might phone Ken and say, 'We've spoken to Andrey and . . .'

'I don't want to know!' he'd interrupt. Most other clubs would say, 'Oh yeah, what did he say?' But that is not how the Arsenal decision-makers do business.

Andrey quite rightly wanted to know about the tax situation. In Russia, he paid 22 per cent. We got to a stage where we were two million pounds apart and I started to think that gap was bridgeable. Phil was talking to Dennis from our Wembley office; I was speaking to Arsène. Lachter did nothing and decided what would be, would be. We had to make all the running. I think he might have had another deal with someone else which wasn't maturing and, in his mind, this was it. He is of Israeli–Russian extraction and he knew their mind-set. They don't negotiate. Unless Arsenal hit the fifteen-million figure, Andrey was going nowhere.

We got to 29 January and Arsenal were hinting that they might go that far but without offering anything concrete. Arsène really wanted the player and Ken Friar was unwilling to go higher. I decided to contact David Dein, the former vice-chairman of the club, with whom I always had a warm working relationship, for his assistance. David is one of the most well-connected men in football and I explained the situation to him. David told me he would speak to Alisher Usmanov, Arsenal's second largest shareholder. Alisher is an Uzbekistan billionaire who surprisingly did not have a seat on the board despite owning 30 per cent of the club's equity. But he had a good understanding of Zenit and Gazprom and the advice came back to tell Andrey to go and see Alexey Miller at Gazprom. Word began to circulate that Usmanov had got involved, which was softening the Russians' position a little. That was proving useful, although I had no intention of telling Arsenal because it could have exacerbated existing tensions between Usmanov and the club's hierarchy.

It was now 30 January and there were soft edges everywhere, so I sensed that if there was a way of making one side take a little step forward, we could open a path to an agreement. Andrey was convinced it was happening because Usmanov had got involved, so he got on a plane to Paris. He didn't want to be seen in England in case the media picked up on it but still jumped the gun anyway and upset Zenit at a time when negotiations remained precarious. He ended up sitting in a Parisian hotel room on his own, waiting to find out what was happening.

The night passed. We were now at 31 January – in theory, this is the penultimate day of the window. However, the weather report for later that day and the following day was worrying. Snowstorms were set to engulf London overnight into deadline day. It was a snap decision and we just said, 'Right, we have to get him out of there. The last thing we want is for this deal to fall down because we can't get him into the country – or someone out to him – for a medical and the relevant paperwork.'

Phil had an arrangement with the Village Hotel in Elstree and we flew Andrey into Stansted on a private jet. We'd now got to thirteen-and-a-half million from Arsenal, solely from Arsène pushing the club to increase their offer. He felt relaxed about it all; the player was in the country, which shifted the balance of probability in their direction.

Andrey came to my house. I gave him one simple instruction: 'Don't go out. There are a lot of Arsenal supporters around here. If they see you, it will be chaos.' Andrey nodded in recognition of the situation and returned to his hotel.

The following day – 1 February – he was photographed in every national newspaper standing outside the Elstree hotel in his bobble hat looking at the snow, texting on his mobile phone. Brilliant, I thought to myself. Now all bets are off. I was expecting a disaster but instead we caught something of a break. After consultation with the Football Association and FIFA, the Premier League announced that the transfer deadline would be pushed back until 5 p.m. on 2 February; the inclement weather had made travelling across the country difficult, meaning a delay in medicals, face-to-face talks and the physical movement of players from one club to another. That relaxed us somewhat, but Zenit still had to move from fifteen million. The extra time gave everybody a chance to pause for breath. Nothing changes overnight.

I woke up the following morning hoping for an email, a text or some indication of progress from either side. There was nothing – Arsenal were stuck, Zenit were stuck. Russia was three hours ahead of us, which condensed the time-frame still further. Mitrofanov told us there was a meeting at 3 p.m. UK time to discuss Andrey's situation.

'You are leaving it a bit tight,' I said, given there were just two hours left to sort things out.

'That is just how it is. You will have our final decision then,' he said.

Arsenal often use outsourced medical facilities – based in Harley Street – and we took Andrey to have his medical so there wouldn't be any hold-ups on that front. The Russians knew he was in London and probably anticipated us having got that far.

Meanwhile, I was trying to get hold of Ivan Gazidis, but his phone was engaged. Everyone else at Arsenal was saying it was his decision. I had been dealing with Ken and Arsène but Ivan is now in situ. And I know him – he asked my advice when Manchester City offered him the chief executive job two or three years previously, back when they were under Thai ownership. We told him to wait on that occasion but, when the Arsenal job came up, we advised him to take it, although, as it turned out, his mind was already made up. He still probably needed time to adjust but, as chief executive, he did not want to sit idly by while Arsenal conducted a club record deal in his first window.

The gap still feels bridgeable but nothing was happening. Yet the buzz was huge. The fact my sons were watching it unfold on TV in the room next to me while I was still negotiating was a colossal adrenalin rush.

'Arsène Wenger is about to meet Andrey Arshavin and welcome him to Arsenal,' blared out the TV as I sat, within earshot, with my head in my hands thinking, It's nowhere near that close.

We tried everything; we suggested putting some of his wages into image rights, save a bit of money and put that into the deal. Alisher was talking to everyone trying to make the transfer happen.

The phone was ringing relentlessly but everyone was saying the same thing: we need to find more money to get closer to Zenit's asking price. The best Arsenal have offered totals £13.8m.

Part of me thought, What are Zenit going to do? Call him back? They have got nearly fifteen million for him anyway. But the Russians were absolutely poker-faced. They were not budging and the clock was ticking. Pavel, the administrator for Zenit, sounded frazzled on the phone every time I tried to work an angle.

We had now reached the final 40 minutes. I rang Pavel again; it was time to act. 'The answer is yes. Let's do the deal at fifteen million.' I couldn't take it any longer. I decided to offer the additional £1.2m myself to get the deal done and sort it out with Arsenal later. It was serious money to me. It wouldn't ruin my life but it was a significant outlay. The commissions might have covered most of it but that's not the point. I'm in this business to make money and protect my family.

Pavel drew up a contract and sent it to Arsenal. Except, of course, it said the money was all coming from Arsenal. Ivan called me with five minutes left before the deadline. 'How much have you cost me?' he said.

'I've just offered them the £1.2m,' I replied.

'Jesus,' Ivan said.

There was a pause which felt like an eternity. 'OK.'

Did that mean yes? Did he finally agree to Arsenal paying the money and not me? I think he just had.

This new agreement was only on a term sheet. We now needed to exchange paperwork between Arsenal and Zenit to confirm the agreement formally. They had to submit a piece of paper that said 'Arsenal offer this and Zenit accept' in an official document. There was enough online traffic being sent for me to see that Ivan and Zenit were exchanging emails. But even though this was 2009, the Premier League still wanted hard copies, not emails. They needed a fax.

So I wrote to both of them in an email: 'Ivan, you have got to fax this over to Pavel.'

We waited.

Pavel didn't receive anything.

'Pavel, you fax them,' I wrote in another email.

Nothing.

'OK, somebody fax me,' I said in a third.

Still nothing.

The Russians' fax machine wasn't working. We were now into the final minute. The clock in my office ticked louder with each passing second. My heart began to race. I sent another email: 'Pavel, Ivan is going to send you something now. Just send Ivan and me an email with the word "Agreed" on it.'

We wait. The clock ticks down into the final ten seconds. I am frantically refreshing my inbox. Jim White is counting down the time on Sky Sports News. I can see Big Ben on the TV. With four seconds left, Pavel's email arrives. Relief washes over me. We have got an electronic trail that we can justify to the Premier League now. That said, it was not a *fait accompli*. Technically, the required forms had not been submitted in time.

Arsenal had to wait until the early hours of 3 February before the deal was formally confirmed while the FA and the Premier League investigated the paper trail. And why did they ratify it? Simply because of that one-word email: 'Agreed'. That was deemed sufficient proof of a confirmed transaction, which might seem like common sense but it did not adhere to the Premier League's strict regulations of the day.

The whole episode was one of a few transfers – Rafael van der Vaart's 2010 move to Tottenham was another – that led the Premier League to introduce a 'deal sheet', which formalises what clubs have to do if they are involved in a prospective transfer that might run past the deadline. I look back on the episode now with joy simply because it came off. I would have been devastated had it not. At one point during the whole saga Andrey was distraught. He thought he'd burned his bridges at Zenit but would have had to go back because the deal would fall through.

My sons Ross and Scott took him out to our games room to play FIFA, essentially to distract him. As they prepared to play a game, Andrey selected the 'Be a Pro' option where you play as one player rather than a team. He chose to be himself, starting in the Arsenal team. He turned to Scott and said, 'Ah, OK, this is my début at the Emirates!'

That could have been as close as he ever got. Such is the pressure of deadline day.

2

Window Shopping

The introduction of transfer windows in 2002 took most people by surprise and they have shaped the conduct of clubs ever since. They encourage a modus of brinkmanship which manifests itself most palpably on deadline day. Clubs operate in this way because the power has seemingly swung irrevocably away from them and towards the player.

Prior to 15 December 1995, clubs had a lien on a player's services after their contract expired. On that date, Belgian midfielder Jean-Marc Bosman won a landmark ruling through the European Court of Justice which was the product of a five-year legal battle that started after he had been denied a move from FC Liège to Dunkerque even though he was out of contract. Alongside his tireless lawyer Jean-Marie Dupont, they successfully argued that a footballer's rights should be considered in the same manner as workers' rights were expressed in the Treaty of Rome: no lien once a contract's end date had been reached.

Bosman won £312,000 in damages over his failed move; together with Dupont, he had taken on Liège, the Belgian FA, UEFA and FIFA and somehow had won. Players were no longer termed 'enforced employees'; they had become employees with rights. Up until this point, clubs always called all the shots. These were also the days when some clubs would declare the official attendance as fifty thousand when it was actually more like sixty-five thousand and the surplus cash went into certain people's pockets. It was a different time. Players' behaviour was shaped by the fact they were always on unsteady ground. Very rarely does a player get punished for a stand now.

Saido Berahino at West Brom in 2015 is a case in point. Upset at the 'outrage' of not being allowed to move clubs just because he wanted to, he took to social media and declared, 'I'm not playing for you ever again.' Eleven days later, he did. Pre-Bosman, players had no firm footing – or the technology – to do anything of the sort.

Bosman himself went on to play at a mediocre level before retiring and later suffered from alcoholism and depression. It is a sad personal legacy but his professional one is profound. Before the Bosman ruling, transfers were much simpler because the concept of player power did not exist. If you go back to the days prior to the Premier League, players often didn't even get paid during June and July when there were no matches. It might seem odd now but, at the time, Bosman's victory was largely greeted with indifference throughout football; most were sceptical that the European Commission would ever allow it to happen. And yet, late in 1995, they did.

I was fascinated by the case and made a point of getting in touch with Dupont. I put together a deal to tell Bosman's life story with him, Dupont and Jerome Valcke when he was Head of Acquisitions at Canal Plus years before he became Secretary General at FIFA. I wanted to learn all about it: the motivations behind it, the nuances within and the ramifications afterwards. There was no question it was the right thing for players on a fundamental level but it created a lot of uncertainty within the game at the time. I remember sitting with Paul Stretford in the days after the ruling and saying to him, 'This is pension fund stuff, now. For the players and for us.' Bosman had greatly expanded the role of agents overnight.

And it was the start of wages going through the roof; rightly so, as they began to receive due recognition for their status as the lifeblood of the game alongside fans. Contracts became really worthwhile because they instilled a timeframe that created leverage where none had previously existed. So, if a player has a five-year contract, the club must now look twenty-four months ahead at the end of year three. There was no lien any more. That's why year three of a five-year deal or year two of a four-year deal are now so important. If a player gets into the last year now, subsequent rulings have allowed them to speak to other clubs during the January window six months before their contract ends. So, in effect, clubs really only have six months to negotiate a new deal as a player enters his final year. The whole world of contract law in football changed for ever after Bosman, creating unprecedented opportunities for players and their representatives. It seemed too good to be true. There had to be a catch somewhere and it came in the form of transfer windows.

Mario Monti was the European Union Competitions Commissioner – he would later become the Prime Minister of Italy – and he argued that you couldn't completely transform an industry overnight as the Bosman ruling had done. The problem was, because Bosman and Dupont had successfully argued their case for footballers' rights, there were many ready to see the Treaty of Rome argument through to what could be interpreted as its logical conclusion and scrap the entire transfer system altogether. Together with his cohorts at the European Commission, Mario suggested a compromise whereby players could only be transferred at pre-designated points during the season. UEFA were in favour because of the confusion that abounded in a post-Bosman world.

By 2000, the European Commission had begun to run with the idea. Negotiations over the length and timing of the windows continued until the system we know today came into effect.

* * *

My First Artist company floated on the London Stock Exchange in 2002 and, despite the evolution required post-Bosman, we had adapted and thrived. But suddenly this new European Commission ruling told us we could only ply our trade for four months of the year. We'd become a toy manufacturer with our Christmas in August. Nobody had any forewarning of this at all; there was obviously some discussion among politicians but it never made it into the general marketplace. It was kept in a little cabal in Brussels and, ultimately, it was only when football's governors realised the real threat of a transfer abolishment from the European Commission that they decreed a new path. Almost overnight, we had to reconfigure everything in our negotiating armoury.

Of course, you could renegotiate player contracts during a season but the bulk of any agent's income always came from trading players. Renegotiations are never as lucrative as being able to buy and sell; the parameters are better established, the margins harder to grow. But a responsible agent now had to advise their client to consider his position in the team, his physical well-being and if he is likely to be a star that year going into the final eighteen months of his contract.

We had Steve Howey at Newcastle. Steve was a lovely lad and a really good player on his day but the most injury-prone guy I've ever met. He would typically get injured in September and reappear in April. Ruud Gullit was Newcastle manager at the time and Steve had two-and-a-half years left on his deal. He was playing out of his skin and Newcastle said they wanted to offer him a new contract. We sat down with Steve and said, 'Take the money now and get your security sorted, because in four months' time you might be injured and this deal might not be on the table.'

A few people around him were saying, 'Yeah, but if he does really well, in a year's time it could be double.'

I said, 'Yep . . . and maybe you are playing Monopoly and you could land on Mayfair. At the moment, you are on Bond Street and that isn't such a bad place to be.'

Greed can cloud judgements, especially when deciding between the angel and the devil on your shoulders. I wasn't sure he would but, eventually, he signed the contract. Three weeks later, he was badly injured and was out for the rest of the season. He came back and did OK but never returning to the same level prior to that setback. It was an occasion when, thankfully, we got it right because there are times you can wait and wait but it doesn't work out.

Players were empowered by Bosman but it meant they also had decisions like this to make. Do you take the short-term security at the risk of long-term decline? Or do you back yourself to move on the basis of your talent earning you a transfer to a top club somewhere down the line?

The changes were more seismic in player transfers. A football club looking at their squad would make decisions either from a long-term planning perspective or an immediate short-term fix for a problem position in the team. For a while, there was a deadline day on 31 March – which acted as a forerunner to the August/January set-up – and by then people were making judgement calls on their team performance, the manager's aspirations and their cash ability. What trading windows did was force the smaller clubs to compete with the bigger ones at a higher level in a confined time period.

For me, that is a major negative about windows; smaller clubs are encouraged to spend resources they probably don't want to within their overall financial management because they are forced to create a contingency plan which may never be called upon. That plays into the bigger clubs' hands because they have greater resources. For example, left-footed players have usually been difficult to find down the years in the Premier League and Football League – that is why there are so many brought in from abroad. So the bigger clubs will decide to stockpile some of them to take them out of the market and ensure the competition can't have them. Smaller clubs can react either by paying over the odds or gambling on leaving themselves short.

In 1990, I remember then England manager Bobby Robson telling my young son Scott as he kicked a football around our garden, 'Oh, you are right-footed? For the next three weeks only kick with your left foot – we need more lefties.' If only Ryan Giggs had been English – he would have gone to many major tournaments, just as his talent deserved, and England would have had the right balance to their team for more than a decade.

There have definitely been instances when clubs have moved in to take a player in a certain position where there was a paucity of talent. Manchester United did that with Luke Shaw in 2014. It appeared they weren't sure about him but knew other clubs – most significantly Chelsea – were keen, so they took him off the market. He cost thirty million but if you are Manchester United, you can do that, especially for a young English player with obvious resale value. It is ironic that several English left-backs have thrived since, including Danny Rose and Ryan Bertrand, but United still feel Shaw is better than them all.

Transfer windows changed the timing of business for clubs. Some people – Karren Brady, David Sullivan and David Gold at both Birmingham and later West Ham, for example – wanted it done as early as possible, taking the stress out of it. Others, typically Daniel Levy at Tottenham, would think the prices were going to change so much he would be happy to wait and wait. Hence, very often he does business on the last day. I remember Daniel phoning my brother Phil at 6 a.m. on deadline day once, bursting with enthusiasm and asking, 'Right . . . What are we going to do today then?'

What often happens is talks might take place at the end of a window on a deal where a dialogue has first started three weeks earlier but nobody was in any rush back then. The pace of business is usually thus: you have a bit of a rush in June, then there are clubs like Chelsea who work on specific targets, progress them through the window if need be and not get distracted by any opportunities appearing elsewhere. And when the window gets to the end, it focuses everybody's mind. Eventually, somebody has to make a decision on a player and a price – as Arsenal belatedly did on Arshavin – but people use the window to see what else is around and there are many clubs who delay that decision as long as possible. Then, there is this mad scramble to complete their business. The consequence is a selling club could lose a player they need to replace. And that sparks pandemonium.

Daniel is somebody with a reputation for thriving in that environment. He has become the silent assassin of the transfer window. He is very bright but some find him extremely difficult to deal with. People will look at the selling club and think, Oh, it's Tottenham. Can we be bothered with all the hassle? Is there another deal somewhere else? I think he is charming and engaging. I've never had a problem with him. But he's very tough. Some people might think that is an issue but I'd rather have that than try to negotiate with someone more duplicitous. He can nickel and dime annoyingly; in any deal, there will be payment schedules, for example, and he'll want those at odd times. In the 2015 deal Spurs put together to sign Saido Berahino, it was reported that Daniel offered them a nominal figure up front and about twenty million spread over six years. Why would West Brom ever agree to that? They needed to spend the money straight away if they sold such a prize asset. But, of course, he had turned the player's head and it all played out in a rather ugly fashion as West Brom stood firm. Sometimes he can overplay his hand but, in most cases, he gets the job done. He always does things with a smile and that way, if he is squeezing your hand, you don't feel the pain so much.

The loan market is a very popular space these days. Everton are experts in this area; they have taken players left behind by managers departing other clubs or players who have not quite found their place in a team. I remember talking to David Moyes during his time in charge and he wanted me to help him sign Michael Essien.

Everton needed bite in their midfield and Essien was sitting on the bench at Chelsea, not getting a game. As it happened, Essien didn't want to move out of London, but it highlights the policy they have had for many years and it has helped them compete with teams on much bigger budgets.

The timing of a club's transfer business is always the product of a compromise between the manager's squad-building requirements and the board's financial strategy. You might have a situation at Leicester in 2015 where Claudio Ranieri came in and wanted to get his group together early. Pre-season is hugely important – even more so for a new manager learning about his players – because it is the design framework for the whole season. There is not a lot of time during a campaign to change things around, although obviously it is still possible. A manager wants six solid weeks to build a unit, exactly as England try to do before a major tournament. The issue becomes whether the financial arm of the club believes conducting early business will ensure accurate market value for the assets required and leaves them in a healthy place going forward. Cashflow will be an issue for most clubs and so, if they are selling players – as is often the case – that may well have to come first.

You might think Premier League clubs can operate a money-no-object policy with the TV cash surpassing eight billion and due to go considerably higher, but the banking industry has affected football, too. For years, clubs invested with local banks that could not be seen to deny the team funds because the community around that club would never bank with them again. The socio-economic globalisation of recent years combined with the fact that, in some cases, Premier League clubs are spending in excess of 90 per cent of their gross revenue on salaries nullified that threat. And so that business practice is perceived for what it is: exceedingly poor management.

So much so that before Fenway Sports Group took over at Liverpool, although Royal Bank of Scotland were not exactly enthralled by the prospect, they must surely have been close to pulling the plug on the club. It would have been unheard of but it must have been a real possibility. Christian Purslow, later a senior commercial executive at Chelsea, was put in by then RBS chairman Stephen Hester to renegotiate the terms of the £350m loan to owners Tom Hicks and George Gillett, which threatened the club's very existence. Bolton Wanderers were another club that nearly went insolvent but owner Eddie Davies kept chucking tens of millions into it so the banks held off.

These days, the banks won't allow a club to get into that position. Hence, financial products have hit the market. Investec, amongst others, have a fund that bankrolls transfers, leveraged against other assets of your club or future income so you don't have to go to your bank and ask for money. Leeds and Everton are among those thought to have looked at this type of securitisation.

The 2008 global financial crash means that they will not lend like they used to, even to such culturally visible and asset-rich entities as Premier League clubs. Those clubs that have mortgaged their gate receipts and television income for two years in advance have found that the banks would not facilitate further expenditure so they still have to sell before they can buy.

That may change in the coming years as the TV money goes up and the worldwide economic situation improves but it is particularly relevant at the time of writing for another reason. Although they are not huge businesses compared to ICI or Shell, Premier

League clubs reach sizeable audiences globally. Every week they engage with approximately one-and-a-half billion people around the world for 90 minutes, so investors want to buy clubs for their own corporate or personal purposes. Clubs like Southampton and Burnley will not want to overly degrade their balance sheets by overspending too early, thereby having additional player commitments on their books. They want to keep in good shape just in case one of the high-net-worth investors comes calling.

They are not trophy assets or a tax write-off. Clubs are now a bona fide marketing tool for Asian and American businessmen who would like to own something with a large outbound reach. As big as we think they are, clubs are not as expensive to buy as multinational conglomerates or large corporate entities. Clubs have more money to spend than ever before but their transfer activity could be caveated by a willingness to remain as desirable as possible to potential new owners. Finishing in the top half of the league on minimal expenditure makes any club a particularly viable target.

But that is an extremely delicate balancing act. Fans demand new signings because it is the ultimate expression of ambition. And that's where agents come in.

3

Negotiating Life

One of the biggest shortfalls in public understanding is how deals are instigated, negotiated and completed. There are more people involved in a single transaction now than ever before.

Back in the late 1980s and early 1990s, it was commonplace for players to negotiate deals on their own with a manager directly. As they began to seek more professional advice and the opportunities to earn serious money grew with the success of the Premier League, agents negotiated on their behalf but still only with perhaps one or two representatives from each club.

Today, there can be more than seven or eight parties involved. If you are dealing with a club in southern Europe or in certain parts of the world such as South America, there can be multiple representatives of that club: one for the board, another for the money behind the club, a third for the interests of a supporters' group that may have a stake in the club. The coach of the selling club may also have a representative present.

On the buying side, there is normally a chairman, a chief executive or a sporting director. Sometimes there is also an agent representing them. The player will be represented as well, often by an agent, a lawyer and a financial adviser. Any of these agents could bring a PA with them or their own advisers. I've seen an agent's delegation total six people, which, in my opinion, is overkill. The quorum should always be as small and tight as possible.

Everyone has to leave with something but they all come to the table with a preconceived idea of their own value – the larger the number involved, the more diffusive talks become. It is very difficult but you get around it by grouping them up. You put a couple of people with mutually aligned interests around a table and get them to agree on a point. You put them into silos and gradually form the building blocks of a deal by piecing the disparate component parts together. That is my one God-given talent – being able to organise people and move them forward in a way they feel is mutually beneficial.

It is not an exact science. In a much more wholesome and important realm than football, peace negotiators have the same task. Sometimes, they can throw in government money to help reach an agreement but I am always working from a finite pot of cash, whichever side I'm on.

At the highest level in the Premier League, more deals happen now the increase in income means more money is available to complete transactions if the will is really there. In the lower leagues, that isn't the case and more deals collapse.

The focus of an agent when representing a player should be entirely around what is best from a footballing, financial, taxation and lifestyle point of view for their client. Those are the four key elements of a good agent's representation contract.

The picture is further complicated by FIFA's decision to deregulate the football agent industry in 2015. Prior to that, there were around 350 licensed agents in the United Kingdom, each one having to take an entrance exam and pass background tests. The exam tested a person's ability to deal with possible scenarios involving a client, sometimes requiring detailed answers and, in other instances, legal questions with multiple-choice answers. It was a difficult exam and the pass rate was low. Now, agents are classed as intermediaries and there are no qualifications required at all. Consequently, the number has exploded; within eighteen months of deregulation, there were more than 1,600 intermediaries in England.

Everyone thinks they can be a football agent and believes it is simply a chance to print money. It isn't. Of those 1,600, only about a dozen make the kind of money that angers some people. A few more scrape a living and the rest just make up the numbers. Some in the latter category are parents simply renegotiating deals for their progeny already settled at a club. But there are many more that exist simply to trip up the professionals and give the whole industry a bad name. They assiduously read anything from Network 90 – a football insiders' website where private information is often exchanged – to the Sunday papers to glean information and bombard players and clubs with bravado, claiming they can finish a deal they have just read is in its formative stages.

These people invariably fail but the waters are muddied. It therefore becomes essential that the professional agent operates with written instruction from either the player or the club for whom he or she is acting. It should include the word 'exclusive', although in some countries this does seem to get lost in translation as, in quite a few cases, I have seen two or three agents turn up on behalf of a player with a so-called 'exclusive' representation document.

I'd like to think that over the years I have been one of the agents responsible for changing the way talks are held and contracts are configured.

In the vast majority of cases, agents are involved in two types of transactions: player contract negotiations and transfers. Both have their own nuances but the methodology is essentially the same. Very rarely is a deal done straight away. Occasionally, a club may offer silly money to get something done but it is unusual. Most clients reach a crossroads two years away from the end of their deal. The chatter over a significant player's situation begins at this time. Control is essential – you don't want other agents talking to your client, quietly suggesting other clubs are interested or proposing moves that they have been incentivised to generate themselves.

Equally, you cannot have a club speaking directly to a player about a potential move or new contract without your involvement, as they can immediately take the high ground and leave your client compromised without the requisite support network.

I grew up in the era where you were either on the side of the player or the club – these days, a handful of influential agents often operate not just for players but also for clubs. This duality is relatively new and something the FA is still trying to grapple with; they are always years behind the cutting edge. But I always believed that while standing up strongly for my player, it was essential that I maintained a good working relationship with most, if not all, the senior clubs around the world.

Bear in mind, when you are a football agent working at the high end of the game, you only have about forty customers. Each one you irritate is a significant blow to your earning potential. If I alienate 20 per cent of that forty, my prospective income has considerably diminished, especially if my player wants to go to a particular club with whom my relationship has soured. It is good to show strength in any transaction but it is also important to make sure that the other side feels that they haven't been short-changed and that, once a handshake has taken place, that deal will stand. On many occasions over the years, I believe we ended up getting more for our clients because the club felt that they were on safe ground moving forward with us based on our reputation of fairness.

Timing is so important. Pick the wrong moment to discuss your player's contract and it will create a negative environment with his employers. Sometimes a well-placed story in the media – nominally about interest from another club – will give you a prelude to open the discussion. If it suits the player, works for the newspapers and enlightens the employer to the possibility of a looming discussion, then all well and good. If the player ideally wants to leave for football or financial reasons then the agent's role would be to professionally solicit other potential employers and ascertain the financials surrounding a potential transaction.

We have always been pretty good at naming a likely asking price so very often it comes down to pitching the financial requests on behalf of your player. Before talks begin, the first thing I do is my research. The secret to mediation is in the minutiae. There is no substitution for preparation. I learn the club's wage structure and bonus policy. Poor agents often get knocked out in the first round by just being way out of kilter with that club's pertinent wage structure.

I try to find out what makes chairmen, managers or whoever is on the other side tick; learn what makes them smile and encourage them to walk down the same road as me by developing what they could perceive to be common interests.

In the case of Roman Abramovich, he is very intelligent – he puts everyone else in front of him and normally only turns up at the very end. But at Chelsea I still had to form relationships with his right-hand man Eugene Tenenbaum, Bruce Buck and, latterly, fellow director Marina Granovskaia – three very tough, bright individuals.

Asking questions is vital. I learnt this with Ken Bates. Ken was a different negotiator to most others. He was just a bulldozer. His starting point was usually, 'No, fuck off!' sometimes with his engaging smile.

Common ground isn't exactly easy to find from there. But you have got to be able to take some of the most powerful people in football into your confidence and get them to enjoy you being there. I would enquire about all aspects of their interests, lives and passions and park the information. If they were interested in, say, horse racing, I'd go back and research it so next time we met, the sixth or seventh question I'd ask would be about horse racing. And then I'd follow up with some facts that I had learned. It is a meticulous process but necessary to reap sizeable rewards.

Of course, you have to hide your apprehension, too. Being successful at these meetings ensures the future well-being of your client and is the essence of your livelihood. It is inevitably unnerving when you meet these senior executives and managers for the first time but I tried never to let them smell any fear.

Ken Friar had been at Arsenal for years and was a legend in his own time when I started. Ken Bates, Irving Scholar, Maurice Watkins – all these guys made it an intimidating place to do business, even though they were all fair along with it.

You have to mark your ground early. Sometimes, this may be with an initial phone conversation, which would necessitate arriving with a lawyer or an accountant to advance those discussions. But you should always be able to handle those negotiations yourself even if the club have their own lawyers and accountants in the room with you. Professional expertise is essential as your facts have to be correct at all times but, sometimes, as in most face-to-face negotiations, the senior principals lead talks.

I try always to remain confident and positive. Everybody is pretty macho in these deals so you can't be seen to be undermined by any other party. I usually drop my voice by half an octave to develop more resonance and never talk for the sake of it; only speak when you have a salient point to make, once you've established who and what you are.

When I want to look someone in the eye meaningfully, I focus on the bridge of their nose because it has the same effect but also means you will never blink when they do. That can be seriously disconcerting for the other party. I often use pauses to lend additional gravitas to a point – three seconds may seem like an eternity but it certainly captures the opposing side's attention.

Inevitably, the club would start with, 'This is what we are proposing . . .' The trick is breaking that down and rebuilding the component parts in a way that works better for your client. It is about creating a journey the other side will take with you and that is achieved by asking questions. And whenever progress slows, I take a step back from the intricacies of the situation and ask general questions about football or the area. Moving away from the subject of money usually helps. When will an English team win the Champions League again? What's the housing market like in Sunderland?

The greater the information at my disposal, the more I can manoeuvre a deal in my favour. When the Premier League money first started dramatically increasing, we operated in an ocean of opportunity. However, as the sheer volume of cash accelerated beyond all anticipated levels, HMRC began to get tough with football and its finances. They reduced that ocean to a pond we could go fishing in and now there is merely a puddle.

Of course, salaries in the game these days are grossly disproportionate compared with the fans filling the stadia but football is an entertainment business and players should be viewed in the same way as movie stars or rock stars. They are, after all, primarily responsible for generating billions of pounds for the Premier League.

Taxation laws are generally more relaxed overseas. In Spain, the highest income tax level is 42 per cent; in Russia it is 13 per cent.

The basic wage never moves too far in a negotiation. For example, if you start talks asking for a hundred thousand a week, the club may offer about sixty thousand. That figure won't change massively but there are plenty of ways to create a package worth eighty thousand. From there, a hundred thousand pounds doesn't feel so far away.

When it is reported 'X player earns a hundred thousand a week', it is invariably wrong. That will be the maximum figure he could receive. His basic is more likely to be sixty thousand and it'll gross up depending on bonuses.

The basic wage is paid through the PAYE system. We developed various methods designed to increase the tax efficiency of a deal. HMRC clamped down ruthlessly but inevitably there was always a settlement. Not many of these cases went to court. And as each avenue was shut down, we looked to explore new ones. This was designed to maximise the income of our clients in order to retain their faith but, of course, it also meant we benefited financially by association, too.

Signing-on Fee

The most common one of all. This is a lump-sum figure paid early on in a player's contract, usually to help them buy a new house in the area they are moving to. The football authorities have always allowed a tax-free sum to assist in relocation which was agreed with HMRC, but it is only worth about eight thousand pounds.

Signing-on fees have become larger as the years progressed, so much so that they needed to be regulated and the rule now is that this sum is divided by the length of contract. For example, if it is a million-pound signing-on fee for a five-year contract, that is paid at a rate of two hundred thousand per year.

Loyalty Bonus

In an attempt to evolve the signing-on fee, we came up with a loyalty bonus. It replaced some of the upfront earnings with an annual payment at the end of each season. It also allowed us to reward players renegotiating contracts rather than transferring to new clubs, although signing-on fees for players extending their existing deals is now commonplace, in addition to a loyalty bonus. Neither the signing-on fee nor the loyalty bonus was originally in the PAYE system but was instead taxed separately as a bonus. That has now changed and become uniform.

We negotiated Peter Beardsley's exit from Newcastle in 1987. Chelsea and Liverpool were interested. It was a difficult negotiation made tougher still with the spotlight placed on us by incessant newspaper coverage. It stalled for a week or so due to a forty-thousand gap, which, these days, could be an appearance fee. We overcame that by creating the first loyalty payment. Newcastle initially questioned how he could receive such a payment if he was leaving but, in reality, the club were happy to accept £1.9m – a British transfer record – and reward Peter for his years of service.

Image Rights

These were created by us and our peers, initially to take into account overseas players coming to Britain with inherent corporate sponsorship deals that were hitherto not taxed by the British authorities.

In the catch-all environment engendered by HMRC over the last few years, it became essential to protect incomes that were not strictly earned in the UK but were subject to UK taxation. This was a legitimate move – tax mitigation not tax evasion. However, like all good things on this planet, it got abused and, in some cases, agents and advisers were claiming over 50 per cent of a player's salary under image rights.

Essentially, that percentage was deducted from the players PAYE and the image right then assigned across to the benefit of the club. After many years and much discussion with HMRC, the completely arbitrary figure that appears to be acceptable if applicable is now about 17 per cent.

Player Bonus Schemes

I might ask a club about their bonus schemes, where each player would get a payment depending whether they won or drew – usually more if it was away from home – scored a goal or kept a clean sheet. These days, contracts are often appearance-led. Anything that alters positively the value of that player to their books is factored in. National team appearances are rewarded, for example. Even selection for a national team squad could trigger a bonus payment because of the enhanced value that recognition delivers to the club's balance sheet. Furthermore, participation in a World Cup or European Championship is often rewarded for the same reason.

Players are more incentivised now than ever before because the overall wage bills are so big. And there is an element of one-upmanship among the players. It is harder here because inevitably everything is taxed, but abroad there are family funds that can be given charitable status. Here, HMRC just see straight through it.

If the player had a great year, starting most games and hitting his goal target, he'd see his maximum one hundred thousand a week. Otherwise, he might earn 70 per cent of that. The very best players have the leverage to negotiate more of their salary as a basic wage. That isn't usually a problem for clubs – it is more the issue of 'wage drag' – where other, less talented players at the club demand a raise because they are sitting next to someone in the dressing room earning three times as much as them.

Alexander Hleb's deal at Arsenal in 2005 was a basic wage which would be supplemented by generous appearance fees. Was that clever? Fortunately, he played quite a lot but, when he had moments out of the side, I felt our team – us and his German agents – got him a good deal but may have let him down in the way that his playing bonuses were constructed.

This practice has become commonplace and has since been expanded to a player playing for an hour, forty-five minutes or even thirty minutes. Fans should look at a manager's substitutions in that context sometimes. Why take a player off after fifty-nine minutes? Why only bring some on after the sixtieth minute? Equally, consider whether a player is declaring himself fit when he might not be because his appearance money is such a significant aspect of his weekly wage that he may feel financially obligated to play.

A different take on this is the stoppage-time substitution; sometimes, late changes are made to protect a lead in matches but, on others, a manager may want to reward a player for performing well in training by giving him a token appearance that triggers a payment in his contract.

There might be ways of making a greater payment to a player in that way rather than taking funds from the basic wage bill. If we dropped his basic wage but added on five thousand pounds each time he scored, that could appeal to a club.

A lot of clubs also pay their players based on their achievements against certain opposition. It used to be that most clubs thought Tottenham were more important to beat than Arsenal because they brought more supporters with them. It felt better beating Spurs as a result, although that has changed over the years, particularly in Wenger's time. So you could pick the six most important matches to a club and say that if the player scored in one of those games, he would get another bonus payment. That would not be offensive to them because it is incentivised money.

I don't like goal bonuses as football is a team game. Although it is great for the goalscorer, he may be too self-centred to offer scoring opportunities to fellow team-mates. This is not necessarily unprofessional, just human nature.

Employment Benefit Trusts (EBTs)

This is another method used to ease negotiations and maximise a player's income. An EBT is a scheme in which property (very often shares in the company which the employees work for, but sometimes also cash) is held on their behalf. In the past, they have been used as income tax mitigation. Legislation has narrowed this avenue sizeably, but EBTs have an entirely legitimate role in companies which operate an employee share scheme or employee ownership scheme.

The problem in football is that a player is unlikely to own a share in the club as part of his deal so, instead, a certain amount of his wages – a cash sacrifice similar to a pension scheme – would go into an EBT alongside the club's administrative staff's share options scheme. That worked well for a couple of years but HMRC attacked it as it became widespread. A small number of clubs came to a swift deal with HMRC before anyone had been punished. They must have been the subject of an investigation and immediately came to a settlement to avoid a fight.

Other clubs were stunned. Ultimately, Rangers were liquidated in October 2012 largely as a result of EBTs because they saw a potential liability of £49m from the scheme and, with everything else that was going on, it would bring the club down. HMRC scored what many described as a landmark victory in July 2017 after five Supreme Court judges unanimously found against Rangers in a tax dispute. It was determined EBTs should be considered taxable income rather than loans; the Government may now retrospectively revisit some EBT cases and similar schemes to claim against all parties involved.

Player Pensions

The PFA have played an important role here in not only getting salary sacrificed into a players' pension scheme but, pertinently, the maturity of a football player's pension is at the reduced age of 35 due to the shortness of their professional career.

Benefits in Kind (BIK)

These are very difficult to deliver in the UK. Often packages in certain territories include free housing, cars and travel back to their home country; our Revenue see that as a BIK and either disallow it or tax it at 45 per cent depending on the circumstances. To my best knowledge, clubs have still resisted getting involved with a player's mortgage. They don't do this any more but an old trick used to be throwing in a company loan for a house.

Bizarrely, a lot of players still go out and buy properties well beyond their need at that moment. Although someone might be earning a hundred thousand pounds a week, they are only – only! – taking home about fifty thousand. If you want to spend eight million on a house, that is a lot of fifty thousands. But their wages substantiate a mortgage. Even if they put down one million pounds, they may well get a seven-million-pound mortgage. I've always thought it would be useful if the clubs had a financing facility which they earned from, but everyone has been a bit reticent about that to date. Perhaps it infringes some sporting regulation somewhere but it may be something worth visiting in future.

Scouting arrangements are not unusual. A club might refer to an agent as a 'scout' in a deal, but the player is taxed differently if, instead, that club chooses to pay an agent as a scout, sourcing the player involved. In reality, if there are four hundred thousand pounds' worth of agent's fees, two hundred thousand could go to the player and two hundred thousand could go to the agent in terms of the tax remuneration. The P11D tax item says that the player will have his half taxed as a BIK and pay 45 per cent of it to HMRC. Incidentally, it might take eighteen months for the tax bill to arrive, in which time the player might have changed agents and won't be too happy. So his current agent will be charged with getting more money for that player to offset the tax bill.

As you play around the edges with all these various devices, you invariably reach a point where the club aren't prepared to make any more concessions. Let's say, for example, eighty thousand pounds a week over four years. In my mind, I think the best I can get is eighty-five thousand. When it appears as though negotiations have been exhausted, the trick is to express disappointment but then keep them waiting. I'd go to the toilet or go outside and make a phone call. When you come back in, you give the impression you are at a loss over where to go. You could keep this going for a couple of days if necessary, but obviously it depends on the situation, who you are negotiating with and the timeframe in the transfer window.

Sometimes, a bridgeable gap could be anything between five million to ten million in, say, a transaction worth in excess of thirty million. That wouldn't scare me. A twenty-million gap in a forty-million deal is a little harder to bridge! Of course, the club could pull the plug and you lose the entire deal. It is about trusting your instincts. I always like to finish a negotiation face to face for the avoidance of doubt as much as anything else.

If the negotiations are still alive and we are not too far away from touching distance, I might say, 'I'd really like to make this work so let's pause for a short while just to buy ourselves some time. Perhaps we could introduce a renegotiation clause for three years' time.'

They normally wouldn't want to do that so I'd make a counter-offer. 'OK, let's try and keep the clause but make it a three-year deal with an option for a further year. If he's played a certain percentage of games, the additional twelve-month period is automatically implemented.'

I've added security for the player albeit at the cost of a potential moving option but also ensured the player will have his contract renegotiated north – for more money – in three years' time instead of four. If the player is good, he'll play all the time so that element should take care of itself. For additional player insurance, the percentage of games required to trigger a further year would be based on periods when he was fit – so injuries would not cost him that fourth season.

So, we've changed the dynamic of a four-year deal completely. Now, the club might accept that or, most likely, they will come back and say, 'Look, Jon, let's keep it as a four-year deal but we'll increase the salary to eighty-two thousand a week . . . ' Hopefully!

I'd continue to tweak things like that. This sort of thing happens regularly in any player contract negotiation. Of course, you have to know the limitations of how far you can push things. Most contracts include healthcare – although BUPA and other private providers are taxed as a BIK – and foreign players sometimes get the concession of a return airfare for their family at the end of the season.

With the ever spiralling number of foreign players in the Premier League, agents increasingly deal with clubs from overseas. It helps to learn their customs. The southern Europeans often employ a tactic which is essentially a staged walk-out. You negotiate and they just respond with, 'No. No. No.' So you park that aspect of the deal and move to another, ask them about that and they say, 'No.' So you change tack and go back to something inoffensive where they can exert greater control – such as the commercial aspect of how you can help promote something – to calm them down and then return to the part where you really want to be. As you hit that point again, sometimes they bang the table with the palms of their hands, claim they are no longer interested and get up to leave. The first time it ever happened to me, I panicked.

But you learn it is often all an act. They get up, spend a lot of time putting things into briefcases, elongating the drama, and you let them walk towards the door before speaking. They don't really want to leave. 'Just before you go,' I'd say, 'I've got an idea.' It has got to be a real idea, though, so it is always best to keep something up your sleeve.

Very often in Latin countries, negotiations stretch endlessly into the night when really a set of hard-nosed answers with a smile could have brought matters to a conclusion much earlier in the day.

In Spain, Italy, Argentina and Brazil, I often finished a set of negotiations for some bizarre reason around midnight only then to be asked to go to dinner. You need stamina in those situations – English negotiators were always relieved to finish and go home.

On one occasion, though, I wasn't invited to dinner but the lead negotiator on the opposing side had frequently looked at my watch before telling me how nice it was, followed by a lingering pause. The message was clear: if I wanted to come back and do more business, I had to forget about buying dinner and give him the watch instead. Thankfully, he didn't like the shirt I was wearing as well.

Over time, negotiating styles worldwide have become more uniform. But in the early days it was more obligatory to engage with a region's idiosyncrasies. If, for instance, you were taking a player into Japan, very often you would have to remove your shoes and wear flip-flops as a mark of respect to the other side. There is nothing wrong with that, of course, but wearing flip-flops with a suit always unnerved me. I struggled to take myself seriously in negotiations dressed like that.

In China, it used to be obligatory that any incoming player had to pass a fitness test which included being able to run one hundred metres in under eleven seconds. We used to bring in stopwatches with a slower second hand to challenge their findings. We were respectful of their local custom but at the same time tried to work an angle.

Transfers are more complicated than they used to be. You never had payment schedules between clubs, for example. Money was transferred at the beginning and at the end of a contract, or at the beginning and at the end of the first year.

There have been managers down the years who have, either officially or unofficially, demanded a percentage of a player's transfer deal. Some managers in the Premier League have been nearly impossible to deal with unless their chosen representative is in the mix. Some of it could be innocent but, again, the possibility for something more sinister is obvious. What should happen is the buying club spends the money and the selling club should receive it, but if they want to disseminate that money to individuals who helped broker the deal, that is completely their business.

The buying club could pay a representative of theirs to bring the parties to the table – that could be an agent, a lawyer or another third party; all of those have a place. And the agents working for buyer and seller have a place. The agent for the player obviously has his own role, too.

For the most part, the selling club should be in charge of any transfer process and dictate the terms. Inevitably, if the player is coming from a part of the world where there is Third Party

Ownership – which is not allowed here but still exists else-where – it will influence proceedings. In these cases, there are ownership stakes that are intertwined with a player's career. It could be his original academy or his former club who want a seat at the table.

There are agents around the world who buy and sell players like commodities. So, they buy the economic rights of a player from Chile, for example. They transfer him to Spain, get paid and then transfer that money back to the club in Chile, where it is much easier to make it work in a different way. There would be minimal – if any – taxation around those funds. So there are conglomerates that buy players, trade them and make money. This is Third Party Ownership and it occurs in many countries around the world, and it happens because the clubs cannot afford to pay to keep their assets.

A report in August 2014 by consultants KMPG found that between 27–36 per cent of players in Portugal's Primera Liga were owned by third-party investors. The most prominent example in England was Carlos Tevez when, in 2006, he moved along with Javier Mascherano to West Ham. Their economic rights were owned by two offshore companies. Mascherano's rights were later bought out but the situation continued with Tevez.

Premier League chief executive Richard Scudamore compared it at the time to what he termed 'indentured slavery'. Tevez publicly stated he wanted to move to Manchester United, Manchester City and then Juventus in turn before returning to his first club Boca Juniors in Argentina. Tevez is a world-class player who can control his own destiny, but it's easy to see how those with a vested interest in a player's economic rights benefit from a nomadic player. So whilst third party ownership works for some, unscrupulous owners can exploit their players with repeated moves.

HMRC has deemed players' agents' income not to be a legitimate claimable expense but a Benefit in Kind, unlike entertainers' agents. So you had the peculiarity in the Beckham household that whenever Victoria went on tour or did anything commercial, her agent was expensed. Whatever costs they incurred were put against Victoria's tax. But if David's agents' fees were paid by the club in any way, they were considered BIK and therefore taxable rather than a taxable expense. In 2015, they applied the same ruling to broadcasters.

The final part – and sometimes the trickiest – of any negotiation is getting paid yourself. This is where acting selfishly in a deal can come back to bite you. A club may have to deal with you because you represent the player but that doesn't mean they can't make life decidedly difficult if they feel they have been screwed along the way. It is part of the reason why agents perpetually fight an uphill battle for recognition.

4

The World of
the Agent

Football's powerbrokers have always marginalised agents despite the vital work we do. We are an easy target; agents traditionally have no formal trade union to fight our battles and the secretive nature of our business creates a vacuum in the public consciousness that is easily filled with misconceptions and downright lies about what really goes on. The time has come for football supporters to be realistic in their examination of how clubs really operate at home and abroad. This is a cynical, cut-throat environment where the ruthless prosper and the naïve are left in the gutter.

When I got involved in the game in 1986, we tried to make success off the pitch dovetail with success on it for the very best players. So football inherently became more of a business over time. Fans want their clubs to be clean, transparent and efficient with their financial dealings because they are emotionally invested. Historically, Britain spread its mores and values across the world through empirical expansion and, as the Premier League has garnered its own worldwide influence, English supporters similarly demand that their clubs act in an unequivocally wholesome manner. (Then again, the creation of the British Empire had its ugly side – some choose not to see it).

This is a sentiment rarely repeated in the wider world. Some may call it 'delusions of grandeur'. The United Kingdom's outrage at corruption within FIFA, for example, is not reflected throughout large parts of Europe, Africa or Asia. In England, fans believe the clubs are theirs and insist on the prioritising of certain principles over pragmatism. That is just not realistic, at least not any more, because of a surge in foreign ownership and the emergence of running clubs for profit as well as points. The business of football dictates multi-billion-pound institutions, as clubs are now, are too important to be run on capricious emotion. It is how business works in the real world; boardroom success is never the product of myopic tribalism.

Therefore, to understand football transactions as they truly are – and the role agents play within them – there needs to be an acceptance of the reality of modern-day business. In the UK, we think we can trade around the world on our own terms and there is still a level of moral indignation if things are done differently. I gave a speech at the University of East London towards the end of 2014 about so-called 'corrupt' practices around the world and the way UK industry was viewing the next major territory for transactions, which was, in their estimation, Asia.

I don't think you can say that the practices of a nation or a continent are 'corrupt' without examining the historical references of where those practices originated and what they mean to the local population. If you go to a bazaar anywhere in the Middle East, or further eastwards, very often it is second nature to barter.

You start from the asking price, you negotiate down and sometimes you give back something in exchange for what you receive. I'm not saying this happens all the time but you might give somebody a watch in addition to a cash sum for something you are buying. That *modus operandi* tends to travel through the entire commercial world in Asia.

The point is different cultures have alternative business practices. A few years ago, I was invited down to a meeting with the South African Premier League to talk about possible marketing strategies. I arrived at their offices in Johannesburg and all sixteen club owners were in attendance, arranged around a vast table. Chairing proceedings was Trevor Phillips, the former FA commercial director, and he introduced me to the group. 'This is Jon Smith, who helped found the English Premier League and develop the revenue streams that are today envied the world over,' he began. 'Before we start, can we all just put our arms on the table.'

I looked around, thinking this request was a bit strange. I leant forward and put my forearms down on the table pointing away from me. Nearly everyone else pulled out a gun and placed it carefully on display.

'What the hell is going on?' I asked Trevor.

'Don't worry, it's a custom here – we are all friends now,' he replied.

It was a gesture telling me I was in a friendly environment – that there were no hidden dangers – but you don't half feel the opposite when confronted with all that weaponry. Thankfully, none of them were pointing at me this time.

In the UK, we take it for granted that you may take a client or associate out for lunch. I might be talking to you but I think your mate next to you is quite important. They could be your friend, your wife or your PA but the important point is that they may be able to bend your ear when I'm not around. So I am going to 'look after' this potentially influential person next to you as well as you.

In other parts of the world you have to 'look after' that person in a different way. That means those people sometimes become a third party in a deal that is no longer a one-to-one operation which, in turn, gives rise to the line of thinking that money is being passed nefariously between parties to deflect the fact a transaction has taken place between person A and person B. That model could be applied to a deal for goods, it could be services, or it could be footballers. Very often, senior officials at clubs worldwide have to be paid for the release of the player, effectively becoming the third party in a deal between two clubs.

Now, who are we to question the validity of that third person's position? In other words, he might be a chairman who has funded that club out of his own pocket or out of his grandmother's savings for many years and he is suddenly thinking, 'OK, I've now got a winner on my hands.' Player X is leaving his club for three million pounds. He might never have seen three million pounds in his life. So he could put two million into the club and take one million for himself.

In pure financial terms, that could technically constitute third-party ownership (TPO) because he is benefiting personally from the transaction. The Football Association abhors TPO for many reasons – primarily because they think it is corrupt – and consequently they have focused in recent years on closing loopholes in a strictly regulated path. In South America, though, third-party ownership is huge; in Asia, multi-party dealings are commonplace;

in eastern Europe, multi-party ownership causes a chaotic fusion in deals given the plethora of people involved in a transaction.

The negative – and not uncommon – view of agents is that we are an unwelcome addition to the table, swelling these numbers to an unworkable level and operating solely for our own financial gain and often to the detriment of the others involved. People don't like the idea of agents taking a cut because it diverts funds away from buying more players, improving facilities or potentially lowering ticket prices. But these amounts are relatively small when considering the overall turnover of even an average Premier League club nowadays, especially with the billions coming in from television companies.

Football is a business and, in business, people are paid to get things done. First Artist played a key role in helping Ken Bates evolve Chelsea in the 1990s. We helped to bring in Gianfranco Zola, Roberto di Matteo, Celestine Babayaro, Ruud Gullit and Petr Cech through European contacts the club could not otherwise call upon. In the cases of Babayaro and Cech, we presented the opportunity to them first because we had a good relationship with the club. Hardly unhelpful, is it? We were welcomed into football by most people in the game and that only changed when we began fighting more robustly for players' rights.

Football transactions are conducted through the unforgiving prism of a business-savvy mind-set now. The parochial days of a manager of one club sitting down with a player from another to discuss a transfer over a beer are long gone. People have to get over themselves.

Moan at the manager if his tactics are bad, complain to the board if the financial management is poor but don't start nit-picking at people who are making a living by carving out a niche and max-imising their expertise. Because that is life. That is what happens in every single industry and I don't see football as any different. And while critics argue agents' fees are monies going out of the game, where are directors' wages going? Are they taken out of the game?

I am one of the people largely responsible for the Premier League existing in the form it does today. That's because not only were we there at the outset, but we brought in the stars that made it the global commercial entity it is now. The top agents facilitated football's trans-formation into a multi-billion-pound industry. So why shouldn't we be paid accordingly? People are happy for, say, Robert Elstone, the CEO at Everton, to receive a decent salary. Robert does a very good job and nobody cares what he earns. But if I made half a million on a deal bringing a great player into Swansea, people would say that is money going out of the game. In fact, there is no difference.

It is understandable that people want greater transparency but don't be fooled into thinking the figures listed by clubs as agents' fees is the full story. It's nowhere near. The regulations as they stand provide a framework that is restrictive. If they are only allowed to pay 5 per cent to an agent but somebody in Milan wants 10 per cent, you have to find ways to structure that properly. And they do. There are different forms of contracts put in place for that agency with the football club which in fact comprises various services. Some of it may be hospitality or scouting-re-lated. I think most reputable agents would be happier to have total transparency. I wouldn't mind. I have earned one-and-a-half million pounds from a deal. So what? I'm paying tax on it. The fact that I have done well is nothing to be ashamed of, especially given the intense rivalry among agents.

Relationships between the main agents are better today. Historically, there were partnerships between English agents and their counterparts in Europe. To a degree, they still exist, although latterly foreign agents are increasingly dealing directly with English clubs – Jorge Mendes and Mino Raiola are prime modern-day examples. English agents reciprocate by dealing with clubs around the world rather than using local partners.

I was probably the first agent to create wraparound lifestyle management for a player. The leading football agencies cater for every aspect of a player's life, particularly when a foreign player first arrives in England. I developed a network of contacts able to facilitate any eventuality. And we did everything for them: if they wanted to go to the cinema in, say, Leeds, players could phone a 24-hour helpline run by First Artist exclusively for their benefit, we would pay for the tickets and leave them at the box office to be picked up. They didn't have to lift a finger.

Nowadays, that is commonplace for a player of any meaningful repute. Agents have to go clubbing with them, look after their families, organise holidays for them and much more. The line I always used to use was: 'You never have to pay full price for anything when you join First Artist because we're a Jewish agency and nobody here pays retail!' And I embellished my income all the way down the line by sharing in their financial and support services. Whether it was legal advice, housing, personal services or anything a player needed, I earned a cut from using a certain supplier. Every time I gave a player to a certain estate agent and they bought a house, I would split that estate agent's commission with him for bringing in the business. I had a deal with a guy who imported Porsches. This was in the days prior to tighter import/

export regulations but, if I could make it worth his while bringing in, say, three cars each costing eighty thousand pounds, I'd split his 20 per cent commission with him. That's twenty-four thousand pounds for putting him in touch with three clients. I must say, I always felt it correct and prudent to tell the client and offer to split that money with them, which I often did.

An agent will have to identify clientele through connections, youth games, coaches or scouts. They will then spend a lot of time maintaining the well-being of that individual, both financially and in their everyday life. Today, it is fairly normal practice for agents to pay potential clients advance monies and, in some instances, even support the family financially, sometimes involving a parent of the player as part of the management team.

Of course, it can be a lucrative existence but also an unforgiving one; current regulations stipulate you can only sign a player as your client for two years. It is quite possible that, during the course of your player's three-, four- or five-year contract you will lose him before your moment arrives to secure him a new deal and yourself a pay day. Now, remember, you might have bought him a house at the front end of your contract so it is necessary to build in security on your investment.

In many cases, the outstanding commission, normally paid over the length of the contract in equal instalments, is lost at the point at which the client leaves you. Agents have very few grounds for appeal. You can only guard against this loss of earnings by doing the best job possible. Most clients are happy to stay if you maintain professional standards but it is inevitable some will have their heads turned by a mysterious stranger turning up with a gold Rolex or fifty thousand in cash for their family. It happens a lot. When you are a teenager uncertain of your future in the game – and especially one from a deprived background – the allure is obvious.

You build a relationship by developing a strategy to grow his career. Occasionally, you protect him from the media. At other times, you place him in the media; it is essential agents are *au fait* with social media but also harbour contacts at Sky Sports, BT Sport, ITV, BBC, the print media and digital platforms. Inside knowledge is power. Charlie Sale's gossip column is one of the best and read throughout the industry, often acting as a notice board for the key participants.

Keeping players out of the press is troublesome. I've had to dig a player out of the media a few times. It is usually the Sunday papers that deliver the most damaging blows. If you have no idea it's coming and they call you for comment at 6 p.m. on Saturday evening, all you can do is soften the impact by negotiating a headline and strapline. Sometimes you do that by giving the player the right to respond in the form of an exclusive interview; the newspaper is happy because their story gets a great follow-up and, in return, we get the chance to begin wrestling back control of the agenda regarding that individual.

If you get wind of something they are planning early in the week, you have a chance to do something about it. Good journalists will accept a trade-off of stories. If he doesn't print what he has, I'll give him something else. Normally with some, though, the trade-off is three to one in his favour! But as long as I delivered, he stayed true to his word.

We got Ruud Gullit the Newcastle job after Kenny Dalglish left in 1998. The papers all thought he was going somewhere down south and I let that circulate because negotiations were at a delicate stage. The day before the deal was due to be confirmed, the papers caught up but I wanted to brief a certain journalist first. I told him what was happening and dropped in that the deal almost collapsed because Ruud's long-term partner, Estelle, really didn't want to go there. The following day, Ruud came to me and said, 'I've reconciled everything with my wife now but, if it comes out that she was against me going to Newcastle, the deal is off.'

I phoned him and asked him to pull it. He said he'd already filed the story to his sports desk. Ruud was a huge public figure at the time and most journalists wouldn't have pulled it but, after an hour's persuasion, he did. Ruud signed his contract and the rest is history. Actually, in my opinion, she ended up being the reason the whole thing didn't work because she insisted on him flying back three days a week to Holland. And it is no coincidence that, after he left St James's Park, he didn't take another management job for five years. But the whole episode would never have happened at all had that original story run.

I've also used the media to my advantage. There was a journalist I never liked to deal with – it would seem unedifying to name him here – but I leaked to him through a writer I did like that we were negotiating a deal to take a player to Southampton. He wrote a story which was picked up and all the focus shifted to the south coast. But, in fact, we were in discussions with Newcastle. Talks progressed well because we were able to discuss the deal without any reporters sniffing around. That is where people should have a degree of sympathy with sports journalists – many argue their job is simply to report the news but, often, they are being manipulated just like many people are in a transfer. The bottom line is that it has to benefit your player because that's the job.

I tried to fill the role of the player's friend and senior adviser who was always to be relied upon in any hour of need. They had their mates and some had hangers-on but generally I stayed out of their lives, aside from the odd dinner together or a trip to watch a game. But they knew that the moment something went wrong, I was the one they called. Players are always told when they get into trouble with the law, the first call has to be to an agent and nobody else. We'll sort the rest.

When Nwankwo Kanu first arrived at Arsenal in February 1999, he was 23 years old and clearly a great talent but needed support off the pitch. He had a hole in his heart and, due to concerns about his long-term fitness, he was only on a temporary deal.

He started superbly and, within six months, he wrote his name into the club's folklore with a magnificent hat-trick against Chelsea at Stamford Bridge as Arsenal came from 2-0 down with fifteen minutes left to win 3-2. The winning goal was unforgettable. He won the ball from Albert Ferrer, beat goalkeeper Ed de Goey – who came out of his box virtually to the touchline – and despite the tightest of angles, he curled a shot past two players and into the top corner.

Fans were raving about Kanu, and his agent, Frank Sedoc, saw his chance to play hardball over a longer contract. Unbelievably, these negotiations ran on for almost three months. I used to see Arsène at the training ground and it became a standing joke. 'How's Frank?' he'd ask me. 'Has he found any new ways of Kanu getting more money from us this week?'

Frank was certainly creative in his demands. I really liked Frank but you had to love Kanu. Janine, my wife, and I loaned him our housekeeper Carol when he moved just down the road from us.

After six months, we told him Carol couldn't look after his place for ever. She was very fond of him and always enjoyed his company – as did Andrea, the interior designer we found to help him make his house a home – but it was only ever a temporary arrangement.

One day I got a call from Kanu at my office. 'Hey Jon, I've got a cleaner.'

Finally.

'Would you like to come over on your way home and see him?'

I agreed, although I couldn't fathom why a cleaner would still be at his place that late in the day. I was held up in traffic and didn't get there until 7.30 p.m., thinking the journey would be wasted as the cleaner would obviously have left. Kanu opened the door with a big grin. 'Hi, Jon! Come and see my cleaner.' He pointed to the hall cupboard.

My mind momentarily darted to the history of slavery in Nigeria. I walked slowly towards the door, starting to prioritise the plethora of calls I was going to have to make if the worst-case scenario played out. He opened the door to reveal a Henry vacuum cleaner complete with all the attachments. We both collapsed laughing and shared a big hug.

As I remember it, he took me out on to his terrace and, as we began talking about the future, he started playing keepy-uppy with a tin can on one foot and then the other. I was mesmerised by his skill. Try it at home – it's virtually impossible.

We acted for Arsenal in the Kanu deal and it's often more fun representing a club, and nowadays more profitable, too. The proposed 3 per cent cap of a player's package does not apply when acting on behalf of a club. In that situation, a deal can often produce a fee of up to 10 per cent.

There are exceptions, though, Tottenham being one. Daniel Levy will often ask you to rebate some of your commission by buying a box at White Hart Lane. I'm an Arsenal fan yet the irony is I see more games at Tottenham thanks to Daniel. He is happy to do it because he often tells me he makes his money back through what we spend on catering when we're at White Hart Lane. He doesn't miss a trick.

When Peter Beardsley moved to Liverpool in 1987, it dragged on for weeks. The deal was front- and back-page news because it involved a record British transfer fee − £1.9m − and during that process, a twenty-three-year-old woman circulated a story to the newspapers that she'd had a liaison with Peter, who was married at the time. He swore to me it wasn't true. But the problem we had was that, if she told her story, some people would want to believe it. No matter whether such allegations are based in any truth whatsoever, mud sticks to a degree. Nobody can give back the pound of flesh taken.

The *Sunday People* planned to run it. We got a heads-up a few days before publication and managed to dilute its strength. She still got paid − presumably her biggest motivation for doing it − but we took control of the story. Instead of alleging an affair, she claimed they 'often chatted for long periods at the petrol station where I worked . . . he would give me a lift home but in the one-and-a-half years we have been friends, there has been nothing more than that to it'. We added the information − which was true − that she had a steady boyfriend who was supposedly a club bouncer − why is that so often the case in a kiss-and-tell story? − and unconcerned by the rumours surrounding Peter.

With Bobby Robson's affair, there was nothing we could do. It was just after the 1990 World Cup and he was a national hero after England got to the semi-finals, where they were knocked out on penalties by West Germany. I was close to Bobby and his wife Elsie but it ran for three or four weeks and all I was able to do was just prepare them for what was coming. It doesn't sound like much but when you have the chance to brace yourself for the storm ahead, you cope with it a little better. Seeing something in black and white for the first time is horrible, so I tried to soften the blow and change some of the pagination. If he was front-page news, I'd try to reduce the exposé on page one and move it to page five instead.

Agents perform an all-encompassing service and, quite unlike the common perception of us holding players and clubs to ransom – again, that does sometimes happen but nowhere near as often as is made out – actually getting paid is often difficult. In 2006, I had the idea of creating an agents' association called the Association of Football Agents (AFA), which sports lawyer Mel Stein helped me bring into practice, designed to bring some sort of unity to football agents in England and achieve a seat at the table for this important sector of football. There is also a European version – the EFA – which brings us together more. Today, I hope we bring uniformity to our dealings and strength in opposing the proposed 3 per cent cap on agents' fees recommended by the FA and others around the world, as in most instances the norm has settled at 5 per cent. The AFA is now in negotiation with various stakeholders about self-regulation.

Getting paid is not as tough as it was in previous years at the highest level but, in the lower divisions, there are disputes all the time. Agents get very little protection. The FA protects the clubs; the PFA protects the players. Agents are protected by no one. We did a deal in Saudi Arabia for a player and we just didn't get paid. The player also had a period of time when his wages did not arrive. We took the whole thing to FIFA where it rumbled on for three years, eventually ending up in the Court of Arbitration for Sport in Zurich. The player got his money and we lost. Why? Because the original contract was in the name of First Artist, not the individual agent, and the licence only supported the latter, not a company. So we originated and completed the deal, but the guy in Saudi Arabia saw a way out of paying us and FIFA and the system sided with him.

Former FIFA president Sepp Blatter concluded the process of licensing agents many years ago with a simple greeting: 'Welcome to the football family.' But we have never truly been invited in as an equal with the game's other stakeholders.

The relationship is similar with the FA. If a club decided they weren't going to pay an agent because they couldn't afford to – it seemed the FA would do nothing. That stance is disappointing because they are the licensing authority that is happy to police and discipline but not protect us. The AFA board discussed one such incident when an agent instigated a statutory demand against a club for lack of payment. It was only when that order started to roll that the club settled the debt. Surely that is not the way business should be conducted if you are a member of a 'football family'.

Technically, a FIFA-licensed agent had their authority to transact so they would be protected. But FIFA gave it up in February 2015? Why? Because it was a stick of dynamite to them. Every time a transaction went wrong, they had to adjudicate and most of the people who sat on that panel didn't have a clue what shape a football was, let alone understand the nuances of a deal. There were issues raised all around the world, with FIFA saying, 'We don't want to be part of this,' so they handed responsibility back to the national associations and deregulated the industry. All the cases that were waiting to be heard simply never were. There were so many people not being paid globally and they couldn't handle it.

You do a deal in, say, Turkey now – and we are talking about some of the top clubs – and you have to be paid as soon as the transaction is completed otherwise it can become extremely tough to get what's rightfully yours. And that's Turkey, who are seeking entry to the European Union!

In certain countries around the world, you have to be very strong-minded and dogmatic. The player's contract is protected by FIFA, so you know he is all right. As an agent, you have no protection whatsoever. Welcome to the family of football! First Artist has never encountered too much of this sort of treatment because we were quite powerful – with a global reach – so there was no point in trying to beat us up. But we were still very cautious about working in certain territories, especially behind the Iron Curtain in the post-Mikhail Gorbachev era. Unfortunately, a lot of smaller agents haven't got a prayer of being paid in South America if they are dealing down there.

The best way you can guard against your security being diminished is to ensure the player stands with you. If he says he won't sign a contract until his agent gets their money, then the club have little option but to honour the agreement. And let's not forget that's what it is – honouring the agreement. Nothing more. One of the ways to do it is to link your payment to one to his family members – parent, brother etc. That ingratiates you to the player because he won't want his family member to be out of pocket. So effectively an agent says to a player, 'You sign a contract with me to represent you, and I will give 30 per cent of my earnings to your father.' It might sound unsavoury but, when there is no protection from any governing body, you have to play every card available to you.

These days, you even have to give the payment to the player up front for signing with you, whether that's cash, a gold Rolex, a car or perhaps a house. Then you may have to build into the contract that when you negotiate his new deal, you reward whichever relative he wants to receive a cut of that fee. Of course, this may be a way, potentially, of the player receiving more money if he has a prior agreement with the family member, as he is earning from your commission.

There are plenty of poor agents or intermediaries, but I have nothing but praise for some of the guys who I'd like to think, alongside First Artist, have contributed sizeably to the success of English football over the years – namely Jonathan Barnett, Mel Stein, Mick McGuire, Leon Angel, Rob Segal, Wasserman Media Group members such as Fahri Ecvet and Struan Marshall, Neil Fewings, Andy Evans, Barry Silkman, Steve Kutner, Rachel Anderson, and Jerome Anderson (my partner a long time ago).

Sometimes, rivalry is driven by the family. Danny Welbeck's brothers were out there doing everything they could to align themselves to agents to help them when he was doing well at Manchester United. After a series of meetings with a variety of agents, they must have pooled an enormous amount of information before deciding to keep his representation in the family!

A similar situation occurred some years earlier with Bobby Zamora and his family, although on that occasion they ended up employing us and we facilitated his move from Brighton to Tottenham. But, suddenly, Daniel Levy decided he didn't like him – he just felt Bobby wasn't the right fit – and wanted to sell. Zamora's father got irate with me and thought I should have given his son more protection but when a club decides they don't want you, it is best to just go because otherwise you end up kicking a ball with the reserves from Monday to Friday. But, of course, we got the blame and then every other agent stuck the boot in. We ended up settling his contract and he left us. Agents often get the blame when a club wants to get rid of a player and that's fine – that's what we are there for – and if Bobby's family thought we had played the wrong card by taking him to Spurs then I guess they had every right to remove him from us.

The AFA has worked hard to bring people together under one banner to fight for greater representation and unity but the influx of intermediaries has only deepened football's moral malaise.

5

Moral Maze

Football moves human beings around the world. It is human trade. Some years ago, you might have considered it slave trading because people were taken from one employ to another for money. Of course, with the wages players earn nowadays, you certainly can't call them slaves but it has a strangely compromised humanitarian feel to it, even now, especially when you are taking African players out of their homeland. They are not the biggest earners and often repatriate a large percentage of their income back to their families. They are on contracts which, fortunately thanks to the Professional Footballers' Association and Jean-Marc Bosman, have been somewhat protected over the years. But they are still at the whim of a serious injury, a manager who views them negatively or a change in tactics that doesn't work for them. At that point, they can be very quickly dumped out of a club, away from a support network and find themselves at the mercy of middlemen who could potentially take them to places they shouldn't be going to in transactions they should not be a part of.

In the wider context of a global migrant crisis and refugees dying in their desperate search for a better life, the prospect of a

Premier League club trying to take advantage of a young African kid shames football. As, from the other side, does a family from a war-torn region turning down three million a year for their boy because they have read the going rate in the Premier League is four million. That happens and I find it astonishing. The levels of exploitation there are among the most shocking I have ever seen.

In the middle of all this, an agent is trying to reconcile the morality of those two positions to do the best by everyone and, yes, ensure he or she is also reimbursed for their services. It is a complex moral dilemma and one I still struggle to resolve; the idea that agents are the only ethically questionable influence on a deal is nonsense.

Not all agents are decent people. No chicken farm produces only good eggs. I have always tried to do business the right way but often my actions come down to a moral judgement, balancing what is right for my client and what is right for me.

We had originally been involved in the deal taking Mikael Forsell to Chelsea in 1998. We'd acted on behalf of Chelsea with Vincenzo Morabitto – a major Italian agent in the 1990s – representing Forsell. However, because we had brought him to English football and liked him as a player, we stayed very close over the ensuing period at Stamford Bridge. Things hadn't worked out for him on the pitch so, in 2004, he went on loan to Birmingham and was a complete hero. But the following year he suffered the second serious knee injury of his career and doubts resurfaced about his ability. Once he was fit again, I had a conversation with José Mourinho, then in his first stint as Chelsea boss, who told me he knew how injuries like this affected players and Forsell couldn't be relied upon to perform at the highest level any more. José told us to find him another club. We circulated his availability and there were two clubs wanting to sign him on a permanent deal: Everton and Birmingham. Everton made all the running. We were quite keen for him to go because it was a good move for his career. The fee was in excess of two million and our commission would have been about two hundred thousand pounds.

Then we got a call from Birmingham co-owner David Sullivan. He told me, 'We love Mikael here. We really want him back. Not only will I offer Mikael more wages to match what he was on at Chelsea, I'll pay you a commission of five hundred thousand all up front, immediately, to make the deal happen.'

I hate to say it but that does focus your mind. The fact that Mikael's financial position was stronger was the important aspect but obviously we would bank half a million in five minutes, which made it a good move for me, too. That just left the football bit . . . did Mikael want to go there? Did Steve Bruce, the manager at St Andrew's back then, want him? We could have pushed him to Birmingham for our half a million but instead told him only to go there if the deal was right for him. There are ways of presenting these choices to a player and perhaps it is in the process of selecting this information that some people question an agent's integrity but, again, this exists in all walks of life. Presidents and prime ministers are given information deemed to be of the greatest significance by their advisers. Influencing the final decision is sometimes inevitable, subconsciously or otherwise – especially if financial gain is involved – but we tried to present the situation to Mikael as plainly as possible.

We walked a line – and we certainly could have pushed him a lot harder had we put our own interests first. Of course we wanted the deal to happen but Mikael had to be happy in football, financial and aesthetic terms. He discussed it with Steve, who told him the team's tactical plan would play to his strengths and he would be an important player. He agreed terms and we did the deal. It was the money that turned all our heads initially, but it had to be right for him on the pitch, too. And it should be pointed out that while some agents might push their client down a certain path, don't forget there are a lot of players happy just to take the money rather than strive to better themselves.

Money is often a factor and I'd be lying if I said it wasn't. But it is not the sole dictator of how you position yourself in a deal. We were being retained by Leicester City when they tried to sign Esteban Cambiasso from Inter Milan in 2014. His brother, Federico, was in the deal representing Esteban and he nearly screwed it up so many times by making ridiculous demands, usually for more commission. It was such a badly handled deal. Fortunately, we had a good line into Leicester's Thai owners at that time through the club chairman Sir Dave Richards, former chairman of the Premier League, whom I'd known for a hundred years. I could throw a few questions to him about exactly where we were going to park Federico, who had become a real irritant, threatening to ruin his brother's next career move. We worked ways around how we could pay him – it was all legal, although obviously it was up to him if he paid tax on his final amount – and in the end we swallowed half of our commission to get that done. We ended up with a hundred thousand. That was hard work, months of it, but we really wanted Cambiasso at Leicester.

Speaking altruistically, we felt he was what they needed and the manager and coaching staff were so desperate to make it happen.

The Thai owners were only going to put in so much money that summer and he was an attainable player – a Champions League winner no less – and the agent was jeopardising everything by trawling him around the world in search of more money. If we could step in and manage him, it would get over the line and this was one of those times when we could make a concession to seal the deal. Ultimately, we were right about the impact Cambiasso would have as he was their star player that season and helped them avoid relegation.

We always thought Andros Townsend was great, too. He was endlessly going out on loan and we just couldn't find him the first-team place at a profiled club that he deserved. It was getting silly, really. He had more loans on his record than NatWest. In 2013, Queens Park Rangers came in for him on deadline day and that seemed perfect because it was a well-known London club where he would play every game. The problem was Aston Villa wanted him, too, and they were offering a loan fee structured in a way that meant we would earn more if he went to Villa Park. He was in limbo for a while, although never to the extent Peter Odemwingie was on the same day; that farcical situation, where he parked his car outside Loftus Road thinking a move from West Brom was inevitable only for the deal to collapse, is something no agent should ever let happen to his client, whatever the misfortune involved.

As the clock ticked towards the deadline, we decided to break the deadlock. QPR wouldn't match Villa's terms with us so we decided to swallow a chunk of our commission – something in the region of eighty thousand pounds – as Rangers was the best move for him. We completed the paperwork with about forty minutes left and Andros, who had been sitting in my office concerned for much of the evening, was hugely relieved. We tried to convey a sense of calm and purpose as we felt confident throughout the process that we were going to make this transaction but you can never be certain, especially on deadline day. Then QPR manager Harry Redknapp kept telling us, 'I'll show him how to get into the England team,' and eventually he got there. We were delighted and I'm glad it happened because it would not have felt right to deny Andros that opportunity for the sake of eighty thousand pounds.

I always refer to the road haulage industry when looking at the business of football. I am sure that most of the transactions completed by the road haulage association members are legitimate. They have to go through trade and tariff barriers and do whatever is necessary to get their goods into stores all over the world. In some cases, I'm assuming, there are some rules and regulations that aren't strictly adhered to. We are also moving human beings across borders and football operates within rules a little like import and export tariffs – there are regulations that exist as dictated by FIFA or UEFA and also that particular country's football association.

Aston Villa wanted to sign midfielder Sasa Curcic in 1996. He had been at Bolton that season but we couldn't get him a work permit because he hadn't played enough games for Yugoslavia. We had to find a way around it. Around that time he was keen to settle down, so we pointed out to him that an English wife would be the answer. Now, an agent's job often strays into something akin to a fixer. The best ones make things happen. So we set about making sure he had an active social life and mixed with a lot of English girls. Sure enough it worked. He met a lovely girl. They got on really well from the start. She was very attractive and engaging company. Things moved on and before long they were engaged, and shortly afterwards they got married at Marylebone Register Office at 12.30 p.m. on 17 March 1997. Me, Phil and a couple of First Artist staff were witnesses, along with Sasa's parents. We were so pleased for him and his new wife. They seemed very much in love for the few weeks they were married.

And of course the FA were happy too and, within a week, the deal was done. We made about £250,000. Sadly, the marriage lasted less than a year but that seems to be the national average these days.

Aberdeen wanted to sign Illiyan Kiryakov from a small club in Bulgaria by the name of Etar Veliko Tarnovo in 1995. Kiryakov was a defender whose career had taken in spells at more established sides including Deportivo de La Coruña in Spain and CSKA Sofia in his home country.

However, Bulgaria were not members of the European Union and so we were unable to obtain a work permit despite the fact he had represented his country at the 1994 World Cup. Kiryakov was desperate to move to the UK, so much so that he agreed to the circuitous route we created to get him here. We found him a club in Cyprus – Anorthosis Famagusta – where we could effectively place him in a holding pattern until he qualified for an EU passport. He served his time there – playing 19 league games – before moving to Aberdeen in 1996.

Most football clubs are actually run quite well, believe it or not. In the lower leagues, where it is really tough, they are making their pennies stretch. If there are a few bonuses here and there for people, I don't see that as a problem. I don't see the indigenous payments being made to facilitators across the globe as a problem either.

Look at the corporate existence of a football club. These clubs are now businesses run as such, not necessarily for the emotional shareholder. The emotional shareholder is the fan and, yes, he pays everyone's wages but so do television, sponsors, sub-sponsors, hospitality companies and anyone else who contributes to that club's financial well-being. David Sullivan and David Gold were understandably frustrated that West Ham's original deal to move to the Olympic Stadium from Upton Park excluded much of the in-house catering income – it is a much underestimated revenue stream.

Many clubs in the lower leagues will only make a profit year-on-year if they sell players. Clubs like Dagenham & Redbridge live for that purpose. Even at a higher level, Watford got into the Premier League in 2015 because Giampaolo Pozzo used the ownership of his clubs to move players around so that the group has a successful financial turnover. Nobody has really pointed the finger and said 'that's wrong'. But it is no different to clubs doing multi-party deals abroad.

At every single level of a club, there is what I call 'corporate support activity'. Top clubs have a Player Liaison Officer (PLO) who, in most instances, will initially be responsible for housing the inbound player. I would hazard an educated guess that a few will have a deal with a local estate agent. The estate agent could give them preferential treatment on the best properties and there may then be a reward to the PLO for helping the estate agent win that business.

Now – how moral are we going to be? Technically that is incorrect, you shouldn't do it. But in any other walk of life, if you have one person offering the other a part of a transaction, they would be rewarded. It may be lunches, dinner, a golfing weekend in Scotland. Where's the demarcation line? What is acceptable?

A golfing weekend in Scotland is going to cost about £1,500 with hotels, flights and food. If that person was just given £1,500 instead of the golf holiday, is that wrong? HMRC, of course, should be informed of a Benefit in Kind or, if cash exchanged hands, tax should be paid on it. It is easier for him to be given a golfing trip because it is more difficult for HMRC to collect on it, but technically he should inform them.

The player may share in this corporate support activity. He may hit it off with the PLO; they may go golfing together. Similarly, he could share it with his staff. Instead of golf, it could be three cases of champagne. He's not going to drink it all. The point I'm making is seeking reward in this way is human nature. There is huge money sloshing around in football and whoever is immersed in that world is going to think, I'd like a bit of that.

It is wrong? By the law of the written word, yes. But questioning the morality of conducting deals in a certain way involving third parties or agents is a completely outmoded and backward way of thinking. Try and do a deal in Asia – you have to pay a variety of people to facilitate anything meaningful. People say that is corruption. It isn't; it is just their way of doing things. Who says they are wrong and we are right?

I believe in capitalism but who says that's right? Communism works somewhere for someone. Some countries were better under the iron rule of a government. I'm not saying that is right, but it's life.

When the FA, FIFA, UEFA or anyone else espouse the need for change to transfer rules it is merely camouflage masking their biggest failing – these authorities cannot do anything about it. This rhetoric is scenery for the public. Of course, the cleaning lady shouldn't receive a kickback because she buys her products from a certain retailer, which chooses to thank her in the form of a Christmas bonus. But it's life. Are the FA going to stamp all over that? Of course not, but there are some obvious places they can look. For starters, they could examine the number of deals transacted by one agent on behalf of a football club. That agent could be supremely professional but it would be naïve to consider it inconceivable there might be more Machiavellian reasons in play. It is a lot easier for money to go missing in that kind of relationship. People will argue, of course, that these larger issues do not make the idea of a Christmas bonus right. But what is right? There is a difference between a PLO receiving a 'thank you' from an estate agent and getting a house themselves. Judgement is by degree. Of course, people feel differently about footballers and clubs because they feel a sense of ownership. But for the amount of business top agents generate for Premier League football, the amount we earn is perfectly proportionate. We have developed and marketed a product that TV companies now deem to be worth in excess of eight billion pounds. These are decisions you make in life and nobody can say they have done everything strictly right by their fellow man. I am a humanitarian but I am still human. And humans are a flawed creation.

On one of my many hotel visits, I was hanging up my stuff and I looked in a drawer. Usually I don't bother as whatever I put there I invariably leave behind, but on this occasion someone else had done just that. At the back of the drawer was two thousand pounds in cash. Now, what would you do? Morally, you should go down to the hotel and give it to them. What are they going to do about it? Are they going to check back with the previous guests of that room? Or are they going to keep it themselves?

I was there for five days. I put it in my safe and decided if anyone came to claim it, I would give it them immediately. On the morning of my departure, nobody had turned up. So I took it home. To make myself feel better, I gave five hundred to charity.

Morally, I was wrong. But I challenge anybody in that same situation today to give that money back to the hotel. Perhaps a few people would, but I didn't. Ultimately, my belief was that the hotel would split it amongst themselves. It would never go back to the person who owned it and also, if somebody had not retraced their steps looking for two thousand in cash, the chances are they are the type of person whose life would not be affected by losing it. I looked upon it as my lucky day.

There will be people reading this muttering the worst about me under their breath. I get that. You can argue it is an inherently cynical view of the world that denies the prospect of human beings evolving past the point of compromised ethics. Perhaps I have become a product of the football world I helped to create.

After all, some agents can also make deals extraordinarily difficult for themselves and their client. We negotiated Gabriele Angella's loan move from Watford to Queens Park Rangers in the summer of 2015. All the Watford players had a clause written into their contracts that they would receive a bonus if they avoided relegation in the 2015–16 season. It was August 2015. Watford had played three Premier League games and Angella hadn't been on the pitch for a single minute. But before he would agree to go to QPR, the question of his staying-up bonus reared its head. It was worth a lot of money. 'Nice try' I thought. But the deal was starting to stall, so we had to work hard to find a way to deal with this. It wasn't easy, but we did it.

Players can be equally precocious. There was a deal once where a lengthy negotiation to bring a Dutch player to Sheffield

Wednesday from a prominent European club had finally reached a breakthrough. The player said he was going to get the train from Germany rather than fly. His agent was confused.

'Why don't you just fly?' he asked.

'Because I want to bring my dog with me.'

'Um, you know that there is a quarantine period, so he won't be able to live with you.'

'What?' said the player, with a mixture of shock and exasperation.

'You can't just bring an animal into the UK. He'll be quarantined for six to nine months. You can visit him every day but that'll be it.'

'Right,' said the player. 'The deal is off.'

He put the phone down and that was that.

In football, we walk a very thin, watery line and occasionally it evaporates. Deals are extremely complex situations with a multitude of diverging interests an agent is supposed to pull together so everyone leaves happy while conforming to reasonable moral standards. And in the midst of all of it, you are trying to make a living.

One of my hardest lessons in life was working out how I teach my children to behave. My parents brought me up to be nice and always do the right thing. At 64 years of age, I have grown to be cynical. I have grown to question my upbringing, whether Noah existed and God created the world. There is a lot of scientific evidence to the contrary but I still believe in God. He just isn't represented by religion for me. I believe in doing the right thing. I have told my kids, Ross and Scott, 'You have to do what is right. But sometimes you have to do what is necessary.' Being just is its own reward for your conscience but there is precious little recompense from the outside world. Maybe I shouldn't need the latter.

I look at my life and think I've done a lot of things right that I got kicked in the backside for. I've been successful but, if I had been even more ruthless, I would have earned a lot more money, without doubt.

Business teaches you these lessons. And people have to view football through the prism of business now. Club chairmen and chief executives live or die by their ability to conduct transfers successfully. A manager's career is so often defined by the players they are able to sign and sell. Agents smooth that process for everyone in a high-stakes poker game where people are not afraid to bend the rules to win.

You have to learn how to read people and I'm pretty good at it now. If you are too nice at the first meeting with someone, a shrewd operator will take advantage of you from day one. If you are dealing with Dimitri in the Ukraine, you are immediately respectful and on guard.

If they show me any weakness or vulnerability, I'll know where I'm going in a deal. I understand people might find that unpleasant but this book is supposed to be about real life. I've not had the success I've had by being altruistic all the time. I think I am a good bloke and believe I have done a lot of good work but I've had to provide for my family. And that is the biggest motivation of all – not the money – although obviously the two are connected. I don't chase money for money's sake. I want to provide for my family and their families. That's my *raison d'être*.

Now I've got a comfortable place in life, I can be even more forgiving in a transaction. I have a reputation for smiling through deals and being very calm but I have always known what I wanted. The issue for many is whether you can get what you want while playing by the rules. An agent has to operate within certain confines as determined by the football authorities. But the reality of the world says they can't, because a situation will come along where there are two or three clubs that want a player and you have to step outside those parameters to get a deal done.

We were involved in a situation with the midfielder Thomas Gravesen made unusual by the involvement of our offices across Europe. Gravesen was going from Real Madrid to Celtic. My London office was acting for the buying club, the Milan office (called Promosport and acquired in 2001) represented Real, while the Danish office, First Artist Denmark, was employed on behalf of the player. Therefore, I was on all three sides. We should have been paid three times. That situation was a consequence of our success so why should we be punished?

The regulations proved hugely problematic. We had to sign affidavits all over the place and ultimately drop one of our offices' commission as the FA argued a duality of interest. Why? There was no reason under statutory law. Our Milan office had legitimately won a contract from the buying club. We had legitimately won a contract to sell the player from Celtic, and all the Danish office had done was represent the player from day one. Why should we be penalised? We weren't opaque with it; we were transparent all the way along and even initially flagged it to the relevant authorities. My public shareholders were being denied the right to 33 per cent of their income on that deal. That would cause outrage in any business, not the erroneous suggestion that we were being paid three times for one deal. It ultimately cost us a healthy six-figure sum.

The regulation either has to be robust enough to be policed or flexible enough to understand the particular nuances involved in moving human beings around the world. Or, you have to rip it all up and start again, which is what the AFA has been saying recently. FIFA couldn't be bothered to regulate agents any more so they gave it back to the national associations, who developed new guidelines during 2014.

The reworked guidelines are fundamentally flawed because they were written by people at the Football Association and in a lawyers' office somewhere who don't seem to understand what goes on in the real world. So much of it is complete rubbish and policed by people who primarily have to justify their own existence. The people who make the regulations just don't think it through. Football regulations are there just to be restrictive rather than assist in the well-being of everyone involved. The amount of paperwork the FA and various Leagues around Europe demand in a transfer now is remarkable. They also act as a clearing house for both overseas transfer funds paid by English clubs to their foreign counterparts and for all fees paid by English clubs to registered intermediaries. The FA claims it is a regulatory mechanism that operates at a net cost to the organisation yet remains an important device providing transparency to money flows.

But we've had funds sit there for up to seven days. Although the FA have told me they do not earn on any interest accrued in that time, vast sums of money pass through this somewhat antiquated system. Within this framework, the man who has to supervise it all, David Newton, does a remarkable job, especially given it feels as though he is operating with one hand and two feet tied behind his back. There are so many tripwires for agents contained within the revised regulations. Even when they try and incentivise themselves and their player, this can be construed as 'Third Party Ownership'.

Your positioning in a deal can leave you open to governance issues in the game that neglect the realities of transfers. Even Jonathan Barnett and my brother Phil have fallen foul of the authorities in this way.

Deals are not, for the most part, done iniquitously. They are a product of a world where football and business are joined by osmosis to create an environment that is unrelenting, unforgiving and not always fair. I don't condone it. I work within it and I hope my track record will show it is possible to maintain a degree of respect for yourself and others while still achieving success.

You might think that is broad-brushing rhetoric from a silver-tongued agent but, believe me, I am fully aware of the significance of each and every word.

6

Communication

Communicating effectively and with appropriate nuance has been the foundation of my career – yet I could not talk fluently until I was seventeen. I had a cripplingly severe stammer – one of the worst of its kind. The word 'stammer' barely does it justice. I could not speak my own name, let alone string a sentence together or engage in conversation.

Simple articulation was beyond me. As a teenager, I felt doomed to an existence of staccato speech at best. Most of the time, I had a complete mental block preventing anything approaching a coherent word. Conventional treatment elicited no improvement. I was trapped in a spiral of frustration and depression. I wanted to run away. It left me unable to release my full despair at my mother's death from lung cancer when I was just fifteen years old.

But in hindsight, her death steered me back from the brink; I promised her – in dreadfully broken English – before she died that I would make her proud of me because she had tried so hard throughout her life to be supportive of both Phil and me. I had to keep my word.

Representing England as a sprinter aged fourteen in a junior international against West Germany in Siegen was a start – I had won local and national championships over 100 and 220 yards and was selected for a one-off team friendly, where I clocked 9.8 seconds for the shorter distance – but I still had to tackle the major hurdle in my life.

My father, Mick, saw an article in the *Daily Express* outlining a new breakthrough in speech therapy originating in Jersey entitled 'Reverse Fear'. The treatment cost three hundred guineas – about six thousand pounds in today's money – and although Dad had always provided for me and my brother Phil, eight years my junior, we were not a rich family. It was a big financial decision but Dad's fashion business was ticking along well enough and he could see the desperation etched on my face each and every day. I was struggling in school and life was passing me by. The time had come for a drastic measure.

I went to a boat-shaped house overlooking St Ouen's Bay and met a therapist named Bill Kerr who adopted a frankly barbaric approach: for two weeks, he would physically beat me whenever I stammered, which was nearly every single word.

Bill's logic was based on the theory that people with a stammer possessed an irrational fear of words. He divided the brain into two categories: the 'back brain' and the 'front brain'. Assuming there was no medical defect in the back brain where the words were selected, the problem centred on the front brain's fear of pushing those words out, like a horse refusing repeatedly to jump a particular fence. Bill went for the whip more than any jockey would dare. He maintained that people who stammered were mild, meek individuals who hid themselves away in dark corners. So he made you face everyone else when it was your turn to speak, stand bolt upright and place your thumbs on the side-press of your trousers. Then you would purse your lips – like a cheap ventriloquist's dummy – and nod your head to every syllable, while thinking about your posture and your thumb position.

The fear was the worst thing. For twelve hours every day – 7 a.m. to 7 p.m. – he would shout out names at random from a class of twelve and the selected individual would stand before the rest and attempt to say their own name or answer other quick-fire questions. Although it was inevitable you were going to be called up, waiting for it left me with a gut-wrenching pain in my stomach. And then it was my turn.

Slowly and nervously, I tried to push words out. 'My . . . name . . . is . . . Jon . . . a . . . than . . . Smith.'

If any of those pauses in between were too long, I made a pro-nunciation mistake or my thumbs moved, Bill would shout, beat, kick or punch me.

My Dad stayed with us and even attended the sessions. It was torture for him, watching his son get beaten like that at the start. He stood up in anger during the first day ready to knock Bill out.

'Trust me, you have got to let me get on with it,' Bill replied.

Dad wanted to take me away from it but I said no. By the after-noon of the first day, I felt myself being able to talk even though I wasn't talking properly at all and it was emotionally and physically exhausting. We only had a ten-minute break in the morning and another stoppage for lunch but we never left each other's company and almost never left that room until 7 p.m. The doors were locked and Bill made it clear there was no escape.

At the end of each day, we went back to Bill's guesthouse, which was run by his partner. What followed was part of the treatment. You ordered food off a menu and if you stammered while voicing your selection, you'd end up wearing it. Someone got a bowl of hot soup tipped over their head. I only ever had a bread roll thrown at me, thankfully.

The youngest boy in the class was eight years old. His dad, who also stammered, was in his sixties. Their surname was Bateman and, because God has a sense of humour, junior's problem was being unable to pronounce the letter 'B'.

Bill had difficulty hitting a kid that young so sometimes he'd hit the father. Every now and again, Bill would warm up and you'd see a flicker of humanity from him. He gave us little tricks. 'OK, so you can't say "Bateman". Can you say "I"?'

'Yes,' the boy replied.

'Say it then!'

'I,' he said.

'Say it again. And again!'

Bill made him repeat it for about three minutes.

'Now, put "I" in front of Bateman and say your name.'

The boy stayed silent. Bill went nose to nose with him.

'Say, "My name is I–Bateman!"'

'My name is I–Bateman!'

'There! Say it again. And again!'

Bill made him say it about fifty times and the next time he came back to him an hour or so later, he asked the boy to say his name.

' . . . My name is Bateman.'

'Halle-fucking-lujah. You've got it.'

I hadn't got it quite yet. I made better progress on day two, though, and, by the third day, he felt we were all doing well enough to go out on a short field trip. It was 2 p.m. 'I want you to go into town and order something and for the first time in your lives, you must not stammer when doing so. Be back here by four,' said Bill.

I had all sorts of problems – Ps, Ds and Ts were beyond me. Dad and I went into town and found a menswear shop. I went straight up to the sales assistant and said, 'I want a polka . . . dotted . . . tie.' I doubled over with laughter. Dad laughed, too, and we embraced. The guy in the shop probably thought we were on something illegal; I remember looking around the shop seeing a bemused expression on the faces of everyone else there. That was my turning point. From there onwards, my brain gradually and completely broke down its resistance to speaking because the need not to stammer was greater.

In the second week, he started to rebuild us and made us bolshie. Not only were we talking but we cured ourselves. He insisted on us pausing so others would wait for our words. They would then have more meaning.

Bill was obnoxious, obsessive and ruthless – he was a bully. But in two weeks, he gave me a new toy. It was called speech. And at the end of the treatment, he broke down in tears. It was the first and only time he became fully human in front of us.

On day one, it had taken all morning to say hello to each other but, as we parted, conversing and mingling fluently, the emotional aspect of our transformation overwhelmed him. He hugged us all and thanked us for being special people; it made me think the bully in him was all an act and this was one brief window into his soul, especially as he had dedicated so much of his life to helping children.

I had to phone Bill every Sunday when I got back home. About nine months in, I'd had a bad week and I stammered down the phone to him.

'You little bastard. I can't have you ruining my life's work, I'm going to come over there and sort you out,' he said menacingly. And then the phone went dead.

I didn't think much of it because he was in Jersey. The following Thursday, I got a phone call. It was Bill. 'I'm at the Regent Palace Hotel. I want to see you. Now.'

I went to his hotel room and knocked on the door. He picked me up by the scruff of my neck and dragged me inside. 'Right, we are going to start again. You stammer at all and you are going to get my fist through your face.'

I was fine after that. We spent an hour together and I have hardly stammered ever since, although it did happen once. I hosted a lunch for my old friend David Mellor, then the newly promoted Culture Secretary, and a large selection of media at the Dorset Square Hotel in the 1990s. I stood up to say a few words and I couldn't talk. The paralysis flooded back through me. I can't explain it.

But that's why, to this very day, whenever I'm doing live TV, I use the tricks that Bill gave me, always quietly visiting the bathroom before I go on set, composing myself and remembering what I was taught. I still revisit him, mentally, searching for the complete control of my environment through the same methods forty years on. Looking at the bridge of someone's nose to stare them out and not blink? That was Bill's technique. Using deliberate pauses, speaking half an octave lower? Some of the most important negotiating methods I have used throughout my career came from Bill.

I was a physical wreck when I left Jersey but I have never resented him since. He cured me. Many years later, I would become trustee and patron of the British Stammering Association (BSA) after speaking out in defence of Bill's methods as a backlash developed against him during the 1990s. That speech gained traction and, eventually, the BSA asked me to become a patron with former shadow chancellor Ed Balls.

So I returned to London after that frightening fortnight a changed young man. I talked to everyone, anyone. Friends and family could not believe it. 'Hello, how are you?' had always been beyond me and yet here I was chatting away without a care in the world. Years of pent-up frustration flew out of me in an oratory overload.

I was so highly energised I had to make up for lost time. I left school and moved out of the family home. My father was near to remarrying and, although I remained close to him, Phil and I thought my stepmother June was awful. We called her 'Cruella de Vil'.

I decided I wanted to be an actor. Why not? I could talk, after all! I joined a drama school and moved in with an old mate of mine from Edgware, where I'd grown up, called Gary Lyons. We were partners in crime but he had a talent far greater than any I possessed. He had started making a name for himself in the record business, working in a studio as an engineer. I formed my first company with Gary called Music Enterprises International, solely in the hope that people would confuse MEI with EMI. They didn't. But through Gary's contacts, we signed the Swinging Blue Jeans, who had already had hits with 'Hippy Hippy Shake' and 'You're No Good' in the 1960s.

I met Luton Town footballer John Ryan at my dad's shop one day. We got talking – because I could – and I suggested making a football record with the Luton squad. We did and it made a bit of money, despite being completely appalling.

I soon stopped working as a travel agent and went full-time in music with Gary – the acting career never got off the ground because I was so proud to be me all of a sudden, I didn't want to pretend to be anyone else – as things started to pick up.

Years later, Gary ended up working as a studio engineer for bands such as Queen and then as a producer for Foreigner. He went into the stratosphere as a producer, earning huge money and notoriety working for a host of big acts in the United States.

I was just the bloke who could organise things. Gary would have an idea and I would make it a reality. Off the back of the Luton single, we made songs with Tottenham and Queens Park Rangers. I'd stand outside grounds and sell them.

We were making money but it was only enough to keep our heads above water. We were slung out of our flat for playing football on the roof and managed to find a cheap shack underneath the flyover that leads to the M1 in Hendon. It cost us fifteen pounds a month inclusive of rates. There was no heating and the bath was in the kitchen. It was crawling with spiders and the noise from cars rattling overhead was deafening. You could lean out of the window and touch the flyover.

We didn't have a phone. There was a garage a hundred yards down the road and I used to pay the bloke who ran it a couple of bob a week to answer the payphone if it rang. He had this gruff, cockney voice and would answer, ''Ello, MEI. Can I 'elp ya?'

We got by. The first winter there it got really cold. We turned the oven on during a cold snap in October and left it on until April. Eventually we got a gas bill for seven hundred pounds, which in those days was outrageous – it would equate to about eleven thousand now. We wrote back and complained saying it was wrong.

The gas company sent a guy around. He checked for a gas leak but couldn't find one.

'Have you kept the oven on for any length of time?' he asked.

'Don't be stupid,' I said. 'We're two lads living together – we don't cook.'

He apologised and gave us an amended gas bill for three pounds. We couldn't play the same trick twice so the following year we planned to leave. By that stage, Gary was becoming the grand producer I always knew he would be and eventually he moved out. He was in America half the time and needed to commit permanently to his other engagements.

Gary and I parted on good terms because I always knew he was the high-flier – I could never resent someone for fulfilling their potential. But now I was stuck in the flat on my own as a sole trader.

Every deal I did in the weeks after he left was only keeping my head above water. I was too proud to go back to my dad. My mates brought Wimpy meals to the flat just to keep me going.

In the routine of trying to improve the situation, I met a guy called Barry Kingston from Spark records. He thought I'd be useful helping with their productions because I had some organisational skills and they saw me as a good talker, which was still about the biggest compliment anyone could ever give me. I took a part-time job with them and kept the production company going, although I changed it from MEI to Greenlight Productions after Gary left.

Then I met Lee. Dad had been a typical busybody parent, attempting to pair me off with one of his friend's daughters after they discussed their offspring's romantic woes at a health club he sometimes attended. My mother's death two years earlier had brought us even closer together as a family. In the hearse with her after the funeral, a single tear rolled down Dad's cheek. It was the only time he allowed himself to display publicly the emotional turmoil he was going through. His strength at that time has always inspired me.

He never wanted me to be alone and, although I had Phil, it felt somehow fitting that Dad found me a partner.

He gave me Lee's phone number. I waited a week or two before phoning her – as you do – and then arranged a date. I was quite taken with her straight away. I tried to arrange a second date but she was busy. I played it cool. I waited another few days before calling again. We made another date but she stood me up because 'something had come up', apparently. I had my doubts but eventually we met up again and things took off from there. Lee had a flat in Finchley and, after about four months of me suffering in another bleak winter, she invited me to move in with her. I couldn't ask her to move in with me because of the state of the place. Lee only ever came to my place twice – she didn't like spiders.

She rescued me in more ways than one. Once we were living together, she took a greater interest in my work. I'd come home struggling to find solutions for certain issues but Lee had a flair for the record industry and production despite working as a PA for an import/export company in Wembley.

I learned a lot from her. We both believed we had wicked stepmothers and that mutual unease bound us closer together. We acquired a big hairy rescue dog called Scruff who made us both feel parental. However, after a couple of years together she wanted to get married. I procrastinated. But one balmy summer's weekend in Devon, in Bigbury Bay, I proposed . . . but later called it off because it was all happening too fast.

Her entire family was angry with me – understandably – and after a few months Lee sat me down and said she felt this was our time. She wanted us to get married. I took a long, long walk during the night. Scruff was knackered by the morning. I realised if I didn't say yes, she'd probably move on. Something awoke within me. It became clear I couldn't live without her. I'd never experienced that before. So I told her I didn't ever want to lose her and I would marry her. Whatever reservations I had as a guy in his early twenties were inconsequential compared with the overwhelming love I had for her. She just needed to open my eyes – something she did in so many areas of my life.

We got married and I didn't stammer at all during my wedding speech! Her family thought I was a bit of a chancer – a view reinforced by me being so non-committal on the wedding plans no doubt – and I guess there were times when I appeared arrogant because I had my speech. I was often impatient and excessively talkative; these are irritating traits viewed in isolation but I felt I was seventeen years behind everyone else. I wanted to be a millionaire by the time I was thirty. It was all that mattered to me before Lee came along.

We went on honeymoon to Thailand and were really happy. A year later, in 1977, our main focus had become trying to find an act that would help Greenlight Productions take off.

Having the allegiance with Spark, who owned their own studios on Denmark Street in Soho, opened a lot of doors for me. I was in Wigan doing a sales run for Spark when I took a break in a café. There was a guy in the next booth behind me talking about this phenomenon sweeping the region's clubs called Northern Soul. I carried on earwigging and eventually introduced myself to him.

His name was Russ Winstanley – one of the DJs at Wigan Casino. His view was that it was beginning to take over the whole music scene and would spread nationwide.

Northern Soul was essentially all-night sessions of ostensibly old American R&B but with a quick beat. 'Tainted Love' – a track later recorded by Soft Cell – was one of our hit records which was a remake of the original Gloria Jones track. We were breathing life back into these tracks; the purists didn't see it that way. There was no alcohol in the clubs but a lot of drugs and sex. The police could probably have arrested everyone in Wigan had they known what was happening.

It was the first time since the Beatles that music had had such a cultural significance in the UK. The Wigan Casino guys would remake the American R&B stuff with local artists and sell them to people populating the dance floors. The Northern Soul purists would say the newer stuff was never a patch on the originals. But they still sold very well. Dave McAlier at Pye Records tapped into it and so did I because Russ had opened my ears to it.

I told him I could distribute Northern Soul through Spark and he took me in to see the manager of Wigan Casino, a guy called Mike Walker. Over a few weeks, we developed a relationship and they started giving me tips on the next big record. I went back to Spark and told them I was planning on borrowing some money to put out Northern Soul records, partly through my production company and in partnership with Spark. We had a string of hit records in a row. It exploded in a way I never anticipated.

As this was going on, David Platz – an industry senior from Essex Music – took me under his wing and we started buying copyrights. I don't know why David took a shine to me. I was lucky enough to get the opportunity and just about clever enough to take advantage. We acquired the music to the TV series *Lily Langtree*, we had a piece of 'Cavatina', which is the music for *The Deer Hunter*. It was like owning real estate. At that time, nobody had challenged the ownership of copyright. In those days, you owned copyright for a hundred years. People like Elton John questioned it a few years later, arguing that, if he signs his rights to a publisher, why should they own the material for a century and not the writer? He rightly stated a writer should be able to renegotiate their position as their career evolves. That later came into being but, at this time, publishers owned things virtually in perpetuity.

I was able to capitalise on that. All of my talent has always been abstract. I don't know where the ability to create corporate structures and work business angles comes from. I think I was born with it. The only skill I ever had was to run very quickly. I wasn't bad at most sports and played the guitar, albeit badly. But in my working life, my success came from somewhere, usually on the heels of others and an ability to join the dots commercially.

Life by this stage was pretty good. It had all come together inside five years. And things snowball in the music industry – success really does breed success. Having spent a while desperately trying to align myself with the right people, suddenly more and more of the right people wanted to align themselves with me.

In 1980, Lee and I went to Miami and she started to get pains in her stomach. She felt as though she was putting on weight. We got back home and went to the doctor, who suggested a couple of routine tests. We both went for the results and the doctor was immediately concerned. He said Lee's spleen was enlarged and proceeded to reel off several possible causes starting from a simple virus and escalating up to significantly more serious conditions. Lee only had those two symptoms – stomach pain and a little weight gain – but she knew she didn't feel right. Her instincts told her something was wrong deep down.

We went to see a haematologist at the Royal Marsden Hospital on Fulham Road. Neither of us wanted to be there but we had to go. Dr Ray Powles delivered the bombshell that Lee had leukaemia. I felt physically sick; I had to leave the room. Sometimes you get terrible, terminal news from a doctor but your mind centres itself on the belief you can make the best of it. I just knew it was cataclysmic. If it wasn't the end, it was the start of a dreadful road we had to walk down together.

I paused, hugged Lee but then had to leave the room. I found a toilet and threw up. I was shaking. I wanted to be in the room with her but my legs were giving way when I tried to stand up. I felt my life was over, let alone hers, and she was the one who was important. I thought of my father in that hearse with Mum. That was the strength I had to try and copy.

Eventually, I gathered myself and went back into the room. Lee was as white as a sheet but holding herself together unbelievably well. Further tests were required. A week passed but our lives were suspended in time. The final diagnosis came: chronic granulocyctic leukaemia. She had three years to live. CGL meant she would never go into remission but it moved more slowly through the body than a more acute strain.

The doctor told us we had to shrink the spleen or remove it. He offered us a pill that would do it. The side effects would knock Lee off her feet for two or three days because it was so poisonous but it would stymie the leukaemic cell growth and give her immune system the best chance to fight it.

There was one downside – if she took that single, tiny pill, she would never be able to have children. We talked about her having children before she died so I could bring them up in her name. The doctor gave us a few days to decide. We tried to be brave but neither of us slept properly. Eventually, she decided to take the pill because there was more living she had to do and we could always adopt.

So the plan was to adopt a beautiful girl – because we could choose now! – and give her a great life. I could manage her singing career and make her a superstar. Lee took the pill. The effect on her was awful. She was immensely brave as the poison took hold of her. It was like trying to watch a human being overcome an internal earthquake. I tried to give her all my strength but she was a very strong and determined woman – focused on living as much of her life as she was granted.

I had scaled back my work commitments by this point to look after Lee full-time and enjoy her company as our time together was now limited. I phoned a mate of mine called Tony Simons. He was working as a management adviser then with the rock band Status Quo but I asked him for a huge favour in overseeing the running of my company.

Meanwhile, we had one more test. Lee could have a bone marrow transplant if she had the right tissue-type match. Her sister Rita went through a very painful procedure and we had a three-week wait to find out her results. Amazingly, Rita was a match – that was a one-in-three chance in itself – but suddenly the odds of Lee surviving swung 60-40 in her favour if her body did not reject the bone marrow.

I had feared the worst all along but here were genuine grounds for hope. It was November; she was scheduled to go into hospital just after Christmas. It was an awful Christmas that year, 1980, but at least there was something to cling to.

She went into hospital on 27 December having shaved most of her hair off as she was going to lose it anyway. She looked beautiful. We had a wedding to go to just before Christmas and nobody could believe she was unwell. I don't look at the pictures from that time very often but she radiated beauty, even then. She was a talented artist and was spending more of her spare time painting to give her an alternative focus and a sedentary creative outlet. Sometimes she would wander off alone to paint whatever inspired her. It was her escape.

The treatment went badly from the outset. The preparation hadn't gone well – she had pleurisy which was very painful – but her condition improved sufficiently to begin the bone marrow transplant. She underwent Reverse Barrier Nursing, which meant she had no resistance to any infection whatsoever. I was no longer allowed to have any contact with Lee beyond talking through a screen.

I wasn't working very much despite Tony telling me a company had expressed a serious interest in buying me out. They were keen on the assets I had as a whole – the copyrights and the publishing rights to my Northern Soul records. I told Tony to handle it as best he could. He ran through the numbers with me and I told him to do the deal. We discussed the details over and over but he ran the deal for me and what my role in life would be post-transaction. I honestly could not have achieved what we did without his caring, professional support. Unbelievably Tony was diagnosed with cancer and died five years afterwards. I'll never forget my very special friend.

The new bone marrow rejected her own body. Her condition

declined radically over the next couple of weeks. Eventually, Lee slipped into a coma and it became clear that she wasn't going to come out of it, so the doctors let me go in to see her.

I held her hand as the inevitability overwhelmed me. Over the next couple of days, her organs broke down one by one. Her heart could not take any more; her breathing became shallower and shallower . . . and then she was gone.

I couldn't believe it was all over. We never really got to say good-bye because we never wanted to admit defeat.

Lee died on a Wednesday. Two days later, Tony completed the sale of Greenlight and my wealth increased - I became a million-aire. I was 29, a few months ahead of schedule. It meant absolutely nothing. How immaterial the material things in life can be.

I have lived my life and while the wound isn't as painful, the scar remains. She made me the man I was and, some years later, my second wife, Janine, helped me become the man I am today.

I was unfair on Janine initially. I still had Lee in my head and my heart for a long time, although I think I've been a good husband to her because I have loved and cared for her in the same way; equally, she has been wonderfully supportive to me over the last thirty years.

When Lee died, I bought the burial plot next to her for me. But when Janine's dad died, my then secretary arranged a plot for him just behind Lee and I. Janine voiced her concern that she would be buried somewhere else and so when we were both dead, our kids would come and visit Lee and I together but their mother apart.

I went to see the Jewish Burial Society and explained the situation. Barney Calo, an angel from north London working for the JBS, told me just maybe he could fit us all in together as, by quirk of circumstance, there was a drain that ran alongside Lee's grave that, if the council allowed, could be moved.

The only problem was that Lee would have to be moved three feet to the right. I had to give that some thought but then it dawned on me that she wasn't there anyway as I believe she was really somewhere better. I didn't think she would mind because she would want us to all be together.

It took months to get permission but that drain was moved. Now, when I die, I'll be buried with Lee and Janine either side of me. You could describe it as the perfect exit from this world.

I believe in life after death. Several times I believe I found my own proof that Lee still exists in some form but I went to see a number of spiritualists for something more convincing. A lot of them are complete charlatans but I befriended one by the name of Owen Potts, who later became a family friend. I went to see him twice a year, once in the summer and again at Christmas time. On one of those occasions, Lee supposedly said to me, through him, 'Do you remember those paintings I did? One of them is of your house.'

It wasn't possible. She didn't know the house because I bought it after she died and it was in Barnet and we had lived in Edgware, which wasn't too far away but not somewhere we ever made a point of visiting.

Owen was adamant, though. 'She says she has definitely drawn your house and the painting is under the stairs.'

This was somewhat unnerving. We looked under the stairs apprehensively. There wasn't much in there – a couple of old empty packing cases – but Owen stuck resolutely to the story Lee was apparently telling him.

Six months later, I went again to see Owen. 'Lee is telling me you didn't find the painting. It is absolutely there.'

I went back home and looked again. There was no chance it was there – the space simply wasn't big enough to lose anything in.

Eerily, four weeks later, I got a phone call from Janine. She was breathless and clearly rattled. 'Jon, a pipe has burst in the house,' she said.

'OK,' I replied. 'Are you all right? Is the house OK?'

'Yes, everything's fine . . . but the flood water has lifted out a false bottom to one of the packing cases. There is a bubble-wrapped painting in there of our house.'

There was a signature. It read: 'Lee '80'.

Sometimes, even the most exquisite communication defies logic.

7

El Diego and the
Premier League

Football was suffering an identity crisis in the 1980s and so was I. The British economy was in decline, our national sport was in the doldrums and hooliganism was rife. The Press called it the 'English disease'. Within the space of eighteen days in May 1985, the situation became markedly worse.

On May 11, there was a devastating fire at Bradford City's stadium which killed 56 people and injured at least 265 more. At the end of the month, Juventus played Liverpool in the European Cup Final but the game was overshadowed by rioting at the dilapidated Heysel stadium as 39 people lost their lives.

All English clubs were banned from European competition for five years, which had a negative effect on domestic football and a worse one on the England national team. Those idiots who saw fit to travel abroad and cause trouble in the name of their clubs were now doing it in the name of their country.

Aggression fuelled by misappropriated patriotism provided an unwelcome backdrop to England fixtures abroad. Domestically, social unease stemming from rising unemployment and political disillusionment manifested itself at football grounds. They were not safe places to be, let alone somewhere to take the family on a weekend.

Initially, I was not in the best head space to notice this developing picture because I'd spent two years at the bottom of a whisky bottle. Life was not particularly relevant after Lee died. My friends and family surrounded me with great love and affection but, after about six weeks, I felt claustrophobic and had to escape.

There's only so long you can spend wrapped in cotton wool before you start to feel suffocated. I went to Acapulco purely because I didn't know anyone there and felt that form of isolation was the best way to grieve. I spent the first day chatting to the barman as he topped me up and the second crashed out on a sunbed listening to a Walkman, waiting for midday to come around so I could have another drink.

Two very loudmouthed American guys came and sat next to me. They were a pain. They were looking to party and meet women but all I wanted was solitude. Neither of them would accept that, finding my indifference intolerable.

One eventually said to me, 'You are a miserable bastard really, aren't you? Who died?' The other one sniggered.

'My wife. Six weeks ago.'

They both fell silent.

'OK, well this is the only sympathy you are going to get from us – we're sorry. Give us a hug. We are going to try and cheer you up. We're Alan and Peter.' I latched on to them and, thirty-five years later, they remain two of my best friends. How many times do you meet someone on holiday and say you'll stay in touch but never do? They gave me the week I actually needed, never allowing me to wallow.

I came back home to sort out some financial investments and went to Los Angeles shortly afterwards, where I had kept a modest place from my record business days.

LA's moniker 'the City of Angels' is apt – an emotional place which engenders love, peace and support when you are down. London tends to pass you by a bit more, lacking LA's soft centre. I started to rebuild myself, falling in with an eclectic crowd. There were lots of drugs circling us. I almost always resisted because, if anything, I was scared of losing control. I didn't know what I might do if I stirred the inner demons still circling within me after Lee's passing.

I took a couple of white pills once which took me somewhere horrible. It was some sort of acid and I'm really pleased in hindsight that I had the worst trip of my life because I never did it again. I felt far more at home with alcohol. One day rolled into another. I had no need to do anything. I had no dependants – Scruff was being looked after back in the UK by a family friend – and money was not an immediate issue as my investments were doing fine in addition to the surplus I had from the sale of my business.

I was purposeless. Almost to help pass the time, friends started taking me to live American sports events. I never got into baseball but I became really intrigued by American Football. I loved the fact the LA Raiders were marketed as the antithesis of good sportsmen – they were the pirates, the bad boys. It looked a bit like Millwall Lite in hindsight but their strategy was sensational.

That approach resonated with me because the record business was all about getting your product out there and making as much noise as possible. It was a merchandise-led enterprise. American Football was always viewed as family fun but here were the LA Raiders branding themselves with pirate patches, associating themselves with dark colours and edgy music. This was the polar opposite of the prevailing trend for fun, bright retail.

English football was demure in this respect and very parochial. Local lads playing for local teams watched by local communities. And, usually, local gangs having a scrap beforehand. I felt there was a way to make sports stars like the pop stars I had worked with in the Northern Soul scene.

A few months later, I was watching TV in my house. Dan Rather was reading the news and, at the end, there was an item about Barbra Streisand and Dustin Hoffman ceasing work together under the umbrella of a production company called First Artist. The name struck me immediately – First Artist. Could I acquire it? I phoned the companies registrar in Sacramento to see if it was available and he said I could have it a year and a day later if Streisand and Hoffman didn't use it. They didn't and so, thirteen months hence, I took control of the name 'First Artist Corporation'.

Bizarrely, back in England, my former father-in-law had been friendly with a guy called Jarvis Astaire. I tracked Jarvis for a while during a period when I briefly came back home to visit friends and family. He worked with Muhammad Ali and was the guy behind Viewsport Ltd, who showed live boxing matches in cinemas. Eventually, we met and I was so impressed with him. I wanted to learn his methodology and, over time, Jarvis took me under his wing, just as David Platz had done. I don't know why. I used to attract father figures and, over the years, women have mothered me, too. Maybe I give off this vibe that I need help!

Jarvis wanted to bring American Football over to England. I told him I thought it was a great idea and wanted to help. I could be Robin to his Batman.

In August 1986, Jarvis arranged an NFL game at Wembley for the first time – Chicago Bears versus Dallas Cowboys. I was involved but only at a nominal level. I just watched everything that happened, how it was designed, what worked and what didn't. People were concerned it should be Anglicised but that would have missed the point entirely; American entertainment was a show, all razzmatazz, glitz and glamour.

English football entertainment was dire. I used to go to Arsenal and watch a military band march up and down the pitch at half-time. It was traditional but hardly inspiring. The half-time scores were dropped into slates by a guy operating a manual scoreboard.

Game B might have been Everton v Nottingham Forest. You would see him shuffling through these numbered slates looking for the right score before putting one up for the home team. I'd turn to my friend and say, 'Oh, it's a one. What's the second number going to be? Is it a zero? Are Everton winning? No, he's gone past that. A one? No, he's gone past that? A two? Oh, it's a zero. He just couldn't find it before.' That was the sum total of the entertainment on offer. It was wonderful in its own way but I saw a transformation that could take place.

By early 1986, I was dividing my time between London and LA and knocking around the idea of intertwining American entertainment with English sport. Everything that I did from then on was with that in mind.

Footballers deserved to be stars. A story involving a former idol of mine inspired me to ensure the game rewarded players in a more wholesome way. Alan Skirton was my idol growing up. He played for Arsenal on the right wing – my position – and enjoyed six years at the club in the 1960s. I adored him and was shocked to hear on the grapevine that, after finishing his playing days, he became a milkman around Highbury. He went from being idolised by thousands inside the stadium to delivering milk to the fans' front doors. How could a star that had shone so brightly have become so dimmed and nobody had noticed it? I spoke with Alan some years later and he told me that this wasn't altogether true, but the story has done the rounds and served as my inspiration.

I met Paul Mariner regularly after Arsenal games and his enthusiasm was infectious. He was starting to think about the end of his career. I told him about this great idea I had seen work in America and my ambition to create a sports agency that didn't just deal in sport. I had this great name, too – First Artist – and had all these concepts to play around with. Agents were the 'dirty raincoat' brigade in the UK at that time; grubby men with a cigarette hanging out of their mouths barking bullshit from the shadows. We could be different.

At our first serious meeting about taking things forward, Paul told me there was an England players' pool, dividing money earned from commercial activities throughout the squad and the coaches. The England team had by that stage been assembled as a collective adopting a basic marketing strategy by a respected agent named Harry Swales. The Football Association, who had agreed a solitary and all-encompassing deal with Umbro, turned a blind eye to the embryonic commercial activity Harry facilitated and did not interfere.

Paul thought he could get us a meeting and I flew off to LA to formulate a plan. Except I got to LAX and the weather was so horrible, I looked at the departures board and decided to go to Australia. It was sunny there.

I ended up in Christchurch, New Zealand. The backdrop was so peaceful there it helped me gain clarity. I remember sitting in a church sketching out my plan. It was the same church that was wiped out by an earthquake many years later in 2011. That, to me, was the birthplace of First Artist.

With my idea now clear – rounding the team into an aggressive marketing tool – Paul managed to get me an interview with Harry, who said he was retiring (although he operated well into his eighties, negotiating Ryan Giggs's contracts at Manchester United until the end of his playing days in 2014). Eventually, Harry promoted our candidacy to the FA, who didn't object. With two other parties competing for the contract, the decision first went to a players' vote. We were so far in front by that time because of Paul's relationship with the players, I felt it was a formality. If it was an 800-metre race, I was already on the second lap by the time the others started. Regardless, we were required to make a presentation to a four-man players' committee, which comprised Bryan Robson, Terry Butcher, Peter Shilton and Ray Wilkins.

I took advice from people involved with the LA Raiders, whom I had befriended by that stage, and a few other marketing people from around the world.

We decided we wouldn't sell stories to the newspapers any more. Eric Hall was making a killing at the time charging everything he could for access to players. I believed we could give it all away for free because I would bring in Burton or whoever and have branded photo opportunities to drive the agenda underpinned by commercial support. As awkward as the other agents were, we would bend over backwards and be as user-friendly as possible. I felt it the best way to ingratiate players to the public, who had to experience another side to the game other than scenes of fan violence and stadium disasters.

The players voted for us unanimously. We then made another presentation to Bobby Robson, who was England manager at the time, and finally a third, more informal one to FA chairman Ted Croker. Bobby was lovely; Paul had played under him at Ipswich and their friendship had endured, which ensured a receptive audience when we met to outline our plans. He was fully supportive of players earning more and bought into the vision I was selling. He knew the constraints of the FA and my task then was to befriend the organisation's hierarchy.

Glen Kirton was the conduit. He was ostensibly the commercial manager but his role encompassed far more, including all team logistics aside from travel. I did my homework on Glen and he introduced me to Ted.

Ted's big problem was the FA's existing agreement with Umbro. He reeled off a long list of things we couldn't do because Umbro owned the lot. From the minute they stepped off the bus for a squad get-together to the minute they departed, Umbro had control of everything in commercial terms: access to players, advertising rights, stadium advertising, marketing and promotional activity. England got cash and the kit in return. I told the FA that made no sense and a huge opportunity was being wasted. They had to partition Umbro's territory.

I asked if there was a way we could explore opportunities within the existing framework. Ted acquiesced but warned me not to upset Umbro or Dick Wragg, chairman of the FA's International Committee, who had to be satisfied we were doing everything possible to create the best environment for England to succeed on the pitch.

We had a second meeting with the players at which, if all went well, we would be formally offered the job. There were no major objections. We agreed a four-year contract which would officially begin for the Euro '88 qualification campaign but I was around the camp, albeit taking a back seat, during the 1986 World Cup in an effort to familiarise myself with my new surroundings.

In truth, it had all happened so fast. Suddenly, within a few weeks of getting properly started, my first client was the entire England football team.

There were obvious obstacles to overcome. The Umbro deal was a massive roadblock. I sensed that several players – and figures within the FA – were uncertain about the direction I wanted to take things but I knew if I could bring in real money, the sceptics would jump on board.

The players would take about 65 per cent of the total income, spread across the squad. Each player would be given a points total based on how often they were selected and the money was divided accordingly. The FA took 10 per cent – although I negotiated this down after 1988 – the coaches took roughly 3–4 per cent with a donation also made to Great Ormond Street Hospital. I took 20 per cent. All funds were paid out at the end of a two-year tournament cycle.

Bobby allowed me to integrate myself into the squad at get-togethers. I'd talk to them in groups or take them aside one by one to outline my plans. I didn't address them as a big group for a year or so because I wanted to get to know them individually. We had just come back from the 1986 World Cup in Mexico, Bobby was rebuilding the squad and he wanted my role to remain on the periphery, which I completely understood. Bobby and I had our first, extended one-on-one meeting on 4 November 1986 once I had my feet under the table and a clearer idea of how to progress.

We retained Harry Swales as a consultant to aid the transition into Euro '88 qualification. He'd walked the fine line between the FA's restrictions and the team's exploitation, which proved a useful guide in establishing the parameters we could work within and then bend to our will. Having witnessed such a dynamic scene around the LA Raiders and the music business before that, I could see so much scope for growth. In England, we existed; in America, they lived. I wanted to bring that *joie de vivre* to English football.

I went to see leading journalists of the day – Harry Harris and Colin Gibson among them – and spoke of my plans, dangling the carrot of open access to players as long as Bobby approved. I would help with everything else but, in return, they had to speak to their picture desks and make sure they were malleable regarding the commercial angles I needed highlighting.

John Dawes was a colossus and a colossal help. He was an eighteen-stone gentle giant who worked as a photographer for the *Daily Star*. He got it completely. 'This is brilliant,' he told me. 'This is how it should be. It takes co-operation to a new level.'

He got all the photographers together and introduced me. John explained that I would give them access but, in return, they needed to ensure the picture desks used a picture of a player holding a Coca-Cola bottle in their hand, for example, even if the paper had an advertising agreement with Pepsi that week.

Bobby helped the media where he could but I represented a back door into the camp. If he wouldn't let them speak to Gary

Lineker, maybe I could arrange it. I wouldn't be able to get a pack of photographers into the hotel but John would come in and take a photo for all of them.

It wasn't easy to sneak him in because he was a big lad. But in any case, I was always transparent with Bobby and he told me simply not to give him any problems by upsetting anyone. I knew it was possible we would anger senior FA officials and Bobby just told me, 'I can only protect you so much.'

Sponsors were beginning to see the benefits. Burton came on board soon after I started, as did Budget Rent-a-Car, Protel Communications, Courage, then run by a guy called Brian Baldock, later to become chairman of First Artist PLC who was suceeded by Matthew Freud's partner Alex Johnston and Jarvis Astaire. The team were also signed up with various brands, initially Carling Black Label, and later Kaliber, a low-alcohol lager, in an attempt to disassociate football and beer given the connotations with hooliganism (which seems painfully PC by today's standards).

The Press were enthusiastic because they were getting unprecedented access. England enjoyed unbeaten qualification for Euro '88, winning five of their six matches and the players' pool totalled almost one million pounds, which was a lot of money for modestly paid sportsmen in the late 1980s. So much so that I started organising FA Cup Final players' pools for clubs. The blueprint was the same. We had people at both semi-finals and would arrange to meet the winning teams the following week and pitched to them. We could organise a clothing sponsor, a drinks sponsor and get their pictures in the papers – perhaps alongside an interview – using the same method we'd employed with England. Cup Finals were iconic, stand-alone events with a week-long build-up in those days.

Newspapers craved content and we gave it to them for a price paid by sponsors, who, in turn, got their brand promoted.

Inevitably, because we did it for England, the clubs gave us the job. We chose the team we thought was going to win and every year – Tottenham in 1987, Liverpool in '88 and Everton in '89 – they lost. Manchester United's 1990 win over Crystal Palace was the first time we'd ever been on the winning side. And even that came after a replay. Thank God nobody realised at the time. I never told Sir Alex Ferguson. We also organised the Welsh rugby players' pool for a while in the early nineties – they didn't win a game either.

Players' pools can create conflicting loyalties; I represented Sheffield Wednesday against Arsenal in 1993 and so the tribalism within me as a Gunners fan was pitched against the emotion I felt for my client. That emotion almost always wins out but it is nevertheless difficult to silence the fan voice within.

The football players' pools usually reached six figures, which for one game in those days was a considerable return, especially as we never asked them to do very much. I rolled it out in Scotland as well, pitching successfully to both Rangers and Celtic. We became very well known throughout the game, to the point the players sometimes sabotaged us.

I pitched to run the Liverpool players' pool one year. We had been running pools successfully by that point so I think they had already decided to go with us but we still had to go through the formality of a presentation. As I stood there talking in the changing room at Melwood after training, Robbie Fowler threw his jock-strap at me. Steve McManaman took off his pants and chucked them on my head. David James stood at the back and stopped me halfway through to say we had the gig – they liked us so what we were saying was almost irrelevant.

I had to expand First Artist as things took off. There were no football management companies at the time, just individuals acting as agents. First Artist changed all that and we would go on to utilise all these unexplored revenue streams over many years.

Another big client entered the picture early on, soon after the England team – Diego Maradona. I had been introduced to Ossie Ardiles and we quickly formed a friendship. He is a really bright guy, very amenable and someone with whom it is easy to find common ground. I phoned him one day because I believed in his abilities and viewed him as a possible client. He lived in Broxbourne and I wanted to visit his house because I thought there were opportunities we could explore if we worked together. He agreed to meet but the traffic was horrendous and I had to cancel, as I did the second time when we rearranged. On the third occasion, I was very apologetic but still Ossie wasn't best pleased, especially as, although I'd actually made it this time, I was late.

He was warming to me when the phone rang. It was Diego. During the course of their conversation, Diego explained to Ossie that he wasn't happy with his current agent. As his best friend, Diego asked Ossie to manage him. Ossie put down the phone and said, 'How do you fancy working with Diego Maradona?'

That was it. Had the traffic not defeated me twice previously, I would never have been there when that phone call came. Instead, I had the England team and Diego Maradona as my clients. For me, it felt like having the Beatles and the Rolling Stones.

Diego moved to Napoli in 1984 and stayed there for seven years, during which time I got to know him fairly well. I remember sitting in Diego's house in Naples one day when he took me downstairs to his garage. He had about twenty magnificent cars – Porsches, Lamborghinis and all sorts – and I said to him, 'You can't even drive these here. The roads are too narrow and there are too many traffic lights.'

Through a translator, he said, 'It's OK. I have special dispensation. I can drive through red lights in Naples.'

I drove into Naples, a very religious part of Italy, and saw huge murals of Jesus painted on to buildings. And next to Jesus, on the same building, there were big paintings and posters of Diego. It wasn't just sport; football was a religion. The team even sometimes trained in the afternoon when Diego fancied a lie-in. He had crossed the divide.

Meanwhile, we were crossing a divide of our own with the England team. There was steady progress in our commercial operations during the two-year cycle up to Euro '88 but the tournament itself was an unmitigated disaster. England's group was tough – Republic of Ireland, Holland and the USSR. To underline its strength, the latter pair would later contest the final. But England lost all three games, scoring only twice and conceding seven. They were unlucky in the first two matches; Lineker missed a boatload of chances against the Irish and England gave as good as they got against Holland, only for Marco van Basten to score twice late on in a 3-1 win which rendered the final game irrelevant as England were already out.

The hard-luck story didn't sit well with the Press. While there had been goodwill towards the side post-'86 after Maradona's mixture of magic and deception knocked England out in the quarter-finals against Argentina, the Press went for Bobby with both barrels this time. *Guardian* writer Dave Hill later described it as 'the most sustained campaign of Press humiliation the national game has ever seen'.

The FA were adamant they wanted to stand by Bobby, which only made the Press more vitriolic. This put me in a somewhat invidious position as the 1990 World Cup campaign got under way and a fresh players' pool began with sponsors hungry for more exposure than before.

The Press had become the enemy. Bobby's natural reaction was always to protect his players and the infrastructure around them. He had a strong personal connection with certain journalists who were still considered to be user-friendly. Bob Harris, of *Today* and later the *Sunday People*, was among them, but those relationships did not stop the concerted campaign to oust him as manager.

Ongoing hooliganism didn't help the wider mood. Bobby felt ashamed when the supporters let the country down. We were under a siege of negativity. Fans were troublemakers, the manager was clueless and had to go, the players weren't good enough. And there was me trying to break ranks and bring the media into the inner circle. I had ongoing discussions with Bobby and senior players to try and keep a dialogue going with the media.

He still allowed me to do it, ultimately because it was positive for his players. He was devastated by what was being written after 1988. And in the next breath I was saying, 'These guys who want to hang you . . . we need to let them in and give them access to the players. Please trust me to manage it. I'll keep within a strict framework of sporting promotion.'

He was concerned that the next stick to beat him with would be all the time spent on commercial activity. You may have the picture desk onside, but then the sports editor could decide it was ridiculous these players were earning extra money while the team was failing and decide to turn them over.

We weren't painting ourselves as whiter than white to the FA but we tried to do right by the players and the game's stakeholders while also – and this is an important point – bringing fresh sponsorship into football.

The backdrop of ongoing violence didn't make the sport commercially appealing. Prime Minister Margaret Thatcher was anti-football, and Minister for Sport Colin Moynihan was Thatcher's man. If she said jump, he'd ask, 'How high?' He was never a supporter of us but I did spend some time with him at a charity event and also in a one-to-one meeting. I tried to tell him how iconic I thought our national team was and how we could all use that symbolism for good rather than just a magnet for negativity. In fairness to Colin, he always listened to my point of view but he didn't do anything. He always just paid me lip service.

I kept arguing to David Mellor, who was a promising younger minister at the time and someone I spotted as a football supporter and continually helpful to our cause, that the upshot of all this was that sponsors were going to put more money into English sport. It needed it. The English game was dying on the world stage.

Money is nothing to be afraid of. That was another entrenched American ideal; being a success was a source of pride, not something demurely to shy away from. Who cares how much players earn if they are successful and make us happy? England's Euro '88 campaign undermined that argument somewhat but these were young men at the peak of their profession, watched by millions.

It helped that we were beginning to get major sponsors on board. Peter Littlewood at Mars was the first one to understand that it was patriotic to support the England team in their moment of need. Mars signed up midway through the 1990 qualifying campaign and we could hint they would go deeper and help bring families back to football – that was a wider missive sports editors could appreciate. The game's governing bodies had taken only nominal steps to broaden football's appeal, including an initiative to section off areas within stadia as 'family friendly'.

I was always completely against that. That strategy transmits the notion that while one designated area of the ground is fine, the rest of it is a toilet. Or at the very least, unequivocally dangerous. Families should be able to go to all parts of the ground, not be sectioned off in a manner that suggests demarcation is for their own safety.

In a sense, it epitomised English football's identity crisis. It was a slow process. If Bobby hadn't been so magnanimous and strong, the increase in sponsorship would not have happened so quickly, if at all. Coke would not have got involved for many years. Bobby was happy to dance with the devil despite everything being written about him and the revolution in English football thereafter can, in part, be attributed to him.

Ultimately, it tempered some of the negativity towards Bobby and the team over the two-year cycle between Euro '88 and Italia '90. It had to – access like this was still a precious commodity and we were trying to be proactive by fighting the negativity, which was a story in itself. Journalists find it harder to turn someone over if they have to justify it to the individual face to face the next day. And we began to churn out positive lifestyle stuff on an unprecedented scale at a time when football's image was in the gutter.

I met Steve Jones, who was the man Coca-Cola sent over with a mission statement to crack northern Europe. His goal was to distribute Coke and its other products across Europe to make the brand as big as it was in the United States. Steve's determination and drive was clear. He told me, 'Everything that goes down your throat that isn't Coke is a rival of mine.'

I loved that line. I said, 'All right, but if I am going to do a deal with you that rules out all these other things that go down my throat – apart from Mars bars – you are going to have to chuck in some proper money and I want to see some real support. I want adverts in newspapers and a concerted marketing campaign.'

They obliged. In return, we had to raise the stakes with England. He needed to know they'd be seen. He wanted Coke on the bench, too. That wouldn't be easy – it has never been the healthiest drink around. We could perhaps do it in branded coolers around the training ground – they'd really be drinking Lucozade Sport and nobody would be any the wiser – but we found very creative ways of dividing sport and leisure to give them more exposure. The squad would train in the morning and then there would always be a period in the afternoon when the players would get bored or training would end – that was Jon Smith time. John Dawes was incredibly imaginative and the pictures were always fun.

The problem, inevitably, was Umbro, because all they wanted was everything. Peter Kenyon worked for them at the time and, although it never got physical, they used to get extremely irate with me. I was Public Enemy Number One to them. But the players were on board and the money was starting to creep up to meaningful amounts.

We always shared some of the money with the FA, too. That justified it further as we could reasonably argue some cash was going back into the system for the future of the game. OK, it was only a small percentage but it was still money they would never otherwise have received. To their eternal credit, physio Fred Street and kit-man Norman Medhurst helped no end. I sat down with them and explained how I wanted to take things to the next level. Although Umbro were upset, nobody had tried to intervene and the sponsors I had brought in were satisfied.

I used to go and see Bobby before games and say, 'Look, Bobby, are you all right with this? Can we do some of this stuff?' If it was an important game, the answer was an unequivocal no. But in a friendly, Bobby would say, 'If we are 2-0 or 3-0 up, then I'll leave it to Fred and Norman.'

Fred and Norman received a cut of the players' pool but Bobby politely declined, I think in part not wishing to take a cut away from the players. That's what Bobby was like. Steve was very happy with what we were doing but he wanted me to scale back other sponsors and gross up what we were doing with Coke everywhere. He told me he wanted Coke on the pitch during games. How could I possibly deliver that?

I needed time to think. A few days later, I met with Steve and told him to buy some advertising at Wembley. It would do Coke no harm to be visibly supporting the team through more conventional methods than the ones I had created. I'd then visit the stadium just before the game and tell the players where the boards would be so that when they scored, they could celebrate in front of them. And that would be Coke's TV time. I broached this with the players and they seemed receptive enough. Bobby was happy as long as the game wasn't pivotal.

Paul Gascoigne was great at it. He'd score, his team-mates would jump on him and then suddenly they'd all be looking around for the right board and they'd sprint over to it. Then Gazza would fall over because when the players were at ground level, the board was in full sight of the TV cameras.

Steve and I used to roll around laughing when they did it because nobody had picked up on it, despite the completely unnatural movement of a group of players sprinting off in a direction away from where they'd scored, the bench or England's supporters.

Steve wanted even more. I sat with Fred and Norman, and said to them, 'When you go on to treat a player, you carry drinks. Let's brand them up. You won't actually be giving them Coke – it'll be Lucozade or water – but the effect will work for a television audience.' It was a mobile advertising board – we'd never done it before.

Fred and Norman were keen. We went to Bobby. He laughed and agreed. By this time, I was having regular team meetings with the squad. Bobby would do the serious stuff, talking tactics, set-pieces and all things football. I would be the cabaret act that came on afterwards. 'Hi, lads. Right – the mission for this trip is . . .' and I'd proceed to list whatever ideas John Dawes and I had come up with, where the advertising boards would be and the latest sponsorship deals. 'We have a deal with Nike,' I once explained to them. 'So, when you enter the field of play as a substitute, run on about ten or fifteen yards and stop. Then bend down and check your boots, or re-tie your laces. Make it natural.'

There were very few alternative camera angles in those days. Replays were scarce. The director had nothing else to do but focus on the player coming on. And if he was checking his boots, there might be a close-up. And in that close-up, there would be a clear advert for Nike. We got paid well for that.

The lads were brilliant but Umbro's anger was rising by the month. They had exclusivity on the field which meant I had to encourage players or staff to make 'mistakes'. Fred would pick up the 'wrong' bag – because I asked him to – and ran on with a medical kit with 'Trebor Mints' written on the side. He did it with a smile because it was so innocuous. It used to cheer up the team and the management because everyone was having fun with it. The sponsors and the newspapers loved it. The BBC – the only real broadcaster around – didn't, but the matches were vital to them regardless.

My deal with Coke also included advertising in publications beyond the conventional realm of football. We used gossip and lifestyle magazines and even tried to expand into FM radio. Sport had been a strictly AM entity but I knew Richard Park at Capital Radio and explored the idea of putting music and football together. Now the two are intertwined *de rigueur* but, back then, there was a lot of opposition.

A few months before the 1990 World Cup, I was phased out from Maradona's inner circle by members of an élite organisation based in southern Italy. They took me aside in Diego's house one day. 'Jon, we'd like to say thank you . . .' one of them began.

'No problem at all. My pleasure,' I darted back.

' . . . we want to say thank you and goodbye.'

'Sorry?'

'Your services are no longer required.'

'Oh. Any reason?' I asked.

'No. They are just no longer required.'

'Is there someone I can talk to about this? Can I have a word with Diego?'

'No. We think it is best you go now.'

These were characters you didn't argue with. I didn't see Diego for about five years after that. It was the start of his substance abuse and a time when things were running out of control. Guillermo Coppola was his hands-on manager and I was cut out. It was a shame because I really liked him.

In 1987, Ken Bates was organising the Football League's centenary match at Wembley and Maradona was invited to play. The FA were trying to talk to him through Napoli but Diego had about twenty people around him on a daily basis. There was a nice guy called Néstor Gorosito with whom I had common ground. I'd sit with him in Diego's lounge sometimes and say to him, 'Look at this. What the hell is going on? All these people around him. What are they doing? Why are they here?' There were so many hangers-on.

Diego listened to me when he wanted to but I was never that close to him. I brought him over in May 1987 to watch the England team play and organised a dinner. Terry Ramsden provided us with a private jet to fly him in and out of the country. I introduced him to Coke and some other people here but Diego principally wanted to shake hands with the England team and let bygones be bygones after what had happened at the 1986 World Cup in Mexico. It was just a PR exercise. He loved to be loved, even after the 'Hand of God' that knocked England out of the tournament.

After that successful trip, I was puzzled as to why the Football League weren't talking to me about Diego's possible attendance at the event they were planning only three months later in August '87. Amid ongoing Press speculation, Ken called me and asked me what I was playing at. Why hadn't Diego agreed to play? I told him nobody had really asked me. 'I'll ask him if you want me to. Is there a fee for him?'

'No,' Ken snapped back.

'Well, everyone says there is a fee, Ken, so what is it likely to be?'

'We shouldn't have to pay him.'

'I know you shouldn't have to, but the problem is people have mentioned a fee in the Press so it looks like it is now being taken away if you offer nothing. The dynamic is all wrong.'

After some deliberation, Ken offered a six-figure fee but the people closest to Diego demanded more and so we spent the next three weeks in negotiations. I felt sorry for Ken and the Football League at this point because all these people around Diego were winding him up.

That happens a lot, even today. Agents are often accused of doing precisely that – and I'd be lying if I said that didn't go on in some cases – but often there are people hanging around a player and they can potentially ruin a promising career because they are blinded by reflected glory. And rarely do they do so in the best interests of that player who, remember, is supposed to be their mate.

Diego's gang was renowned for it. Eventually, Ken comes up with a number – about £250,000 – and it was time for me to have a frank chat with Diego. 'All the good PR you did before is being undone so, for the sake of what we've built, come to England. The money is good but I know that isn't important to you. Bring your daughter Dalma and make it a family thing.'

He was such a warm guy around his family. God must sprinkle some magic dust on certain people because Diego would light up any room he was in. He stood about 5ft tall but had the presence of a Goliath.

Diego saw my point of view and decided to play. When he

arrived in London, I had to answer questions on his behalf. 'He loves England, he's always wanted to come and experience the culture here – and the Football League is fantastic,' I told journalists once his participation was confirmed.

We were in a car afterwards and he asked me, 'What did I say? Did I say the Football League was great?'

'Yeah, you did. It's OK – don't worry,' I said and he beamed that wonderful smile back at me.

He played in the game and we held a press conference at Wembley afterwards which went off without incident. Diego would usually go to a nightclub called Tramp whenever he was in London but he had Dalma with him so he asked to go somewhere in the English countryside. For years, we had been frequent visitors to a very popular restaurant called Villa Rosa in Brookman's Park. A really lovely guy called Michelli ran the place; he was a huge football fan and Maradona-obsessed. When he found out I was working with Diego, he used to give me free meals just because I'd shaken the great man's hand.

It was a Saturday night and I phoned Villa Rosa and asked for Michelli. The bustle of paying customers bubbled in the background as he came to the phone. 'Hi, Jon. It's mad here tonight. What's the problem?'

'I've got a party of people looking to eat after the England game. We'd like to come in – can you find us a table.'

'Er . . . for you, OK. How many people?'

'About thirty.'

'Don't be stupid – it is Saturday night.'

'Sorry, but there really are that many of us . . . and one of them is Diego Maradona.'

Michelli paused. 'Really? Are you serious?'

'Yes.'

'No problem then. See you shortly.'

We got there about an hour later to find the vast majority of diners knocking elbows as they ate, crammed into one end of the restaurant to accommodate us. Diego walked in and Michelli welled up immediately. We had a wonderful night. Gary Lineker was with us and very gracious as always, especially given Diego commanded so much attention throughout. Everybody came back to our house at the end of the evening as cars home were arranged but Gary stayed with us, not before posing for a photograph with Diego, Janine and me. It is a treasured memory.

Relations improved a little between the England team and the Press during World Cup 1990 qualification. England were unbeaten – although a 1–1 draw against Saudi Arabia prompted the *Daily Mirror* to run with a headline 'GO, IN THE NAME OF ALLAH, GO' demanding Bobby's head on a platter once again.

They went seventeen games undefeated and performances were promising in the build-up to Italia '90 but the domestic game suffered another shocking tragedy. The Hillsborough disaster in April 1989 claimed ninety-six more innocent lives and thrust football into the spotlight for all the wrong reasons once again. Although the England team were being viewed in a more positive light, the work we did could obviously never outweigh the public anguish at such human suffering or prevent further negative headlines if the Press wanted to hound Bobby.

The players were earning money, major sponsors were coming on board and I was a bridge between the media and the team. I did my best to blunt the knives that were out for Bobby where I could.

Gazza was exciting fans and, although England lost to Uruguay in May 1990 for the first time since Euro '88, there was something tangible to build on. However, just before the 1990 World Cup, a story emerged claiming Bobby had agreed a deal to join PSV Eindhoven after the tournament and the Press targeted him again, arguing he could not possibly be committed to England's cause with another job on the horizon.

Thatcher's Government had even talked about pulling the team out of the World Cup because of a series of hooligan incidents which, in fairness, reflected well on no one. Gazza was also involved in a bar fight on the eve of the tournament. Asked if he would sue, Gazza, in his own inimitable way, said, 'Nah, I whacked the cunt, didn't I?' England left for Sardinia with a nearby jet running its engines on the tarmac so Press questions could not be heard as they boarded.

We were still the back channel that kept a relationship going when, publicly, Bobby and the Press were at each other's throats. Things were really bad after this latest flurry of negativity. It had become a national sport to have a pop at the England team. We had to operate under the radar. The FA didn't see it that way but Bobby appreciated the help.

I was able to deliver some information into the camp through my relationship with sports editors. The FA press officer David Bloomfield, Michelle Farrah and I became good mates eventually. He was an interesting guy and had a certain appeal. I made sure people at the FA were involved – particularly Glen Kirton – and if we did something with Burton or Top Man, I'd always include them so they got a new wardrobe out of it.

David came up with the Italia '90 song. He was friendly with someone in New Order but I had to get the team to agree to do it. They thought the one we did in 1988 was rubbish – entitled 'All the Way' – and it was. But when they heard 'World in Motion' for the first time, everything changed. Gary Lineker was still quite opposed to it but I played it to John Barnes and told him he should do the rap. He was really up for it. It was clear to me that track would change the way football songs are created and received. 'This is good music and, believe me, I know,' I told them.

I think the squad saw a lot of what I was doing during Italia '90 as a welcome distraction. It was a very long tournament – although not quite long enough for England – and we were sitting in the hotel in Sardinia desperately trying to find ways of amusing the team. We organised a shoot featuring Peter Shilton jumping into a swimming pool catching a ball with a T-shirt emblazoned with Coca-Cola. It was a perfect encapsulation of the team's vibrancy. That made all the papers, too. It blew Coke away, which was just as well because they were putting in hundreds of thousands of pounds by now. We had twenty-six lads sharing over one million pounds during that tournament – on top of their wages – which was big money.

Sometimes we took advantage of it. Mars and I had a conversation one day in which I told them there was a marketing company inside First Artist that was best placed to facilitate further progress. Of course, Mars had their own marketing department but they didn't understand what we were doing. We were breaking barriers. I hired First Artist's marketing services out to Mars and was being paid another income in addition to my cut of the players' pool. I was very open about it and made good money.

We started a gag with the England team during Italia '90 that whenever one of the players did an interview, they had to get a song title in one of their answers. Each player would pull one out of a hat at random and be forced to work it in somehow. It is a tradition that continued throughout the '90s and beyond, but I will always remember Graeme Le Saux drawing 'I've Got a Brand New Combine Harvester'. We were sitting there watching him and somebody asked him about the tactical patterns England used in their previous game.

'Well,' said Le Saux, puffing his cheeks out, 'it was difficult in that game. It was a bit like I've got a brand new combine harvester but I don't know where I'm going with it.'

That was magnificent.

I was very friendly with the players but I did make one big mistake. I received the same training kit and leisurewear as them so I walked around the place in an England tracksuit. You should never cross that line. I took stick for that and rightly so. I overheard one of the Press pack – not a regular covering the team – say, 'Look at this agent, wearing the same gear as the team. Who does he think he is?' He was right. I should have always worn a suit or smart-casual clothing. An agent should always know their place, which is in the background, not to stand alongside the talent as an equal in their domain. Umbro probably didn't take too kindly to me wearing their gear either.

The groundswell of public support for the team grew on an unimaginable scale throughout Italia '90. There were riots around some of the games – most notably before we played Egypt – but the team's performance captured people's imaginations and it reached fever pitch at the semi-final stage. Gazza cried, Lineker scored, Pearce and Waddle didn't. England lost to West Germany on penalties. The players were obviously devastated.

I told them, 'Despite what has just happened, you are so loved and celebrated back home. You have done so much for the well-being of football in England. What you have done in four weeks has helped put right perhaps a decade of pain which the game has suffered from the Bradford fire, the Heysel disaster, Hillsborough and everything else. You have put the smiles back on the sporting faces of people in England. We should have a bus parade even though you didn't win it. We'll position it as the England team saying "thank you" to the fans for all their support, not a celebration.'

That idea was met with significant scepticism. After all, we hadn't won the tournament and cynics would argue we were celebrating failure. There were many who thought England should come home quietly and let the plaudits for their performance permeate the public consciousness.

I kept persevering. 'We'll get the sponsors to chuck in some more money and give some to charity. This is a big moment. When you come back, every newspaper, television and radio station in the country is going to want a piece of you. If nothing else, let's say thank you to the people who have supported you.'

They acquiesced and I got my way. I flew back to England and sorted out the logistics in tandem with Janine while the team stayed on for the third/fourth place play-off, which they lost to Italy at the Stadio San Nicola in Bari.

I got Luton Airport to let me on the tarmac when the team landed so I could brief everyone on board about what was going to happen. The plan was simply to do a loop around and return to the terminal.

The turnout on the day was astonishing. The bus driver was worried for the safety of the public because hundreds of thousands of people crammed into every conceivable space along the proposed route. It was overwhelming. The team were amazed as they stood on the bus but it was all getting a bit too much for Liverpool midfielder Steve McMahon, whose mind was racing to the possibility he could be witnessing a second Hillsborough. I put my hand on his shoulder and left him to gather his thoughts.

It was party time. Gazza wore that now famous pair of rubber breasts on his torso and lapped up all the adulation from the human walls that lined the roadside.

The connection between players and fans had never been so visibly realised. It was the beginning of a new era in football. Those images were used to visualise the future of the game in this country – this is what it could be. You can co-habit with sponsors, make money and redistribute it to people in the game but still retain football's soul. I really believe it was a seminal moment in time that lifted our national sport out of the gutter and into a new consciousness as entertainment.

Football had crossed the divide. Not only had it found an audience on FM radio, thereby collecting non-football and, more importantly, female supporters in significant numbers for the very first time. It absolutely blitzed that medium. It was everywhere; we even had a number 1 record at the time with New Order. We had great component parts: Gazza's mesmeric football and his tears after being booked in the semi-final, knowing he would miss the final if England made it; Bobby Robson, who'd had a heinous time at the 1988 European Championships, suddenly reviving the team in a way few thought possible; the dramatic victories; the agonising penalty shoot-outs. We had sponsors thanking the team on behalf of a nation after a decade of people dying in football stadiums. We were trailblazers too; a lot of European nations looked at our players' pool and the way the England team were marketed and followed suit.

People just wanted to be part of something that felt so real to them. I don't care what anyone says, I think the way we managed that squad off the field played a big role in it. It was so much bigger than I ever imagined it could be; the LA Raiders could not have achieved that level of publicity even if they had won the Superbowl. Italia '90 touched an entire nation. The England team had put me back on track, too, but this was just the beginning, not just for me but for English football. Nobody could have predicted the revolution that was to come next.

8

Monarchs and
Kingmakers

The 1990s began amid growing momentum for change in English football. There had been reluctance to tackle the issues blighting football in the previous decade but the Hillsborough disaster altered the prevailing mood. It was a tragedy that politicians and public alike vowed would never be repeated. After years of condemning the consequences without tackling the cause, Westminster realised it was time to act.

The Taylor Report, published in January 1990, recommended that the biggest stadia became all-seater, a requirement the Football League demanded was enacted by August 1994. But there were plans already afoot to revolutionise the game long before then. Informal and intermittent talks began in the mid-1980s among senior executives at the top clubs, then labelled the 'Big Five': Arsenal, Tottenham, Manchester United, Liverpool and Everton. There was a feeling that the remaining eighty-seven clubs – but more specifically those outside the First Division – were living off the successes of the élite. The Football League's one-club, one-vote system restricted the Big Five's ability to make changes in their favour. They wanted greater control while remaining part of the fabric of English football.

Simple changes were blocked. A motion to increase match-day substitutes from one to two was voted down because smaller clubs complained they would have to travel in a bigger bus to matches. The big clubs wanted to put names on the back of shirts as well as numbers but the move was opposed by the rest because of the additional laundry bills.

Money was also, inevitably, a factor. The Heysel disaster prompted a five-year ban from European competitions which, further impacted the Big Five's revenues. That ban began in 1985, which was also the year television companies decided to drop live coverage of matches. The negative environment prompted further talks among the Big Five over breaking away and forming a league independent of the game's current structure but strong opposition from the other clubs curtailed their ambitions. Although no agreement was reached, it was beginning to dawn on the game's powerbrokers that the real financial power lay with only a handful of clubs.

Greg Dyke seized upon this sentiment. By 1988, the Big Five had been offered one million pounds each by Dyke, then a senior executive at ITV, as part of a four-year package worth a total of forty-four million. At the time, each club had previously received twenty-five thousand pounds in television revenue; Arsenal's entire turnover was just one-and-a-half million pounds.

The Big Five had their heads turned but there was a problem – the other Football League clubs had voted in favour of a deal with BSB, an emerging satellite company. The Big Five lobbied hard against BSB, claiming that ITV were the established broadcasters and there was no guarantee their rivals could pay the sums they were promised. The Football League clubs reneged on their initial decision and voted for ITV, meaning the Big Five stayed in the existing set-up for the time being.

But then came that fateful day at Hillsborough in 1989. It is impossible to underestimate the impact those horrifying pictures had on a nation already examining its uneasy and often unedifying relationship with football; the injustice lasted for far too long but I am delighted the families of the ninety-six finally won their case in 2016, defying forces that obviously didn't have their interests or the truth at heart.

The fences caging in supporters at grounds were removed. Prime Minister Margaret Thatcher visited Hillsborough in the aftermath and could barely disguise her despair. She wouldn't accept that football could ever change, reflecting the view espoused by the *Sunday Times* after the Bradford fire in 1985 that it was 'a slum sport played in slum stadiums increasingly watched by slum people, who deter decent folk from turning up'.

The Taylor Report was a damning indictment on the state of football. Poor leadership, dilapidated stadia, insufficient policing, an excessive drinking culture among fans and the failure of authorities to learn from past mistakes all added up to a toxic mix in dire need of cleansing. Football had to lift itself out of the gutter. Government funding, local authority grants and further financial support from the FA helped clubs pay for the stadium renovations required to drag them into the twentieth century.

ITV's eleven-million-a-year deal was the biggest boost to the clubs' coffers but the Big Five, now able to compete in Europe once again, believed the distribution of wealth was at odds with the relative contributions of English football's top sides. A now infamous secret meeting took place on Friday 16 November, 1990 between six men: David Dein (Arsenal); Martin Edwards (Manchester United); Irving Scholar (Tottenham); Sir Philip Carter (Everton); Noel White (Liverpool); and host Greg Dyke. It was decided that this was the moment to form a new league. They believed the Taylor Report had driven the winds of change sufficiently to sweep enough clubs and the FA along with them.

Liverpool were the pre-eminent club and, as it happened, White was on the FA Council and, along with Dein, the pair took their plan to the FA on 6 December 1990. To their astonishment, Graham Kelly, formerly of the Football League but now chief executive at the FA, welcomed them with open arms. Kelly was in the midst of writing the FA's blueprint for the future of the game and he believed a new Premier League aligned with his vision of the future – the essence of the Premier League had to be entertainment. Some of the Big Five members were already looking to American Football as a possible template as the future marketing of English football.

That's where I came in. England's performance at Italia '90 was the antidote to the domestic dismay that engulfed the sport. The bus parade which greeted the team showcased the depth of sporting passion among the English public. My work had highlighted the positive aspects of the heroes they came to worship, and had resonated with football's revolutionaries who were desperate to alter the common perception of the game after years of controversy. My reputation had steadily grown in the years leading up to the moment when I was invited into the clandestine inner circle plotting English football's regeneration.

First Artist's player-management portfolio was steadily growing. Diego Maradona had been our headline act and that association made me useful to senior figures at various clubs. In 1987, Peter Ridsdale was the chief executive at Top Man and also involved at Leeds United. I knew him from their sponsorship of the England football team and he invited me up to Leeds for a chat. Leeds had just missed out on an FA Cup Final and promotion to the First Division under Billy Bremner that summer and, little did I know, the club's hierarchy wanted to shake things up. Their managing director, Bill Fotherby, joined us at lunch. I thought I was just chatting amongst friends before the conversation took an unexpected turn.

'How's Diego?' asked Peter.

'He's fine. We're doing a few bits and pieces with him. We helped get him his Coke deal – the black stuff, not the white stuff – and although we aren't that close to him, we're inside the camp.'

'OK. Think he'd sign for Leeds?'

I was taken aback. 'Er . . . probably not. The weather isn't quite as good as Naples for starters.'

'Yeah, but if we paid him a lot of money? And we arranged a big house, spared no expense, that sort of thing, what about then?'

'I don't really know. Maybe.' I thought no more of it.

But from that one answer, they leaked story after story to the press about how Maradona was weighing up a move to Leeds. I vowed never again to put myself in that position.

The journalists I was talking to knew I would be speaking off the record because, if they breached that, they wouldn't get the considerable access I was in a position to provide them. Equally, I knew they had deadlines and a power far beyond anything I could achieve, so I looked after them where I could. It was a symbiotic relationship in that respect.

Perhaps I became a bit too trusting of people as a result. Bill completely turned me over after that lunch and put his name in lights. We kept saying it was unlikely to happen; Napoli were irritated by it and I had to phone Diego to explain the situation.

Leeds continued briefing the press to the effect that talks were ongoing when, in reality, whenever I did speak to them, it was always about something else. I put out statements to the contrary, which Leeds then countered by stating that I was only saying that to protect my client! We denied it tirelessly and, eventually, the story petered out, although Bill did his best to revive it with the *Yorkshire Evening Post* as long as he could. The deal may never have materialised – or even got off the ground – but the intense media speculation around Maradona's future only thrust me further into the limelight by osmosis.

I had become very publicly visible, not least because I made sure my mates in the media were writing nice things about me, showcasing the groundbreaking work I felt we were doing. First Artist was receiving enquiries from all over the world as we pressed ahead on various fronts. In June 1989, I got a phone call from an official in General Wojciech Jaruzelski's Government. I was told Mikhail Gorbachev's Soviet Government was cutting financial ties to the satellite states. Many teams at that time were owned by the state. Legia Warsaw, for example, was actually owned by the Army but they reported up to the state; the supply line of cash ultimately came from Gorbachev. *Perestroika* had many aspects to it but one of them was about countries outside Russia not paying for anything in the Soviet Union.

So the Jaruzelski Government got in touch and asked me to come to Warsaw to have a conversation about selling their players, as they owned the registrations and could generate money through their sale to put back into the system. We sold them all around Europe and two came to the UK. Dariusz Dziekanowski went to Celtic, where his claim to fame was scoring four goals in a European Cup Winners' Cup tie against Partizan Belgrade but his team did not win the game. That had never happened before. Weirdly, another client of mine, Andrey Arshavin, did the same thing in the Premier League many years later as Liverpool drew 4-4 with Arsenal in 2009. Dariusz Wdowczyk also moved from Legia to Celtic and stayed there for five years.

After 1990, I had become 'persona more grata' at the FA because of what happened at Italia '90. I did feel somewhat bomb-proof at the time. The connections with the FA had been getting better as time went on and the FA were more inclusive of me during Italia '90. There wasn't a great squad overhaul after 1990 and I had the confidence of the players. The players' pool was paid out to everyone in September, which did relations no harm at all, given it had topped one million pounds.

I suggested adding more entertainment at Wembley matches. We laid on big pre-game shows but the crowd never really took to them. The FA rightly believed these days were all about the football, so why not organise charity games? It was a great idea. We had a host of celebrities agree to play – stepping out on the hallowed Wembley turf was a sufficient draw in itself. Rod Stewart played once and was somewhat nervous. 'You've played in stadiums like this all around the world, Rod, why is this affecting you so much?' I asked him.

'This is different,' he said. 'This is football.'

I played in one because they were a man short. Bobby Moore was on my team. The moment he passed the ball to me was a seminal moment in my life. I played the most careful pass I was capable of to ensure I didn't give it away.

The FA asked me to organise friendly matches for the England team – by that time I was licensed by FIFA and UEFA to arrange matches. Having been considered something of a pest for a couple of years, now I was being given official duties regarding team logistics. It felt like a vindication of my work to date. So I set the wheels in motion to arrange a game with Cameroon in February 1991 and, later, against Brazil in May 1992, both fixtures greeted with approval from the FA and the players themselves. Cameroon was a particularly attractive fixture, evoking memories of England's quarter-final victory during Italia '90, but also because Roger Milla's performance was one of the tournament's most captivating stories.

He was thirty-eight years old yet scored four goals and each time he celebrated with a dance around the corner flag that became a signature move for fans all over the world. We inserted a clause in the contract with the Cameroon team that Milla had to play – he did and the game was a sell-out.

I began to spread into other sports, primarily managing their players' pool as well. The Welsh rugby team never won a game while I organised theirs either. For a while, I thought I was cursed.

The England cricket team did well, however, getting to the final of the World Cup in 1992. I phoned the new marketing director, Terry Blake, at the back end of 1991 and explained the work I was doing for the football team and thought it was easily transferable to cricket. The authorities agreed and I got involved, but the Test and County Cricket Board (TCCB) were much more controlling than the FA ever were. Sponsorships were vetted and they took a keen interest in my activities, probably in part because they weren't providing the same integrated support to the team as the FA did in football. I was used to an existing infrastructure around the England football team, with everything already organised for the players from transportation and accommodation to individual dietary requirements. The cricket team had no such luxuries. After the World Cup Final at the Sydney Cricket Ground, I found myself outside hailing cabs for Graham Gooch and the others. Nothing was laid on. They had to get themselves home having just lost the World Cup Final.

They would later seek divine intervention. After my wife Lee died, I set up the Lee Smith Foundation – run by a fabulous woman named Karen Rauch aided by two of my closest friends Andrea and Julian Margolin – and I accepted an invitation to sit on the board of the Institute of Child Health at Great Ormond Street hospital. One of the other members said he'd spent some time in Calcutta praying with Mother Teresa. After one meeting, I approached him in search of a contact number for her because I was due to travel there with the England cricket team in early 1993. He gave me a number of the Mission there, which I rang after arriving with the team at my hotel in Calcutta.

'Hi, my name's Jon Smith,' I began. 'I'm the agent of the England cricket team. You might know that we are in town for a Test Match with India. Is it possible for us to have a meeting with Mother Teresa?'

This little voice almost whispered back, 'You are speaking to her.'

I said: 'Sorry?'

'I am Mother Teresa.'

'Oh. Hi. Um, do I call you Mother?'

'You are very welcome to join me,' she said, ignoring my question. 'I pray at 6 a.m. every morning. Come and join me tomorrow.'

I called her Mother anyway. I turned up at 5.45 a.m. and she opened the door. She remembered me, took my hand and led me inside. She had bare feet and I remember her toes were bent out of shape. And she was very, very small. We held hands and prayed together before she signed a prayer card. I told her a few members of the team would love the same experience and, a couple of days later, I took Phil DeFreitas and Neil Fairbrother back to see her.

Religious experiences notwithstanding, I really believed the core philosophy wasn't any different from sport to sport. It had to focus on entertainment, garner financial support from sponsors, generate a sizeable television audience and gain traction in print media. It was a transferable template. Although there were smaller networks who might give something a good showing on prime-time, it was preferable to be on ITV at 8 p.m. My philosophy had worked and I wanted to be more than a football agent: I wanted to own things, which is why I became an event promoter.

Football was second only to sex in terms of the British public's interest – and maybe chocolate. As long as I had the England football team, my stock with the media was always going to be incredibly high. I could trade off access to the football players in return for greater coverage of other sports I was promoting to grow an embryonic audience. The five years from 1989–94 were sensational for me.

Jon Holmes and Dennis Roach were my contemporaries and they managed people very well. Jon was one of the forerunners in the agent world for whom I have always had great respect, but I was building the definitive sports management and marketing business of the 1990s. Player management was about 40 per cent of what we would do in any typical week. England get-togethers occurred intermittently throughout the year and we would spend time setting those up a week or two before. There were also strategy meetings with sponsors but I had a marketing department to deal with all that.

But what really underlined my ability to deliver a vision of the new Premier League was running the London Monarchs in 1991. Helping Jarvis Astaire bring the NFL to Wembley in 1986 had lit a fire within me that I was able to stoke early in the 1990s. I wanted to bring other American sports to the UK and my relationship with Jarvis, who was on the board at Wembley, afforded me that opportunity.

I was involved – only on the periphery – as Jarvis brought the NFL to Wembley in 1986 and 1987 but my growth as an agent and promoter in the intervening four years prompted Jarvis to give me a major opportunity. Some of that growth came courtesy of luck more than judgement. I won the contract to run the British American Football League and brought in my mates at Coca-Cola as sponsors but still needed help with the day-to-day management.

There weren't many people in promotions I could call on who even knew what shape the ball was but my brother-in-law, Raymond Jaffe, was an expert. He was American Football mad and had the passion to grow an embryonic enterprise such as this. There was only one problem – he worked as a baker for Janine's father. He had no promotional experience whatsoever, but I just thought his passion and versatility could extend to this challenge so I took a huge gamble on Raymond by asking him to run the league, supported by a management team that we supplied.

He exceeded all my expectations, so much so that our success catapulted us into prime position when London was granted the eighth World League of American Football (WLAF) franchise.

The NFL came to Jarvis, understandably, to discuss the details. Jarvis graciously passed them on to me – which I took as a welcome further sign of my progress – but we decided to take the project on together. The NFL retained a controlling stake but we were given a sizeable equity and virtual autonomy to run the new London Monarchs team as we saw fit. Jarvis took a back seat and I was designated CEO; I had become Jarvis's protégé by this point. I used to call working for him my 'Alma Mater', but he would always correct me by saying he was my 'Alma Pater'.

I named the budgets but the key to the whole operation was Larry Kennan. We brought him in as coach after his work as an offensive co-ordinator for the Indianapolis Colts, where he had developed promising young quarterback Jeff George and running back Eric Dickerson. He had won the Superbowl with the LA Raiders during his spell there as quarterback coach and jumped at the chance to lead his own team. He brought two or three advisers with him but Larry's knowledge was so impressive, we backed him completely.

Marketing it was the big challenge. Although the WLAF was underwritten by twenty-six of the twenty-eight NFL team owners, the League was effectively funded by the fifty million dollars paid by ABC and the cable station USA Network.

In February 1991, we commissioned a survey which revealed that only 0.3 per cent of Londoners were aware of the Monarchs. The situation required a serious PR drive. We ran a few publicity campaigns which helped improve things but it took Ellery Hanley to really make things take off. Hanley was the big star in Rugby League, which at that time was vying with Union as the sport's pre-eminent code. I asked him to come and play for the Monarchs. He really fancied it and came to our training base in Hertfordshire.

The story got unbelievable coverage. It featured everywhere from the tabloids to *News at Ten*. Even the BBC, who had been reluctant to acknowledge gridiron as a credible sport in the UK, covered Hanley's potential move on *Sportsnight*. He agreed in principle a contract which enabled him to combine playing rugby league for Wigan and American Football for us.

That moment launched the Monarchs into the public consciousness; another survey in March told us the Monarchs had jumped up to an astonishing 97 per cent recognition factor. As it turned out, Hanley never played for the Monarchs as the appearance fee became too prohibitive on top of late-stage contractual complications at Wigan. But, in effect, he had already done his job – we ended up paying him a small fee as a thank you for propelling the Monarchs on to a bigger stage.

We opted to play at Wembley Stadium, obviously facilitated by Jarvis. It was a brave call given there were no guarantees we could fill the eighty thousand seats, or even get close. We drew fifty-one thousand for the first match by giving away tickets to schools but, by the end of the year, we sold out with each fan a paying customer.

The media bought into it as we went along. The *Evening Standard* gave us great coverage and Capital Radio shared my vision – we were going to make sport cool on the streets, not a catalyst for violence on the streets. Capital Radio programme director Richard Park put the Monarchs on FM radio – it was bold but exactly what I had seen in the States and something I knew would work here.

Everybody wanted to be at a Monarchs game – from Chris Evans and Danny Baker, Duran Duran and Danni Minogue to Chris Tarrant, Steve Davis and Paul Gascoigne. We created a rock 'n' roll atmosphere. We played 'All Right Now' by Free every time there was a touchdown, there were cheerleaders, a laser show, fireworks and even stilt-walkers; the sense of fun in the air was palpable whenever the Monarchs were in town. We released a single entitled 'Yo-Go Monarchs' which sold well.

Monarchs fans chanted my name. One weekend provided the perfect example of the dichotomy my life had become: the Monarchs played at Wembley and I was front and centre, a personality celebrated by many inside the ground. Two days later, England played at Wembley and I was back in the shadows – anonymous to most and the pesky, meddling agent to the rest.

But the ratings in America were poor from the outset which gave the NFL a problem. We won the Worldbowl against the Barcelona Dragons but nobody in America cared. The American management of the League decided to change the rosters for the following season and, although there was no hard evidence they were going to downgrade our team in favour of the Americans, the head coach, Larry, Jarvis and I were all concerned our winning team would be broken up. So we decided to leave on a high.

My events team were distraught and divided. A lot of them were on seasonal contracts which were not renewed, as the NFL brought in their own people, many of whom were American, to run the team thereafter. It was a hugely difficult decision at the time but one made easier by what had been bubbling under the surface for some time and was now coming to the boil.

I had known David Dein for many years through our connections at Arsenal. He joined the board in 1983 and I represented a couple of players there, which put me in frequent contact with David.

Conversations between the Big Five had intensified in 1990 and, by the following year, the FA's support for the formation of the Premier League had gathered pace. The Football League were furious with the FA for their stance, arguing they were railroading through the most significant change in English football history. While the public and media debated on which side of the fence they should stand, secretive meetings were taking place throughout 1991 as the Big Five fleshed out their vision for the future.

Rick Parry was a management consultant at Ernst & Young and had spent time in 1985 orchestrating Manchester's bid to host the 1992 Olympic Games. Rick was hired in an attempt to ensure the formation of an élite league would succeed. He and the Big Five executives had begun to look at American sport as a possible template for the future.

I met Rick for a Chinese meal – coincidentally, the same venue where John Cleese picked up his gourmet duck dish in the famous *Fawlty Towers* scene – over which we discussed just one thing – the Premier League. We talked about how to make English football more enticing to foreign players. And we agreed unequivocally that its essence had to be entertainment – everything I had believed in since witnessing the LA Raiders almost ten years earlier.

My experience elsewhere put me in prime position to help convince a sceptical media of the new league. I could also convince players to support a promotional campaign by endorsing the formation of a new division. My relationships with sponsors could help bring some serious companies on board to part-finance the process. And I could deliver the marketing campaign that would be the antithesis of the widespread disillusionment with our national game prevalent at that time.

I also had Noel White's ear because he had been on the FA Council after Euro '88 when I was searching for people sympathetic to the promotional work we were doing with the England team. Noel saw the model we were putting into effect and thought I could add value to the similar ideas they were formulating around the Premier League. I was the guy already delivering it in other sports while transforming the lifestyle image of the England team.

BSB and Sky merged to begin operating as BSkyB in 1990. I met Rupert Murdoch a few times and he bought into the vision of football as entertainment. Every time I saw him, he was eating a bowl of carrots. 'Is that what I have to eat to get your brains?' I once asked him. He smiled without answering but instead introduced me to Sam Chisholm, whom Sky had hired partly in anticipation of winning the television contract for the new league. I began to exchange ideas with Sky over a sustained period and, as a result, I found myself with links to all sides as the Premier League gradually edged closer to existence. First Artist was the only multi-purpose agency in the UK at the time and it put me at the epicentre of this football revolution, albeit intermittently as progress was slow. I knew it had potential and made sure I stayed close with it, especially given other agents were beginning to try and do what we were and I didn't want to lose out to them through any complacency.

David Dein was the main architect of the Premier League and I believe he saw me as an ideas man. They wanted an innovator to help realise an ambitious goal which was still meeting resistance from all sides. The Football League contested ownership of a new Premier League with the FA in a case which went to the High Court in the summer of 1991. They lost. It was determined that the FA was responsible for the Premier League and, with that objection laid to rest, a fierce bidding war began between ITV and

BSkyB's successor, Rupert Murdoch's Sky. On 18 May 1992, Sky and the BBC agreed a five-year package worth £214m. It gave Sky the rights to the Premier League, the FA Cup and England Internationals for the contract's duration.

After it was confirmed, Sam, who had been appointed chief executive, phoned me for a chat about how to launch their live coverage. I turned up expecting a one-on-one meeting and, instead, he ushered me into a room where his entire production team was waiting.

'Lord Smith,' which is what he always used to call me, 'this is the team that will run Sky Sports. And, boys, Jon is going to tell you how to do it. Away you go.'

Some warning would have been nice. I waffled for about an hour – thankfully without stuttering – and made partial sense, I think. The ideas were all in my head because I'd seen them with the Raiders and worked on it in the UK, most recently with the Monarchs, but also from going back and forth to America to assess first-hand what was successful and what wasn't. I'd had no time to organise my thoughts but I told them how tribal it needed to be. And we had to combine marketing and anti-marketing; take the good and the bad and celebrate both. Hooliganism is obviously abhorrent but bad boys on the pitch are nothing to be afraid of. I wanted dancing girls on the pitch and fireworks. The production team looked back at me with a degree of bemusement but went along with it.

I wanted to introduce the concept of Monday-night football to England having seen it in America. Very few people went out on a Monday but it was a dead night on television because broadcasters saved their best programming for later in the week. And under the lights, we could really push the razzmatazz.

Public opinion was divided on the imminent new league. I remember sitting on a fans' forum panel once trying to convince a particularly angry individual that this was the greatest time to be alive as a football fan. 'When I was growing up, I had no chance of seeing Zico play unless he came with Brazil to play England at Wembley or the World Cup was somewhere close by,' I said. 'Now, you can expect to see the best players in the world here. They will all want to be a part of this. It will happen over time, trust me.'

As it happened, the big sponsor I thought I could deliver to the Premier League opted out. Mars got in early as one of the sub-sponsors but Coca-Cola limited their involvement to the England team. They later chose to sponsor the League Cup and the Football League but I couldn't convince them on the Premier League. It didn't reflect well on me because I had played up my relationship with Steve Jones an awful lot. I didn't know what to say to the Premier League clubs to be. We had delivered Mars and helped soften the media but Coke was a big snub I had to overcome. So I threw myself into Sky's presentation and positioned myself at the front of their vanguard movement.

Raymond Jaffe had been such a hit in promoting American Football in the UK that I put him in charge of that and once again he thrived; years later, Sky wanted to take him from me and it was a tough day at the office when I had to let him go. He later went on to launch his own very successful promotions business – The Promotions Factory – which Sky hired to work on their behalf in the UK and Italy.

The first *Monday Night Football* broadcast involved Manchester City and Queens Park Rangers. I was in the stand at Maine Road and when the dancing girls – the Sky Strikers – came on, the punters sat around me all stared at each other quizzically.

We went ahead with fireworks, too, although they were dropped after a few months because it didn't work well on TV. I arranged for the first match ball to arrive on the pitch in the arms of a guy dropped from an helicopter above the stadium – his parachute was sponsored by the *Sun*.

Dave Hill was the Head of Sport at Sky and, quite simply, a revolutionary. So much of what makes Sky's coverage popular is down to Dave – he later went on to launch Fox Sports and, for the first time in 2016, he produced the Oscars. He was a real inspiration to me – he taught me a lot about different presentational styles for TV.

Sky insisted on seventeen cameras from the outset. The BBC used to use three. Nowadays, Sky use thirty-five cameras, sometimes more, depending on the stadium facilities. Sky's growth has been truly staggering and it happened by chance. Their original business model was based on HBO in America, the principal hook centring on a perceived audience appetite for movies. In those days, you had to wait three years before a movie played in the cinema would be shown on terrestrial television.

Except it didn't work. Sky was losing two million pounds a week by June 1990. BSkyB merged with Sky but, in February 1991, they agreed a refinancing package with the banks totalling £4.2bn. That gave them the platform to bid for the Premier League, which they had by this time identified as the product that could save them. And my, how it did. They made a £62m profit in 1993, £170m in 1994, £237m in 1995 and £315m in 1996.

None of the Big Five or I could ever have imagined how big it would become. But it was the product of a perfect storm:

disaffection among England's top clubs at the restrictive nature of the one-club, one-vote system; the series of disasters and abhorrent level of hooliganism prompting government support for change; and Italia '90, which simultaneously highlighted this country's passion for football and we promoted it in a way that stood as a prototype for the future.

It wasn't completely altruistic. Of course, the money played a part but those involved had a genuine desire to create a lasting legacy. But football is a professional game. Mansfield shouldn't receive the same proportion of centralised income as Manchester United. Those that formed the Premier League would point out that a Founder Members' Agreement is still in place today which distributes television money equally. It has never been challenged. Unlike in La Liga, where Barcelona and Real Madrid have negotiated their own TV deals to the detriment of the League's competitiveness, the Premier League's original agreement has stood the test of time.

A few years ago, I know several chairmen discussed the idea of producing the host signal for these games themselves and selling it internally rather than doing a wraparound Sky deal but it is to the credit of Richard Scudamore, the Premier League's chief executive, that it never got off the ground.

Back in 1992, the Premier League's story was just beginning and before it became the colossal enterprise we now know and love, I had time to explore life beyond football – and even sport.

Jon, Phil, Mick and Rosemary, Majorca, 1964.

Lee and Jon, 1977.

Jon, Boy George, Phil
Smith and Marilyn,
1983.

Gary Lineker, Jon, Janine and Diego Maradona, 1987.

Jon and Peter Beardsley, having completed the record-breaking transfer from Newcastle to Liverpool for £1.9 million, 1987.

Alan 'Fluff' Freeman, my Vintage Nash Metropolitan and dog Scruff, 1989.

Jon and Bobby Robson, 1990.

Jon and John Barnes on the celebratory bus organised by Janine to welcome the England Team home after a successful World Cup, 1990.

Jon and Raymond Jaffe walking around the pitch at Wembley after organising the pre-game entertainment, 1991.

Jon and Graham Taylor, 1991.

Jon and Mother Teresa at her Mission in Calcutta with Neil Fairbrother and Phil (Daffy) DeFreitas during the England Cricket Team Series in India, 2001.

Claudio Ranieri whilst he was Chelsea manager at Jon's 50th birthday, 2002.

Ruud Gullit, Steve Howey, Freddie Fletcher (deceased) and Freddy Shepherd, re-signing Steve Howey at Newcastle, 1998.

Jon and Seb Coe, 2008.

Jon's speech at the
Variety Club tribute
for Jarvis Astaire, 2008.

Jon on completion of the North Pole marathon, 2011.

Jon with Gorbachev and Victoria Charlton, 1993.

The piece of paper used by Francesco Becchetti, Barry Hearn and Jon during the deal to sell Leyton Orient from Barry to Francesco, 2013.

Jon with his son Ross during the Paris to London Bike Ride, 2014.

Jon with his father Mick and son Scott, 2015.

Scott, Janine, Jon and Ross in New York, 2016.

9

From Russia with Love

My involvement with the London Monarchs was over but I still had an appetite for American sport. I went to see the NHL and the NBA to talk them into bringing teams to London. They were keen on international expansion and saw London as the logical host city, not least because of the absence of a language barrier.

The NHL were the first into action; the Chicago Blackhawks and the Montreal Canadiens contested a two-game series at Wembley Arena in September 1992. We branded it as the 'Molson Challenge' – after lead sponsor Molson Breweries of Canada – and the games were the first warm-up outings for both sides ahead of the 1992–93 season.

The Blackhawks had a player called Stu Grimson who was nicknamed the 'Grim Reaper' because he fought opponents regularly on the ice. If anyone ever got past him, he'd take them out. We wanted to focus a promotional campaign for the games on his 'Grim Reaper' image and lined up an interview with the *Sun*. A double-page spread had been agreed – significant coverage back then – when I got a phone call from Stu in his hotel room.

'I can't do this,' he said. 'I can't talk to the *Sun*.'

'Why?' I asked.

'They have naked women in the *Sun* and I am a Born-Again Christian.'

'How can you be a Born-Again Christian when you kick the crap out of anyone that moves in a game?'

'That's a different matter. It's my job.'

I have always thought that distinction was a real dichotomy, one that resonates today when I consider where morality fits into working as an agent. Stu thought it was all right to knock seven bells out of someone but not to look at a picture of a woman. He was 6ft 5in, 220lbs and an animal on the ice yet, meanwhile, he was studying for an Economics degree at the University of Manitoba. Perhaps it all added to the intrigue.

We had to pull the *Sun* article to keep him happy and, instead, set him up with the *Daily Express*, a much tamer publication.

The games went well. I described them in the event programme as the 'greatest hockey spectacle ever witnessed in Great Britain', given it was thirty-three years since the NHL had visited our shores. The two sides were among the six NHL founders and the gravitas of the teams involved only helped strengthen our case for a repeat in future years.

The New York Rangers and the Toronto Maple Leafs followed in their footsteps with another two-game series in September 1993. It was then I learned an invaluable lesson for any promoter – you need backups for absolutely everything.

I had bought a brand-new Zamboni – a device which cleans the ice to remove any divots or indentations on the surface from the players' blades – but it broke down just before the first game was due to start. We were broadcasting live in the UK. Gary Glitter was the warm-up act, chiefly because his 'Hey Song' was a staple at NHL games in the States. He finished his act and came off stage moments after the Zamboni packed up. I grabbed him and said: 'Gary, go back on and do the whole thing again. This time it'll be live on TV, too.'

He set aside his initial bemusement and agreed. We wasted about eight minutes of live television time with Gary Glitter instead of a sports event while the Zamboni was fixed. ITV were furious. Not having a backup Zamboni was indefensible. They screamed at me but all I could do was apologise.

We added a pre-game light show when Gary went on the second time which helped promote a sense of progression for those inside the arena while the audience at home hopefully thought it was an unusually long introduction but entertaining nevertheless. Gary came off stage the second time and said to me, 'It's a good job you had a pro booked tonight.'

I had to give ITV a discount. It was a huge mistake and I feared what the impact would be on First Artist's reputation but we avoided any lasting damage, not least because the event was still a big success but also as the television commentators covered manfully on the night to minimise the confusion surrounding such a significant departure from rehearsals.

Luckily, the NBA were already signed up so we could move on quickly. A month later, in October 1993, the Orlando Magic and the Atlanta Braves flew over for a two-game series of their own which we called the 'London Games'. We got luckier still because Shaquille O'Neal had signed for the Magic in 1992 and Pepsi signed him up after becoming Rookie of the Year in his début season. The Magic had the first pick in the draft and Shaq, fresh out of Louisiana State University, took the NBA by storm.

I spoke to Pepsi just before they launched their marketing campaign and told them to put Shaq front and centre in the UK. Tickets sold out almost instantly as a result. It was pretty much the start of cool black culture reaching a mainstream UK audience.

Shaq was 7ft 1in, colossal in stature, with size 22 feet. At the first press conference, some idiot asked him, 'You are so big with such massive shoes. Is the rest of you as big as that?'

Shaq was clearly offended as the rest of us squirmed with embarrassment. We had to remove that journalist – if that's the right word to describe him – from the room. The interest was huge – that weekend, it rivalled English football as the big sports show in town.

The logistics weren't easy. They had to stay in a Sheraton hotel because the NBA had a sponsorship agreement with them. We had no leverage to negotiate as a result and the costs spiralled; we had to buy in special beds because they were too small for the NBA players. I ended up collecting 900,000 Air Miles because I put the entire bill on credit card.

The players had to duck down in the corridors at Wembley Arena because the ceilings were too low. There wasn't much I could do about that. Still, despite a few teething problems, everything was coming together well and focus turned to the opening night. The games were live across America on NBC. Timings had to be extremely precise also to coincide with the NBA players' regulations regarding pre-match preparations. The players go through their warm-up and then there is a twelve-minute countdown until tip-off. If there is any delay, they have to begin their warm-up all over again with another twelve-minute countdown at the end of it.

Doing the whole thing twice was not an option for us because this was a live broadcast. The players came out for their warm-up to a great fanfare – the sound was deafening, the lights dazzled and the crowd were slowly being whipped up into a frenzy. Then, in my communications earpiece, I heard a pop. I turned to Nadia Raibin, our superb and very experienced event co-ordinator, and asked her what was going on. 'We've lost power in a certain sector of the hall,' she said.

I looked up and a section of the court was darker than the rest. A runner told me a heater by one of the team's benches had switched off.

'OK, it can't be that difficult to fix,' I said, trying to keep calm. 'Where is the problem?'

'We don't know,' said Nadia. 'It could be anywhere in the wiring.'

At this point, the players left the court and the twelve-minute countdown began. Except that countdown had now doubled as a timer to a televisual catastrophe.

I knew it would be the end of my event career if we didn't fix it. However I dressed it up, whoever I blamed, the buck stops with the promoter. I would never have done anything in America again and everything we had in the pipeline would have collapsed with my reputation in tatters. I might even have been left facing a huge financial compensation payout if the insurance company didn't come to my rescue.

Two NBA event co-ordinators approached me seconds after the players left the court demanding to know what was happening. They told me the court was unplayable given the lighting shortage.

That pain you get in your stomach when something goes seriously wrong was causing me to panic but I kept trying to tell myself to be calm. As the minutes ticked by, everyone started shouting at each other in my earpiece which didn't help. Nobody could find the fault and I could feel my blood pressure rising. The NBA guys didn't leave my side as I stood at the control booth co-ordinating the search. They repeatedly stressed the importance of fixing the lights, as if I didn't know the gravitas of the situation already.

'Everyone needs to stop shouting,' I said simultaneously to the NBA and into my comms piece. 'We have to get someone up in the rigging. We've checked all the inputs into the building so it must be up there.'

'There are only a certain number of people allowed up there at any one time and they have to be licensed because it is dangerous to work that high up.'

I told Nadia we had to get an army up there. The clock was ticking down and I was desperately trying to mask the fact we were no closer to solving the issue. By now, NBC had seen the court and were asking why the lighting wasn't right. Internally, I was panicking. I doubt the stadium crowd knew anything was wrong – it is not unusual for lights to drop before a main event – but I knew a critical aspect of my career was on the line. It was an inverted storm – all around was calm but the eye was a maelstrom.

Nadia's lighting team were very experienced – they had worked on gigs for The Who and the Rolling Stones – and she was relatively calm, which gave me an inner belief we might just find a way through it, but time was running out fast.

After what seemed like an eternity, one of the guys up in the rigging found a plug which had come loose, knocked against another and fused. It took three minutes to fix it and, by the time the power came back on, we had fifty seconds left before we had to pull a national broadcast across America. Until now, the wider public never knew what really happened – or very nearly didn't happen. The event thankfully ended up again as a huge success.

There was only one pre-eminent American sport left to crack and that was Major League Baseball (MLB). I had an idea to put baseball on at Lord's Cricket Ground. It was the perfect venue, juxtaposing quintessential British tradition with a sport only just starting to gain traction in the UK. I had discussions with the Marylebone Cricket Club (MCC) over an eighteen-month period and, eventually, they agreed to a meeting with MLB in the Long Room at Lord's. I think what eventually convinced them to consider it was that between the moment I floated the idea in 1992 to late 1993, I had been involved in so many other events that gave me a track record worthy of an audience at the MCC.

Three MLB officials arrived in London and one of them – the players' representative – was a woman. We got to the Long Room and the MCC wouldn't let her in. We walked up a few steps, then there were two commissionaires flanking the door. They looked at each other, then back at us and robustly stated that she couldn't pass.

It was, of course, utterly absurd; only in March 1999 were women formally accepted as members upon the creation of the MCC's first women's team. But before then, only the Queen was allowed in. Anyone else required a quorum of members to make an exception and nobody had thought to ring ahead, least of all me, because I had had no idea who the MLB would send. I was only dealing with the MLB at that point and not the players. Mind you, even if they'd told me, I don't think I would have thought of phoning Lord's because the rule belonged to a different century.

It was a miserable day, pouring with rain, and the MCC made us stand around outside the Long Room while they tried to assemble a quorum – comprising six people – so they could allow her to join us for lunch. She was furious. The MCC continued making calls and, after an hour, the MLB reps quickly formed a huddle and one of them declared, 'Forget it. We're going home.'

And that was that. I took them for a nice dinner to try and smooth things over. By the end of the second bottle of wine, they were able to take a distance from it and laugh at the absurdity of such an antiquated local custom. I tried to get them back to Lord's but they dismissed the idea out of hand. Part of the problem was the timing – the MCC wanted it to take place in September or October but the MLB insisted it had to be a pre-season game, meaning a March scheduling. There was enough interest on both sides to continue a dialogue and, eventually, after months of persuasion, I managed to get an MLB game into the Oval. It rained virtually the entire day and only one pitch was possible. The batter missed it. That was the sum total of live baseball in the UK.

American sports had otherwise proved hugely popular but I still had ambitions closer to home. I wanted to breathe life into the *Evening Standard* five-a-sides. It was an event which top-flight teams had taken seriously but had lost its way in the early 1990s, partly as the revolution in English football began to gather pace elsewhere.

Dave Hill at Sky was keen – they took highlights while Carlton TV had it live – and we transferred our business model on to that tournament for three years beginning in 1993. Wycombe Wanderers won it the first year, which didn't help with promotion, but I had no intention of interfering in the sport as the NFL did with the Monarchs a few years earlier.

Arsenal won the European Cup Winners' Cup in 1994 and agreed to show off the trophy on one of the five-a-side nights. Tony Adams walked in with this giant cup wrapped in a black bin liner, unwrapped it and lifted it up to an adoring crowd. As the players were leaving, Tony turned to me and said, 'I'm off out now and don't have anywhere to put this trophy – can you look after it and bring it in to Arsenal tomorrow?' So I kept the European Cup Winners' Cup at my house – complete with bin bag – for a night. My son Ross took it to bed with him. Imagine something like that happening now.

That tournament became a victim of our success elsewhere because the money was becoming so substantial in the Premier League that clubs lost their appetite for a five-a-side event where they were paid a pittance to enter and received £10,000 for winning it. There wasn't much more we could do with it as the game had simply moved on so, when Wembley contacted me and asked me to be the promoter of the Horse of the Year show, I thought it was a departure from our regular work but still worth a crack. Again, we imported our business model, changing the music and putting personalities around the ring.

I was in a reception line to meet the Queen one year at a Met Police event I was invited to as part of the Horse of the Year crowd. Prince Philip came past and, as I shook his hand, I said, 'I'm the promoter of the Horse of the Year show and I'd like to invite you to the event.'

He looked at me witheringly and said, 'Why would I want to go to that?' and walked off. His equerry behind him bolted up to me and said firmly, 'Don't do that again! Only speak when spoken to.' To date, that is my only brush with royalty.

Prince Philip may have given me the brush-off but First Artist's success was exponential and I felt like Superman. There were setbacks, of course, but the company was at its zenith and I had become somebody worth knowing. Work was better than I had ever imagined and my personal life had settled down thanks to Janine. In truth, there was a considerable crossover; she played second fiddle to my gallivanting around the world for years. Lesser women would have not had the patience to stick with me.

I met Janine in 1982, about a year after I lost Lee. Janine was very friendly with my stepbrother, who was getting married. We were both invited to his wedding and Janine later told me she walked into the reception and decided there and then she was going to marry me! She changed the wedding table plan so we sat next to each other. We hit it off straight away and began dating.

The strangest thing was that Janine used to spend a lot of time at my dad's house and although I would often go there, too, with Lee, we never once met, in part because she was ten years my junior so tended to spend time with my younger stepbrothers. Lee and I knew everybody in that crowd except Janine. It was bizarre; sometimes we must have missed each other by minutes when leaving or arriving at the same party.

It took five years from that first moment before I asked her to marry me. You could describe it as an on-off relationship in so far as Janine would have always said it was on and I would often say it was off.

I was very selfish back then. I'd go off for a few weeks whenever I wanted, not least because I hadn't entirely moved on from Lee and didn't need a stable income because of the record business sale. I had the financial freedom to act as a free spirit, which is fine if you are alone but not if there are significant others to consider. I'd disappear off somewhere randomly, phone Janine and say, 'Guess where I am . . . I'm in Australia.' I thought it was clever but she wasn't usually impressed.

Over time, our relationship suffered from a dichotomy of progressing towards marriage while I spent increasing swathes of time away. I needed some time out to consider my future and, sadly, Janine and I split up for a while.

I continued to lead a silly, largely meaningless life. My lifestyle was great but I wondered if that was really it. The love I had for Janine never left me – it just took me time to see it clearly. In my defence, when you lose someone as painfully as I had with Lee, you think long and hard about ever opening yourself up to someone else and risking a repeat. Many years later, when my dad died in 2015, the emotions I felt for Lee came flooding back – I don't think that will ever stop in moments of great loss.

The world was trying to tell me something back then. I was down in Rottingdean at the cottage I had bought with Lee mulling over what to do about Janine after forming First Artist in 1986. I still used a list Lee had compiled of things to do to secure the cottage because it was infrequently occupied, written on pages torn out of a diary and dotted around the place. I was weighing up whether to try and get Janine back and, as I was about to go out, one of Lee's notes caught my eye. The paper was headed '17th April' – Janine's birthday. I realised I'd been here before, prior to marrying Lee. I took the same dog for another long walk, mulling over the same quandary and eventually coming to the same conclusion – Janine was the woman I wanted to marry.

We talked about starting a family. My first son, Ross, was born in

1988 and Scott duly followed in 1991. That latter year was a huge one for me with work really taking off in so many different areas. Janine began working within First Artist as an event co-ordinator, having acquired her knowledge in the field from the catering business owned and run by her parents Bernice and Martin. That helped with our work–life balance and she played an important role in the most prestigious project I had ever undertaken – organising a lecture tour for former Soviet Union leader Mikhail Gorbachev.

Gorbachev redefined the world map for ever. His policies of *glasnost* and *perestroika* brought down traditional political barriers and redefined relations between people and state. He was one of my heroes. The only other person who had reshaped the map to the same extent was Adolf Hitler and we all know he had rather different motives. I felt Gorbachev had made the world a safer place for my children to grow up in. Little did I know at the time.

I was emotionally invested in the whole enterprise but my corporate ambition was to show Britain that we were the biggest promoter in the UK. Gorbachev had received hundreds of invitations to deliver lectures in the UK after leaving power at the end of 1991 but did not accept any of them.

I had developed a close relationship with David Mellor, who had earlier asked for my help in getting the England team to front an anti-drugs campaign prior to Italia '90. It was good PR for the team and it also showed the tide was beginning to turn for politicians, who had previously disassociated themselves from football but were beginning to see the reach these top players had. David was a dynamic thinker. I enjoyed his company and thought process.

Through him, I was introduced to a woman named Victoria Charlton, who had a business with links to Russia's highest political circles. Victoria had a long history of working with Russian theatre and ballet and she connected me to people close to Gorbachev, most significantly his right-hand man Pavel Palachenko. We began initial conversations in October 1991 to stage a lecture in the summer of 1992. Pavel invited Victoria and me to Moscow and we had to be heavily vetted by security before walking through several beautifully ornate rooms in a palatial residence only to arrive at a dingy squat at the back with four white walls and three chairs. There were an awful lot of questions to answer and a great degree of suspicion to overcome. He had his detractors in the old Soviet Union at the time and here was ostensibly a sports promoter and agent pitching up with a desire to bring him to Britain.

'Why are you here?' . . . 'Why do you want to do this?' . . . 'How do you view Mikhail Sergeyevich?' (They always called him by his first and second names) . . . 'How do you want to portray him?'

I wasn't duplicitous in order to convince them – I was genuinely a fan. There were millions like me who felt extremely thankful towards him and wanted an insight into his decision-making. Gorbachev later declined for a number of reasons, not least that the timing didn't suit his schedule, but also as I don't think Moscow took us seriously.

My original idea had been to set up a marquee in Hyde Park with twelve thousand seats. I even found a huge marquee to stage it – something commonplace now yet very rare back then – but it was becoming clear that December 1993 was a possible option and other venues, such as the Guildhall in London, were available, which made much more sense given the cachet they offered.

A second meeting in Moscow passed without reaching an agreement but I felt we were edging forward. John Major had replaced Margaret Thatcher by the time I met him at a Rugby League Cup Final in 1992. He agreed to write a letter welcoming Gorbachev to the UK and seal it in a diplomatic pouch, which gave us the gravitas we needed after being invited to Moscow again in the spring of 1993 to try once more. This time, Victoria and I brought over Sharon Ely as our event manager. Victoria spoke a little Russian, which helped no end, and a path gradually presented itself which we could walk down. We had to make a donation to the Gorbachev Foundation and produce paperwork to that effect so we employed Russian and UK lawyers to formalise the framework of our agreement. By this stage, they were more relaxed, but I insisted on meeting the man himself before signing a deal.

Gorbachev appeared for the fourth meeting. It was a big moment in my life. He walked in and the first thing I thought was that he seemed a lot smaller in real life. You think beforehand, This is the man who changed the world, he must be 6ft 6in, but he was not much taller than me.

I tried with every ounce of my being not to stare at the birthmark on his forehead. Of course, you know it is there prior to meeting him but the mark is so striking and you become conscious he must be tired of everyone he meets focusing directly on it rather than looking him square in the eye. Maybe it helped make him a great negotiator.

He had very dry hands and gave me a firm handshake – not too firm but the balance of authority was clear. We walked gently through the schedule. Pavel translated simultaneously – it was a thing of beauty watching him listen in one language while talking instantly in another.

Gorbachev liked Victoria, which smoothed things along. He

stayed with us for about ten minutes to sign off on our proposed programme and left Pavel, Victoria and me to continue conversations. The lecture tour details had been meticulously prepared long before that point. Gorbachev had previously visited the UK in 1989 and we had to be very selective about planning a route that was inclusive yet not exhaustive.

After lengthy deliberations, we settled on Aberdeen, Edinburgh, two nights in London, Bristol and finally Oxford. Each night would begin with a short video outlining Gorbachev's achievements followed by his lecture, translated on a big screen, with pre-submitted audience questions to round off the evening. Attendance was primarily by invitation only, focused on individuals and businesses with a keen interest in Russia – the CBI supported us and also hosted a breakfast during his stay.

He made a keynote speech at the Guildhall, three days prior to Russia's first free elections. It was a quasi-state banquet – a supremely elegant affair which Janine organised. John Major and Baroness Margaret Thatcher were among the guests, both of whom were scheduled to have private meetings with Gorbachev, and the media interest in his tour was very significant.

Due to the timings of broadcasting live into ITV's *News at Ten*, the dinner and the speeches had to be over just before 10 p.m. Various corporates and dignitaries had paid £500 a head to be in the room for an iconic night in political history. It was a huge amount of money at the time but we were running very late before dinner had even started and it was clear we were going to have to drop a course to get everyone into the right positions for live television later on. It couldn't overrun because guests would be making noises with their cutlery which would hamper the sound and we would end up broadcasting a meal rather than the interaction of modern-day political titans.

Everybody wanted to talk to Gorbachev before sitting down to dinner. Thatcher spotted me talking to Janine out of the corner of her eye and raised her eyebrow in my direction. When I walked past shortly afterwards, she stopped me and said, 'Is everything all right, Jon?'

I debated not telling her because, well, it was Margaret Thatcher and dropping a soup course probably didn't rank very highly in the crises she faced as Prime Minister for more than a decade. 'Um, Mrs Thatcher, we have a little issue on time because of *News at Ten* so we need to get on with dinner and make sure we have the speeches over,' I said, a little sheepishly.

'Leave it to me,' she replied. Thatcher carried on talking and began to lead Gorbachev by his left elbow into position to start dinner. He never resisted. Everyone followed. She drifted past me, turned around and winked at me before saying, 'See? Grandma knows best.'

By and large, Gorbachev was his own man, though. I was treated to a rare flash of his ruthlessness when he refused to do an interview I had lined up for him. He looked at me and barked, '*Niet!*' with a menacing tone that put me firmly in my place. The immense power of the man in that moment was striking.

Oxford loved him – the university had invited him to speak three-and-a-half years previously and his lecture on political, religious and economic tolerance went down very well.

Children were very important to him. During the tour, we had a free evening. In what was a hugely pleasant surprise, Mikhail and Raisa asked Janine and I for dinner. We went for a meal at the Oriental restaurant in the Dorchester.

The two boys responsible for abducting and murdering Jamie Bulger had been found guilty a month earlier and he spoke movingly about how appalling he found the whole situation. Raisa was distraught by it, no doubt mindful of their daughter Irina.

But he took the conversation to another level when explaining how he'd been kidnapped during an attempted coup in August 1991. Worse still, he heard his death sentence on the radio.

A small group of Russian military took him while Boris Yeltsin began making damning speeches about the future direction of the country.

The Russians had a coded expression for 'the president is dead' and while he was imprisoned, the only available radio channel was the BBC World Service.

During one broadcast, the newsreader read a statement which contained the coded message. It was meant for a different audience but Gorbachev heard it and knew his time was up.

He was caught up in a mini-revolution at the Kremlin attempting to assume power but Yeltsin had popular support and helped negotiate Gorbachev's release. Of course, a bitter power struggle developed between the pair thereafter and Gorbachev resigned on Christmas Day 1991 but he had avoided an ignominious end at the hands of kidnappers.

It was a fascinating dinner. I asked him if *perestroika* had been the success he originally envisaged. 'You must understand the power I had,' he said. 'I decided. I started a peace process. I woke one day and said to Raisa, "This is ridiculous – we are paying too much money to these people." So I went to my office, I phoned Hafed al-Assad in Syria, Yasser Arafat and the other leaders, demanding they all came to Moscow. They did so in three days.'

He told them he wasn't going to be their banker any more. He wasn't going to pay for their war. He would support them politically but vowed if they didn't begin talking to Israel, Russia would. He contacted Ronald Reagan and informed him of what was happening.

It was difficult to get my head around the idea that he lay in bed one day and suddenly decided to reorganise the Middle East. And what's more, he had the power to actually do it. It was a gobsmacking moment for me – we were talking to living history.

He had a profound impact on me personally and the tour was thankfully a great success. The Gorbachev event was a statement to the corporate world on my part – look who I can get. It was a tour de force that I brought him over after many had tried and failed. It opened up huge opportunities for me to meet with senior political figures and gave me a bandwidth of business much greater than before.

The effects lasted for years; and because of the public success of my events team, we were hired to run the World Sports Awards, a lavish event the brainchild of Dietrich Mateschitz, who had taken over the planet with his Red Bull brand and wanted to give something back to sport.

The inaugural event took place in 2000 at the Royal Albert Hall with a star turn by Bryan Adams and appearances from Arnold Schwarzenegger, one of my all-time heroes Buzz Aldrin, and Muhammad Ali among others.

It so happened that Ali's 59th birthday was the night before. Janine and Laura, her business partner, organised his birthday party at the London Hilton Park Lane hotel. At this time, Ali could still talk comfortably and although increasingly suffering from the ravages of Parkinson's disease, he communicated with plenty of his old sparkle.

Janine, Laura and I went to his suite to collect him for the party, attended by various boxing greats including Chris Eubank Sr, Prince Naseem Hamed and Lennox Lewis, but he invited us to sit with him for a while, regaling us with jokes and stories.

He drew several pictures as he spoke including a cartoon of himself in the boxing ring, which he signed. His wife Lonnie, Janine, Laura and I took him downstairs with Prince Naseem and as the lift door opened to a cascade of flashing lights, reporters and fans showering him with love and affection, he turned around to us, flashed that wonderfully engaging smile and said, 'Hey, not bad for a nigger from the hood.'

Life is all about timing – and post-Gorbachev was the time to return to my grass roots.

The Premier League-led revolution in football was well under way and those in the game were grappling with another new frontier – transfers.

10

The Holy Transfer Trinity

There is a wonderfully astute line in the song 'If I Were a Rich Man' from the musical *Fiddler on the Roof* which reads: 'When you're rich, they think you really know!'

I was a millionaire from selling my music business but, the truth is, I had no idea what I was doing when first dabbling with player transfers. I had grown into someone who could hold my own in most forums and took that song lyric as reality – the fact that I was rich meant football executives would think I knew what I was talking about. I didn't. But I could bluff enough, look someone in the eyes and convince them I was the best person to represent them. On the other side of it, I was trying really hard to develop a rhetoric that was not demanding but co-operational.

The big deals of the 1980s tended to revolve around English football's best players going abroad; the ban on our clubs competing in Europe following the Heysel tragedy aligned with better wages on the continent made moving overseas a very attractive proposition at the time. Ray Wilkins, Mark Hughes, Ian Rush and Chris Waddle were among those to take the plunge and there were only a handful of agents around who negotiated moves of that size.

Football was only emerging from a period in which there was no ability to negotiate whatsoever. The clubs had been totally dominant with regard to player contracts. Transfers were determined between chief executives – although back then the UK chief executive hadn't been invented, instead they were called 'managing directors' – based on a clear market value. Relatively speaking, there weren't many deals of any description done back then so the market rate was easy to identify. The sheer volume of transactions nowadays – combined with so many differing income streams – makes identifying value a more subjective conversation.

Peter Beardsley's move from Newcastle to Liverpool in 1987 wasn't the first transfer I negotiated but it was by far the biggest up to that point. In those days, deals weren't that complicated for the most part. Contracts carry significantly more inherent clauses now than in the 1980s. I'd been around football for a couple of years and I was quite friendly with a number of players, which helped me to establish the going rate. But the Beardsley deal proved to be a minefield.

The thing that really fazed me was the media. I was used to doing music deals that were always conducted under the radar. It was only when they took off that reporters – almost exclusively in the modestly read music press – became interested or even aware.

Football was a different animal entirely. Deals were played out in the public domain through an aggressive mainstream media. I had to learn very quickly how to say something without saying anything of any consequence. Being around politicians – as I later was in the 1990s – made that a lot easier! But back in the mid-1980s, it was a steep learning curve and one made more fraught by my desire not to aggravate those members of the Press who had become mates during my work with England.

Access to players has different dynamics. It is one thing for me to invite selected journalists in to speak to a player for a sit-down interview to give them an exclusive and enable me to satisfy a sponsor but there is a delicate balance to strike when passing on sensitive information. You want to control the message but not appear unhelpful to people you know you will need in future. My mates in the Press would expect me to provide newsworthy information to them on something that everybody else wanted kept quiet. But at the same time, journalists need to be in front of the story to make it worth their while. I had a raft of people who would rely on me to put them in front of the rest. It was a talent I developed very rapidly I think, although I tried to keep a lot of the detail on Beardsley out of the Press as I learned the ropes. Liverpool were quite a leaky club from memory so I often had to react to stories emanating from elsewhere. What I didn't know – and it was probably why the Beardsley deal took so long – was where to apply pressure and how to identify the softer points of the money involved to bridge gaps.

Peter Robinson was essentially the man who ran Liverpool at the time. I lovingly called him 'PBR' and he was a distinguished figure of great stature, both figuratively and physically. That said, it was disconcerting sitting in a meeting with him because his ears were very big. If I brought anyone with me to mull something over, we had to whisper very, very quietly.

He knew the game backwards and, although I remember him being very tough, Peter was malleable enough to understand it was important that the players arrived at the club with the right mental attitude. His belief was to pay players the top market rate to ensure that. It got a little difficult when we wanted more but

I was being guided by others inside the club who believed Peter Beardsley should be getting a higher wage than that initially on offer from his prospective employer.

I was being pointed to an array of people who were more experienced than I was at the time, including a number of local lawyers who dealt a lot with Liverpool regarding tax positions. Liverpool Football Club is institutionalised to the extent that I felt, whatever we did, from whomever we sought advice, we should source it from the region.

It was a baptism of fire. Regulations were elementary back then and you were still not to speak until spoken to but everybody knew Liverpool wanted Peter and that he was interested in a move. The agent was still someone in the 1980s who was just part of the mechanics of a deal. They were often obstructive influences working – in theory – in the best interests of their client, negotiating a player's package. An agent's role had not evolved to a situation where their wishes superseded those of the selling club – as sometimes happens today – because they were always already manoeuvred out of position.

I tried to be the most adaptable, amiable guy in the room. The tone would be: 'We're so delighted that Peter could come to Liverpool. He really wants to be here but I need your help, just a little, to move things along to a place where the terms exceed what Newcastle are throwing at him.'

The transfer created national headlines from the outset. I had to make out to everyone that I knew what I was doing when I really didn't. I had to hug my player and make sure he retained confidence in me while, behind his back, seek out the best possible advice so I didn't make a fool of myself but, more pertinently, didn't undersell him.

If I'd been more experienced, things would have moved a lot quicker. Initially, there was scepticism from both clubs towards me but, over time, my relationship with both grew when they saw that I was trying to deal in a professional way just to make things a bit easier for everybody. I wasn't an obstacle – I was an enabler. The Newcastle board, led by chairman Stan Seymour Jr, had always said that if they got the right price, he would go. Ideally, they wouldn't sell but they knew Peter's head had been turned and would acquiesce to his wishes. There was no emotion in it.

If you ingratiate yourself to all parties, you can use their positivity in the deal. As long as you keep people thinking you are on their side, you can perpetuate a dialogue and manoeuvre all sides into a place where a compromise feels comfortable. The hardest aspect of that in a way is dealing with the buying club because you are going to have to come up against them at some point in a negotiation.

The Beardsley deal taught me that, in future, I'd aim to do the player's contract first. I knew then that we weren't going to fall over our bootlaces by getting the buying and selling club into a place only for the player's personal terms to prove an insurmountable hurdle. Technically, that is the wrong way to do a deal – and contravenes agents' regulations – but the stumbling block in the end wasn't Liverpool or Newcastle, it was Beardsley's financial package.

We got PBR to offer Newcastle £1.9m – which wasn't easy in itself – but Peter loved being on Tyneside. If he got the right salary, he'd move, but it wasn't just about money because he was genuinely torn. Wages are often the decisive factor but he was being advised by his wife, Sandra, a proud Geordie with strong local ties. It wasn't easy for him to up sticks and leave. But at the same time, he wanted to play for Kenny Dalglish.

We reached such a stalemate – forty thousand pounds apart – that I even asked Kenny for some tips on what would be acceptable to Liverpool and how we could improve Peter's deal. I believe we invented the loyalty bonus. It was an idea born of Kenny Dalglish and I having a chat. Kenny told me, 'He's been very loyal but Newcastle are the ones selling if the price is right. They could have dismissed it out of hand.'

We looked at each other and I said, 'Then why don't we charge them for it? He's earning them £1.9m by leaving having been originally on the books valued at zero because he came through the ranks.' Those things did not exist back then. There was a salary, usually only minimally negotiable with the odd bonuses thrown in.

The problem for Liverpool was that every time they edged forward, Newcastle edged back. That happened three or four times until Liverpool's patience wore thin but, to Peter Robinson's credit, he never pulled the plug or issued an ultimatum; he always tried to be helpful. Once things were very far advanced, Kenny and I worked closely together and we came up with a variety of ideas to help bridge the gap. Bonuses and add-ons were relatively new back then. Footballers used to turn up, play, get paid and go home. We were trying to create things like loyalty bonuses. We tried to insert an appearance fee but PBR told me, 'We're paying him to play, not to sit on the sidelines.' So that was a non-starter.

He was very tough. We spent all day on 9 July 1989 in meetings with PBR and that was when we made the breakthrough. Although we termed it a 'loyalty payment', Liverpool agreed to pay the additional forty thousand pounds. Five days later, Beardsley's £1.9m move was officially confirmed – the highest fee ever paid by a British club. He became one of the highest-paid players in Britain.

We ended on good terms with Liverpool despite the protracted nature of Peter's transfer. In fact, I ended up getting on so well with PBR that I was later able to renegotiate Steve McMahon's contract over the phone. It took about two days. We started quite close and ended pretty much exactly where Steve wanted to be financially. It was quick and painless, which made everyone very happy.

'Here's my commission, Steve,' I said, handing him a piece of paper with fifty thousand pounds written on it.

'What? You didn't even bother to come up to Liverpool – you did it on the phone,' he said.

'I didn't need to! You got what you wanted and, because of my relationship with PBR, things moved so fast that a face-to-face meeting was redundant.'

The few agents that were around at the time believed they sat on one side with clubs on the other. Clubs were the enemy. I never saw it that way. It comes back to that point about only having a handful of clients at the top end of the market – why make anyone the enemy?

I was one of the toughest guys in the marketplace but I did it with a smile. Nowadays everyone smiles but, back then, you were expected to be tough and hammer people. I think I helped create an environment where difficult conversations could be undertaken in a different environment because we had first engendered an understanding of the bigger picture – i.e. this is one deal but we could work together on several more, so there is an underlying acceptance of each other's positions. By being more amiable in my approach, I was able to create sufficient goodwill to take the opposing side to a place they would not otherwise have gone yet they'd feel comfortable in doing so. I broke pay barriers in most clubs as a result and yet was still welcomed back the next year. They knew that when we did a deal, we wouldn't try and undo it two years later. We always respected the integrity of that initial deal.

Yet Steve felt I had somehow neglected him by not getting on a train to Liverpool, because the agent *modus operandi* of the day was to try to beat clubs bullishly into submission. 'I can't pay you that because you didn't even get out of your chair at home,' he said, defiantly.

So I had to downgrade my commission to keep him happy. I had to take a hit because I didn't take a hundred-pound train trip, but I respected Steve's position because he was a great guy. He was like Stu Grimson – a warrior on the pitch but the nicest guy away from it. To me, that juxtaposition has always been one of the most intriguing things about elite sportspersons. It is almost corporate schizophrenia. Maybe it is one of the reasons why they become successful; they recognise the relentless combative qualities required on the field of play yet leave that element of themselves in that sphere to allow their humility to shine through elsewhere.

Anyway, it was another lesson – always be there. There is nothing like a physical presence. All the modern-day devices are great – email, SMS, Twitter and all the rest of it – but when it comes to doing a deal, be there to shake the guy by the hand. That seals it.

I was still learning the nuances of negotiation, yet getting Beardsley over the line ensured my stock rose to the extent that other players approached me to help achieve similar results. Tony Cottee sat me down at the first England get-together in September 1987. He told me he was ready to leave his beloved West Ham there and then but they were adamant they wouldn't sell. Tony could see his position in the England team was potentially threatened if he didn't take a big offer.

West Ham's chairman at the time was Terry Brown – a powerful guy from the east end of London; he kept telling me Tony was off limits. Meanwhile, Tony was adamant he loved West Ham but needed to leave to further his career.

Arsenal and Everton expressed an interest and we thought West Ham might then sell but they held a board meeting at which they decided to wait until Christmas. December came and they decided to wait until March. Then it was deferred until the end of the season.

Something had to give and I took the conscious decision to play this transfer out in the media. They had kept him against his will for almost a year and, by using the media, the pressure became too great. It was one of the first times anyone had pulled this trick and we used it to the maximum. Tony was good fun – he enjoyed being in the Press and his family was great. When West Ham eventually allowed everyone to talk, Colin Harvey was manager of Everton and we decided to go there first because we thought he'd go to Arsenal. I had a Bentley at the time and, as my chauffeur Marcus drove us up to Liverpool, I tipped the media off about our visit. We took in the training ground, spoke to Colin and his team, and they offered a reasonably good deal. It wasn't the biggest we thought we could get, but we were going to see Arsenal next so it didn't matter as they would top it up.

We met George Graham at the West Lodge Park Hotel in Cockfosters. I liked him but the problem was he offered well below what Everton had put on the table. I kept telling him, with respect, Everton were an inferior team but a long way north of Arsenal financially and urged him to help bridge the gap as Tony was keen on moving to Highbury. But he drew a line in the sand and wouldn't budge.

'His career will be much better at Arsenal, I know I can get the best out of him but, if he wants to go to Everton for the money, then so be it,' said George. Maybe he didn't believe the size of Everton's bid. We would have taken a little less money at Arsenal to go there but George was so far below the offer at Goodison Park, it wasn't feasible.

The whole saga took its toll on Tony. I kept saying to him and his father Clive, with whom I became very good friends, 'It will happen ... it will happen ...' every time things took a negative turn. I even wrote him a note once with those three words written on it and left it at his house.

Eventually, I contacted Colin and told him to get down to London because Arsenal weren't the clear frontrunners everybody thought and the deal was on if he could hit certain numbers. Colin never thought it was going to happen because Arsenal were the more attractive option so he got in his car almost instantly when it became clear that wasn't necessarily the case.

The notion of negotiating a record British transfer deal in a service station in full view of any passing supporter is ludicrous now but that is precisely what happened with Tony. We met at South Mimms service station on the M25, for no other reason than the logistical convenience of being near the M1. Cottee was the story of the day and I was receiving phone calls from sports desks across Fleet Street. We were negotiating his terms on a napkin in the middle of this service station with fans coming up to the table, peering over his shoulder and saying, 'All right, Tone? Is that what you're going to get paid? Oh, right, mate. Nice one!' It was just ridiculous.

We were left with Everton at two million pounds. Gazza had been sold to Tottenham by Newcastle for two million and West

Ham had publicly said by this stage they wanted in excess of that. The modern-day equivalent was Arsenal's £40,000,001 bid for Liverpool's Luis Suarez in 2014, but that particular offer didn't treat the situation with the delicacy it deserved – Cottee's fee ended up being £2.05m based on West Ham's valuation and Everton's decision to chuck in an extra £50,000 on top to keep everyone happy. It had taken almost a year, but Everton ended up paying a British record fee on 26 July 1988.

A few days later, Tony sent me a plaque on a wooden frame emblazoned with the words: 'It has happened'.

I earned around one hundred thousand pounds each from these deals, which, in those days, was very good. In the Cottee deal, we were paid by the player and Everton, the latter in the form of a scouting agreement for sourcing the player. If I was in that situation now, with two clubs bidding on a big player, I'd be getting sizeably north of a million pounds, easily. That's how agents' fees have jumped since those days. First Artist was making a high six-figure profit back then – Tony's transfer represented about 10 per cent of our annual turnover in one deal. It therefore had to be the way forward for us. The Premier League was still a few years off and the marketing side, by comparison, was small beer. Transfers were the future and so I actively went out and sourced clients.

This was seminal for me. I realised that I could bring my business expertise to the transfer market. Having stepped into the unknown, I now realised I could not only keep my head above water but really thrive in it. I saw Gary Pallister as one for the future – he had just got into the England squad and I unashamedly used the advantage I had of a seat at the top table to mingle with the players. I was looking after them, giving them money and nice things to adorn their lives – they were always happy to support me. I went to see Gary one day and told him I wanted to work with him. I felt he should be at a bigger club than Middlesbrough. He agreed and we moved forward together.

Some months later, United manager Sir Alex Ferguson phoned about Pallister but Middlesbrough boss Bruce Rioch was adamant he didn't want to sell. He never took a phone call from me. Alex was under pressure at the time at United and desperately needed a centre-back. He told me Pallister was his first choice but they harboured some reservations, namely that he needed beefing up physically. Alex felt in his present state, Pallister had the required frame – standing 6ft 4in – but was too lightweight and consequently they baulked at the kind of figure it would take to get Middlesbrough interested. Money was starting to talk in football and perhaps Bruce realised that a potential deal could improve the club's financial future.

Alex said to me, 'I can't believe I am paying over two million for a centre-back.' He must have been close to a heart attack years later when he paid Leeds United £29.1m for Rio Ferdinand.

We got the deal done in the most comical of circumstances. The meeting took place in a pub car park near Scotch Corner, where the A1 meets the A66 in North Yorkshire. It was a rain-soaked Sunday and the pub was closed.

Two cars pulled up and faced each other with headlights on, spearing through the driving rain. I stepped out of one with Alex while Bruce emerged from the other. It felt like a scene from *Gunfight at the OK Corral* as we slowly walked towards each other. Mind you, I don't remember Burt Lancaster or Kirk Douglas speaking with same candour in that film as Bruce did here. 'You . . .

Fuck off!' Those were the only words he ever said to me during that transaction.

Alex, to his credit, said, 'He's with us, Bruce, he's not going anywhere.'

Eventually, they came to an agreement on price and I was sent away to discuss Pallister's personal terms with Maurice Watkins at United and we did the deal. It was quite big news at the time – a national record fee for a defender, the highest fee between British clubs and the second highest ever paid by a British club (behind Ian Rush's £2.7m return to Liverpool from Juventus).

Whereas I thought I did really well for Peter and Tony, although the deal for Gary was substantial, I felt a little disappointed with the final numbers on his package. Maurice was a ferocious but gregarious negotiator. I had a conversation with Alex Ferguson at the end of it and I said to him, 'I think I've done a reasonable job for the lad but there is a little part of me that wishes I could have found a turnkey to go a little higher. We ticked all of Man United's boxes and pushed them as far as they could go but I pride myself on finding loopholes in the system and I couldn't do it this time.'

Alex said, 'He's a thin lad. I'm going to have him in the gym every day bulking up. As he gets bigger, you are going to come back here asking for a new contract which will be even better than this one.' Beef him up for a beefier contract.

Some years later, Bruce turned up at Arsenal as manager (1995–96, his only season at the club). I was at Highbury one day and Bruce saw me. As he walked over, I'm thinking, Christ, what is he going to say now? as I remembered those three little words he said to me, which remained the sum total of my dialogue with him.

He said, 'You . . . Come here.' He put his arm around me. 'Let's talk about some commercial opportunities and what you can do for me.' We had a good relationship after that. Alex also stayed close – I later managed Manchester United's players' pool for the 1990 FA Cup Final.

The day Pallister's deal was confirmed – 29 August 1989 – the *Sun* ran a profile piece on me headlined 'SOCCER'S MR FIX-IT' in recognition of three record-breaking deals in as many seasons. It was mutually beneficial. I kept them ahead of the story but, in return, I wanted a piece showcasing my achievements. I wasn't publicity shy – no businessman worth his salt would have turned down the opportunity as it was a palpable chance to grow First Artist and develop my reputation.

And when you are in the media a lot – a bit like when you are rich – people think you know what you are talking about. Except, by now, I did.

11

We're All in This Together

Our mission was clear: the best players had to move to England for the Premier League to become the greatest division in the world. We had successfully rebranded football as entertainment with the 1992 launch but the show's cast list only boasted a smattering of A-list stars from the world stage.

Sky's coverage was superb and many of the promotional ideas First Artist had implemented were paying dividends but everybody at the top end of the game knew this momentum was only sustainable if a stream of top European talent came into the Premier League.

I was one of the propagators of that philosophy. But sourcing and acquiring the best overseas players was easier said than done. The United Kingdom had a 40 per cent top-end tax rate in the mid-1990s but there was unearned income tax to consider as well, and a variety of barriers that made it extremely difficult to compete with the financial incentives offered elsewhere. The tax regimes in southern Europe were bizarre. Sometimes other people paid your tax bill, or an entire transaction would be completed in cash. It was a different world. It can still be difficult to operate in that region even now but taxation rules are a lot tighter since the global financial crash of 2008.

In the Premier League's formative years, the top salaries readily available in Italy and Spain were anathema even to England's biggest clubs. For the first time, a new word emerged in our vocabulary – 'netto'. Previously, we had always talked about wages in terms of gross figures but the Europeans spoke of net earnings because tax was a much less prohibitive issue. Netto quickly became a prominent byword in international transfers as a result.

Finding a way of competing was exceptionally difficult, especially given the necessity of making wages tax-efficient. Bringing a player to London and giving them a house, for example, would have been taxed heavily as a Benefit in Kind. Those taxation barriers did not exist elsewhere or, if they did, they were more malleable and some people were able to work around them.

Convincing players to join a rebranded fledgling league with technical inferiorities and rubbish weather for less money but more tax was a mammoth task. Identifying players was the first issue and, although my work with England, my transfer market success and position at the centre of the Premier League launch gave me due prominence in the UK, I had little reach overseas and had to align myself with the experts on the continent.

Vincenzo Morabitto was widely regarded at the time as the main agent carving up European football, alongside his partner, Venicio Fioranelli. Vincenzo speaks seven languages fluently; he has a Danish wife and consequently spent a lot of time there moving Scandinavian players all over the place. They were highly regarded players back then, not least with Denmark winning the European Championships in 1992 but also because of the success of individuals including Brian Laudrup, Peter Schmeichel and Tomas Brolin. They travelled well and usually weren't too expensive. Vincenzo then opened up Turkey and Greece in a relentless expansion of national markets, working seven days a week and never off the clock. He was the Jorge Mendes of his time so I had to buddy up to him.

He hadn't signed a large stable of players but the connections he created at clubs throughout the world made him the go-to guy if they wanted to buy or sell anyone. As agents gradually grew in prominence, the clubs increasingly opted not to speak to each other and preferred the use of intermediaries. In some cases nowadays, agents often get in the middle of a deal to act as a conduit in the monetary deal flow, especially in Europe. Most Premier League managers have favoured agents for almost every transfer. Certain deals are of course genuinely facilitated by that alliance – perhaps they trust the agent as he has assisted in securing good players on reasonable terms in the past – but because of all the secrecy such closeness naturally leads to suspicions that some deals are entered into because the proximity of their friendship affords greater possibilities for remuneration. This is exactly why we should have greater transparency, then these suspicions could be laid to rest.

Vincenzo was a regular at meetings of the European Football Agents Association – a collective of pan-European agents who came together to create some sort of law in the jungle – and I always made sure I sat next to him. These gatherings used to last for hours and inevitably people would drift off and start their own quiet conversations with whoever was nearby – that gave me valuable one-on-one time with Vincenzo to help me establish a friendship.

I felt like I could learn from him. English football was an emerging market at the time and Europe's more established leagues were keeping an eye on us without being convinced of our merits. Rupert Murdoch's involvement made everyone take notice but they were still on a watching brief for the most part, and sceptical about actively engaging.

What Premier League chief executive Richard Scudamore and his team did effectively over the ensuing years was sell the division to so many territories across the world. I would argue that was one of the Premier League's four pillars of success: attracting players; sourcing licensing revenues; selling the TV rights; and, finally, the packaging and presentation of the league as sporting entertainment anyone could enjoy. By pushing it into so many countries, it became the omnipotent footballing property.

In the beginning, there were a few older players who came over for a payday at the end of their careers but that wasn't as prevalent as you might think. We still weren't paying as much as they could get away with in Italy or Spain. That was the case probably right up until the summer of 2016 when Manchester United broke the world transfer record by signing Paul Pogba from Juventus for eighty-nine million pounds. The latest TV deal has finally enabled clubs to offer the biggest players a salary package rivalling that available in Europe. It also now means that the going rate for an average Premier League footballer is now ten million pounds when not long before it would have been five million. Top shelf players now begin with valuations north of twenty-five to thirty million.

Back in the late 1990s and 2000s, First Artist was able to find a variety of creative ways as discussed in earlier chapters – image rights, Employment Benefit Trusts, and so on. Over time, they were shut down one by one and, after the 2008 crash, the top tax band went up to 50 per cent. It later came back to 45 per cent but HMRC had closed a lot of the loopholes.

Those first few big names were hugely important for the credibility and growth of the Premier League. Ruud Gullit arrived in England after Vincenzo alerted us to his availability and we helped take him into Chelsea on a free transfer in July 1995. Immediately, I saw him as the stepping stone to the next place which was to make these players iconic brands in their own right, just as I had witnessed in America. Ruud was not the first big name we helped bring over but he was the first player – and later manager – we tried to Americanise as a brand. He was the guy I chose to take on a journey that would see sportsmen and women based in the UK evolve beyond the conventional boundaries of their particular discipline.

Ruud's credentials were palpable – he was over 6ft tall, handsome with striking dreadlocks and effortless style on and off the pitch. He had a wonderful grasp of languages and his smile lit up the room. I remember having dinner with him and my brother Phil one night and he talked about detailed tactical plans, such as how to combat going down to ten men with your opponents stretching you breadthways across the pitch, zonal marking and diamond-shaped systems. He spoke with an enchanting rhythm reminiscent of music. That's what made me want to help him become a manager and also, later, a television pundit. He spent his first season at Stamford Bridge as a player but, when Glenn Hoddle left Chelsea for the England job after Euro '96, Ruud took over as player-manager. He was the first Dutchman to manage in the Premier League and became the first foreigner to win a major trophy in England a year later with the 1997 FA Cup – Chelsea's first major silverware in twenty-six years. That success only made Ruud more marketable off the pitch. I launched his clothing line, 'Ruudwear', with a lovely guy called Lance Yates, who was one of Mick Jagger's best mates. He led his life like a saint – he ate right, told me off for eating Mars bars, rarely drank and exercised like a champion. He died of stomach cancer when he was 51 . . . and I'm still eating Mars bars. Life is strange and sometimes very unfair.

Ruudwear took off. We promoted it through most of the distribution sources in the sports world – wholesale, retail, mail order, all advertised in various supportive media outlets. He carried himself through the whole process with that Dutch cool that remains his trademark. He was sexy football 24/7. It was an easy sell.

'We can expand your reach here to: (a) make you more money; but (b) give you longevity,' I told him. 'There are only so many years that you can keep playing. After that, then what? You are so charismatic that I can't see you opening up a restaurant on the King's Road. You should be global. You have a passion for football so let's manufacture that in the world that you are in but we can also expand it into fashion, lifestyle and other areas.'

Some people might argue that was exploitation on my part but I disagree. Ruud never did anything unknowingly and I wanted to give him a platform to maximise his own talents. I thought I was also doing a great job for the game. Again, look at America – as I have done in so much of my working life – they were twenty years ahead of us over there. Their gridiron stars were household names. Up to that point, our footballers were still compartmentalised. That mentality still prevails in some form today; people ask, 'How can a footballer earn that money?' Well, it is because he earns tens of millions for his employers. So why shouldn't he earn a few million himself? Nobody questions a rock star's income and that's because people widely accept they are entertainers performing a show charging a fee proportionate to market demand. Football is no different. Music fans are often equally as loyal but they rarely have the inherent sense of ownership that football supporters possess. Therein lies the root of this difference in perception.

Perhaps their skill is under-appreciated by those who believe footballers just kick a ball about. Do you know how difficult it is for a teenager to negotiate the fraught path from messing about in the park to playing at Anfield? It is a tumultuous journey battling against thousands of other young hopefuls, many of whom are cut adrift and told they aren't good enough in their early teenage years. Sport is one of the toughest professions around; not many plumbers are told at a young age they will never be any good at their chosen profession. It is exceptionally difficult to reinvent yourself in football. Perhaps nobody collectively channelled that rejection better than Leicester City in the 2015–16 season – Claudio Ranieri took a team of cast-offs and won the Premier League title. Those who hurl opprobrium towards football stars for the vast sums they earn would do well to consider that inevitable struggle to reach those heights, in addition to recognising that, without these big stars, the game would not be the product it is today. Significantly, if the top players didn't earn what they do, that money would not then filter down to the next generation.

And yet, Ken Bates didn't like what Ruud had become. Ken and I fell out over it, sadly, I believe because he felt Ruud's iconic image was threatening to overshadow the club. He thought the position of Chelsea manager should be filled, not outgrown. That may have been my fault in part because the attention he attracted was unprecedented but Ruud never once blamed me for what came next.

Relations turned sour. Ken and Colin Hutchinson, Chelsea's managing director, decided they wanted to see the back of Ruud and sacked him in February 1998. They claimed it was done to end a contractual dispute after Ruud had kept them waiting for months to sign an extension to his deal which expired that summer. They said they needed to end the uncertainty.

But there were no major meetings. Ken knew I was wrapped up with Ruud but he never called me. There was no more than a short conversation between Ken and Ruud – they decided to pull the trigger and there was nothing anyone could do, even though I did my best to make them reconsider.

'I didn't like his arrogance,' Ken once reportedly said of Ruud. 'In fact, I never liked him.' Ken publicly declared that because Ruud had never managed before, Chelsea had to create a framework around him where Ruud just coached and picked the team. There was some truth in that but I maintain Ruud began the Chelsea revolution that continued apace under Roman Abramovich. He changed the coaching perspective there and evolved the nutritional and lifestyle aspects of a player's career in a continental way similar to that which Arsène Wenger effected at Arsenal. Sir Alex Ferguson achieved the same in his own style at Manchester United and, while I'm not putting Ruud in the same company as Ferguson and Wenger, he was the catalyst that made Chelsea the forward-thinking club they would become.

However, Ruud did have trouble with several players, Gianfranco Zola among them. We were in both Ruud and Gianfranco's camps during their time together and Gianfranco's unhappiness at Ruud's management put us in an uneasy position. We advised both as best we could but it would have been difficult to steer Gianfranco to another club because the Chelsea fans loved him and Ruud's position would have been undermined. The common consensus among the players became that Ruud was a good coach but a poor man-manager.

Ken may have been critical of having to create a network around Ruud but they clearly liked the continental management structure because they went straight out and appointed Gianluca Vialli, who was exactly the same type of character but without Ruud's level of exposure.

Ruud wanted to stay in England and it didn't take us long to find him another job. Newcastle had sacked Kenny Dalglish and were keen on speaking to Ruud about taking over. The big problem was that Ruud's wife Estelle – Johan Cruyff's niece – didn't want him to go. She was adamant she wouldn't move and Ruud was at his wits' end. In the end, Ruud said to Phil, 'You talk to her.'

She turned to Phil and said, 'OK, tell me about Newcastle.'

Phil said: 'Well, it's a fantastic, well-supported club in what has become a very cosmopolitan area. They have a new Metro centre now with great shops and the town is a really vibrant place to live.'

'So you like it there, do you?'

'Oh yeah, it's great,' Phil said.

'Well, you live there then.'

Ruud could hear every word. In the end, we reached a compromise. Estelle had a fear of flying at the time so we hired a hovercraft to take her across the North Sea to see Ruud in Newcastle. In addition, he would go back to Holland two or three days each week.

Things didn't go well for Ruud at Newcastle. By the time

Alan Shearer was causing him problems and the fans were turning against him in 1999, he knew he had to quit. Ruud's infidelity had come out in the newspapers so he said he either had to resign for personal reasons because his wife wasn't going to move to England or blame it all on Shearer. We offered to negotiate compensation for him but he wasn't interested. He used to call Phil and me 'the lovely boys'.

'Lovely boys, don't worry about it – I'm going to walk,' he said.

'What, with a big round zero in your pocket?'

'Yes – it is the right thing to do.'

Newcastle United chief executive Freddy Fletcher was in tears at the time, and chairman Freddy Shepherd had never known anyone in football be so selfless when it came to money. Ruud was on a good contract so he gave up at least one million pounds, perhaps nearly twice that much had negotiations gone well.

The 'poor man-manager' criticism followed him at Newcastle. Phil had said something in the press on the eve of a huge derby game against Sunderland, claiming Shearer had been a divisive figure and that Ruud deserved greater support. Ruud dropped Shearer and his strike-partner Duncan Ferguson. They lost 2-1. Phil saw Alan in the tunnel after the game and he just stared right through him. Three days passed and then Ruud resigned. Years later, Alan and Ruud sat next to each other on *Match of the Day* as if they were the best of friends. Phil saw him that week and asked how they could stand to be in the same room after what happened.

'Time moves on,' Alan said.

Vincenzo delivered so many players to us – Roberto di Matteo, Petr Cech and Marcel Desailly to name just three – and we became one of the pre-eminent deal-makers for a lot of overseas agents wanting to place their players in England. Paul Stretford's Proactive agency and Jerome Anderson were the other prominent figures, with Jonathan Barnett just getting started.

In more recent years, foreign agents have increasingly gone to clubs directly; if they have an inbound player, they will connect with the manager, scouting staff or chief executive whom they know at the player's desired club. Modern communication has advanced to such an extent it is so much easier for agents to expand their network of influence.

Back then, the overseas agents relied on their English counterparts being part of a deal. We had a good relationship with Swedish agent Roger Ljung. He called me and told us to look at Freddie Ljungberg. Vincenzo had been friends with Roger for years and he agreed Freddie had the quality and charisma to become a real star in England. We talked with Arsène Wenger about taking him into Arsenal. Arsène had been aware of Freddie previously and felt positive about a transfer; there were twenty or thirty players they were tracking at the time and he was one near the top of the list. The player is the most important thing but sometimes the environment around him is taken into consideration and we were able to help facilitate Freddie's deal in a way that appealed to Arsenal. They knew by aligning themselves with us the deal would be easy, and it was. In the summer of 1998, he signed from Halmstads BK for three million pounds. One of the most alluring characteristics of the Premier League – aside from the money – has always been the passion demonstrated by fans, and the unique characteristics of the game in England. It was something that drew Claudio Ranieri to Chelsea in 2000. He was another one of Vincenzo's clients and came to see us at our office just prior to starting work as Blues manager. Claudio hadn't been in the UK long but he was quickly warming to our idiosyncrasies. 'One of the reasons I love England so much is you only have to see the sun somewhere behind the clouds for everyone to take the roof off their car,' he said. 'In Italy we don't touch the roof unless it is 25 degrees.'

We became very close with Claudio during his tenure at Stamford Bridge. He worked hard to improve his English and oversaw an overhaul of the squad including some signings we were involved in – Boudewijn Zenden, Jesper Gronkjaer and William Gallas – and others we weren't, including Frank Lampard and Emmanuel Petit.

Roman Abramovich arrived on the scene and Claudio was given more than one hundred million pounds to spend on players, which he used to sign Damien Duff, Hernan Crespo, Adrian Mutu and Joe Cole, among others. But despite our best efforts to control it, speculation that Roman wanted to replace Claudio bubbled along under the surface throughout the whole season, even though Chelsea reached the Champions League semi-finals.

We tried to ingratiate ourselves with Roman and director Eugene Tenenbaum when Abramovich bought the club; I always made it my business to engage with potential new owners but when I found out who Roman really was – because he was relatively unknown at that time – it became clear that he was someone who would change the dynamic of English football club ownership and on balance, in spite of his public silence, I think Roman has been one of the best things to happen to the Premier League. There was a key meeting during that season in which Claudio outlined his transfer strategy going forward. He identified signing Didier Drogba as the top priority, gave them a detailed breakdown of who to buy and sell and how to make it as cost-effective as possible.

After we left the room, I said to Claudio, 'You've just given them your exit script. The likelihood is you won't win the league and they will want to replace you.'

'I am a professional,' he replied. 'I love the club and this is the best path forward. If they fire me, so be it.'

Peter Kenyon phoned me a short while later to tell me they were parting company with Claudio at the end of the season. We told Claudio to keep smiling even as things were nearing their conclusion with Roman adamant he wanted José Mourinho to take over, but that was his natural demeanour. He was always great fun, and nothing had changed years later in the 2015–16 season when Leicester won the Premier League title, a success he thoroughly deserved.

Everyone thinks contracts contain indeterminable payments but most of them have a mitigation clause in the small print. That means a manager continues to be paid at his current salary until such time as that contract expires or he finds another job. That manager usually has to actively pursue another job, however; think of it like an extremely high-end Jobseekers' Allowance. There isn't normally a sizeable pay-off included on top – beyond a little *ex gratia* in certain instances – and so that is usually the point of negotiation when a manager departs. Talks continued over a couple of days regarding Claudio's exit terms. In the end, we weren't that far apart – about £250,000 – and so I phoned Eugene and threw a line at him that it 'equates to a few tanks of petrol for Roman's yacht'.

He went berserk. It hit a nerve; I don't know why. Probably because it was true. It was only a whimsical comment but I had to withdraw it. Claudio and I spoke later during the day and we decided it might more productive for him to speak to Eugene directly at home that evening.

Claudio called me the next morning saying he just wanted to draw a line under the whole thing. It wasn't a great success for me in getting him a fantastic deal but it is interesting when I see the Chelsea managers come and go now – I'm guessing the same exit-payment formula is adopted each time as it seemed to work for them back then.

Chelsea played Newcastle when Claudio knew he was leaving. The Newcastle fans started chanting, '*You're getting sacked in the morning.*' I was about five rows back and I heard Claudio turn around and shout, 'No ... end of May.' He subsequently left the club on 31 May.

I very rarely dealt with Roman directly. It was always usually Eugene or Bruce Buck. Eugene can be an extremely tough person to deal with at times but for the most part he is a very good guy. Bruce will try to do the best by everyone and he has obviously won Roman's confidence because he does a lot of his legal work now.

Football isn't a major part of Roman's portfolio, given his reach and influence in Russia, but I believe he enjoys it. His entry into the game was swift and decisive – typical of the man. I understand that he had bought a hockey club in Russia, in a city where his oil company worked a few years previously, and had hired a number of Czech Olympic gold-medal-winners to play. So the move into football was logical. He had the idea to buy a football club early in 2003 and, within three months, he had shaken hands with Ken Bates.

His advisers initially drew up a list of clubs across five European countries and thereafter Roman gradually whittled it down to

England. They were left with a shortlist of five clubs: Manchester United, Tottenham, Chelsea, Arsenal and Liverpool. Roman already owned a house in west London near Harvey Nichols, which made a London club the more logical choice. United were looking for around £500 million at the time, which while not financially prohibitive made them far less appealing.

I was told Roman's camp held preliminary talks with Daniel Levy at Tottenham, but a formal offer was never tabled. They also enquired about Arsenal but were instructed that the Gunners were not for sale. Chelsea were more receptive. Although the club wasn't going bankrupt as had been widely reported – there were players in the squad with a good transfer market value, if push came to shove – it wasn't in a healthy position. My understanding is that an offer was made at 40p per share at the first meeting with Trevor Birch, and that evening Roman and Ken met at the Dorchester for the first time and shook on the deal.

Those close to him speak of a man who doesn't rush his decisions. It looked for all the world like José Mourinho would be sacked long before December 2015 given Chelsea's bad results but Roman genuinely hadn't made his mind up until the Leicester game. Then, at once, he was gone. The board process at Chelsea is not a conventional structure - Roman has advisers he trusts, takes information from a variety of sources and then comes to a conclusion. There is no need for haste when you are that wealthy but once his mind is made up, there is no negotiation or review.

It is perhaps a shame he is not more visible to the public but conducting interviews wouldn't be in Roman's interests. His responsibilities include investing and allocating money in Russia so how would it look if he talked about the merits of spending

£30 million on Cesc Fabregas, Andriy Shevchenko or Fernando Torres while people in his homeland struggle to make ends meet?

Roman has his detractors, so did Ken Bates . . . and I can understand why. I always thought Ken tried to do well by his club as a chairman – operating with great passion – without necessarily agreeing with many of the decisions he made. His uncompromising manner often left you with a bitter taste.

In 2000, Chelsea wanted to sell Norwegian striker Tore Andre Flo. After weeks of negotiations between David Murray and Ken Bates, we got twelve million for him. It was widely reported as a generous fee at the time and we felt Chelsea had been well remunerated for an unwanted player who saw his future elsewhere. He wasn't playing regularly and Rangers fans wanted a big signing so everyone was happy once we got it over the line. I was delighted with the outcome and phoned Ken the day after it was completed. 'Hi, Ken. We got you twelve million – how about that!' I said.

'It should have been twelve-and-a-half,' he snapped back, and then hung up. But I rather liked Ken and his lovely wife Suzanna. We had fall-outs – regularly – but he is fundamentally a good man who cares and we were always able to move forward one way or another.

That deal happened independently of Vincenzo and, of course, we weren't solely reliant on him to bring in players from overseas. Mark Goldberg formally took over at Crystal Palace in 1998 but was involved in brokering deals for the club before then, including the ambitious transfer of Attilio Lombardo a year earlier. Lombardo was thirty years old when he moved to the Premier League but was an Italian international with an impressive pedigree comprising spells at Sampdoria and Juventus.

Mark had earned his fortune in the recruitment industry and was a lifelong Palace fan living the dream as chairman. As Mark became more involved, he called us because of our reputation within the game and we provided him with a list of players we thought we could deliver. Attilio was among them because we were dealing directly with his representatives out in Italy. I remember him telling me he had no idea who Crystal Palace were but 'they sound like a nice club'. He was keen to come to England because he could see how the League was taking off. The hardest thing we had to do was keep it quiet because Mark wanted to tell the world. It was one of the first times we hired a private jet to complete a transfer.

We flew Attilio into Biggin Hill airfield and agreed terms. Palace agreed to pay him fourteen thousand pounds a week – a huge figure for a club of that size at the time – which helped things progress quickly. It was an eye-catching deal and one that earned Mark kudos among Palace supporters, especially when he scored on his début and celebrated by mimicking an aeroplane. 'LET'S ALL DO THE LOMBARDO!' screamed one paper the next day.

Mark left Palace after a disappointing spell as owner but not before appointing Terry Venables as Palace manager. I always got on well with Terry but we never did much business with him. He once said to me, 'You are so shiny, people could skate on you.'

We were involved in hundreds of inbound player deals from overseas in subsequent years, continuing to work with Vincenzo and others like him. As clubs increasingly sourced more players from abroad and other big agencies began to catch up with First Artist, our percentage share of big transfers declined but we still had a hand in many major transactions. Vincenzo had an arrangement with the representatives of Emmanuel Adebayor and, as a consequence of being closely tied to Arsenal at the time, we were involved in the deal taking him to north London from Monaco in 2006.

Three years later, Manchester City's then Director of Football, Brian Marwood, phoned us to express an interest in signing Adebayor as a fall-back position because they were struggling to prise Samuel Eto'o from Inter Milan. City were in the first phase of their squad development having been purchased by the Abu Dhabi United Group in 2008. They wanted to land a marquee striker early that summer as a statement of intent for the future. I had a previous relationship with Brian having first met him when I was England's agent in the 1980s; Brian had earned his one and only international cap in 1988.

Phil phoned Arsène Wenger. He told me they would consider a deal if the right offer came in, immediately indicating fertile ground for further talks. Manny spoke with his agent, Stefan Courbis, and he greeted the idea positively but with the caveat that he was happy at Arsenal and 'everything would need to be right'. That essentially meant he wanted to be made to feel very important and paid handsomely, which was not a surprise because he had been somewhat marginalised by Arsène and had ambitions he felt weren't being matched at the Emirates.

I talked to Ken Friar at Arsenal, who gave us permission to arrange a meeting between the player and Brian's team. The first meeting was actually between us and Man City at First Artist House. Negotiations took place over three hours but they were left in abeyance as an agreement could not be reached – Stefan wanted too much money for Manny.

Next up was a meeting with Manny and City's representatives at his house one day after training. If ever there was an example of a player dictating terms, it was this – he had a strict regime that meant he slept after training, so despite all of us turning up to discuss a twenty-five-million-pound move, he went to bed. For four hours. We sat around and drank our bodyweight in coffee, testing the confines of small talk to the limit in various north London backwaters. Eventually, he woke up and we returned to his house to resume negotiations. Things progressed well – it was clear early on that City saw him as an important part of their future.

The third meeting took place at Arsenal's training ground. Strangely, a couple of other agents had been in contact with Arsenal claiming they represented Manny, which just goes to show how unprofessional some of them can be. They obviously had no part of the deal whatsoever but had read about it in the daily papers.

Progress in the deal had slowed so I removed myself from Ken's office and went to see Arsène, who suggested a couple of negotiating points. He really is an exceptionally bright man and would have made a great football agent had he not been one of the game's leading managers. He is also one of the most enjoyable human beings it has been my pleasure to associate with. His knowledge across so many areas of human life, not just football, is vast and, despite some people believing he can be somewhat aloof, I've always found him to be warm, amusing and engaging.

Talks were stuck because Manny had had a change of heart and wanted to stay. Both clubs were now frustrated. Each conversation cost City more money as Manny's demands kept rising.

Something that initially seemed fairly simple had become excessively complicated. Arsène put his arm around Manny and politely but firmly told him that the bridge has basically been crossed now. Of course, if he stayed he would be welcome but he might just end up playing some of his football in the reserves at Barnet's Underhill ground. There's nothing like the power of suggestion.

With Manny reading between the lines, the deal was back on and Stefan had moved on to asking for certain conditions to be met in his Arsenal contract before he left. Arsenal decided that, as the price was good – City had started at £20m but ended at £25m plus a few bits and pieces in add-ons – and the payment terms were excellent, they would accommodate some of the requests. We were nearly there.

The salary package was a huge outlay – the media widely reported as £180,000 a week – but Manchester City felt that they were getting a quality player whom they needed at that moment in time to be the catalyst for further growth.

Only the agents' fees were left. Unlike in most cases, the issue had arisen earlier than normal during talks and we tried to round them up as part of the overall financial numbers. After another forty-eight hours of discussions, the terms were agreed and Manny said goodbye to his team-mates. Janine arranged a private jet to take him to his party in Manchester and City announced the deal shortly afterwards.

Private jets are commonplace now. Deals were once done in motorway service stations and pub car parks because, in those days, managers and staff used to frequent pubs.

We did a lot of our deals in a small restaurant called The Potting Shed, now the basement of the Dorset Square Hotel, before the world found out and we had to vacate that venue, too. People used to know that it was where I liked to meet and greet. It stands on the site of Thomas Lord's first cricket ground in 1787. Terry Venables always used his club named Scribes West in Kensington (he sold it in 1997) because he could shut the doors and nobody else could get in!

It was a great little bolt-hole which provided the setting for many major football transfers. The antithesis of that venue is the Waltham Cross Marriot on the M25, which became known among agents as 'transfer hotel'. It just happened to be in the perfect spot geographically for so many clubs and agents to meet. If you go there any time between the 25–31 August and just wander around, you will see a plethora of people in clandestine conversation. We tried to make friends with the hotel staff during the rest of the year so that, in the latter days of a trading window, one of them might just let slip to us who was in which room with whom.

But increasingly, big deals are often negotiated in private suites housed within restaurants or lavish houses – that is how far footballers have come. The Premier League is now the epicentre of the global game. Which was the plan all along.

12

Brothers in Arms

Player management has always required a personal touch and I felt if we were going to grow the First Artist football business, I needed to be there 24/7. But that simply wasn't possible because there was so much going on around me at the time. I had to bring in someone else I could trust, and my brother Phil was an obvious candidate. Life was treating him well as a promotions executive at MCA Records but, by the beginning of the 1990s, he had outgrown his position there and, with little immediate prospect of further advancement, he agitated for a change.

Phil had worked with artists who are masters of their own destiny in all aspects of music; big acts owned their commercial, sponsorship and branding rights in most cases.

Football clubs were different. A player was part of a club and that club had their own sponsorship agreements which the players were required to adhere to. Phil's skillset was perfectly suited to helping players take greater control of their own destiny just as many musicians did. I knew a thing or two about that from my own record business days but Phil had a more contemporary understanding of the marketplace and could simultaneously sate his desire to become more involved in football.

I knew he would deal with personalities and not be star-struck – always an amateurish trait – but most importantly he felt like a very safe port in any storm; I had people working for me previously who were duplicitous or had decided to leave to compete with me commercially, but Phil would always be loyal.

He came to my house one late summer's day in 1992 to discuss terms. We sat in deckchairs bathed in glorious sunshine in a field at the back of my house discussing what would work for one another. Negotiating with your brother is unusual but we were pulling in the same direction; he wanted to come on board, I needed him and wanted him to be comfortable. He is a really tough negotiator but it has always been easy between us. We're soft when we negotiate with each other.

Phil came on board and began to join me at England gatherings. Graham Taylor had replaced Bobby Robson by this point but I still had a great relationship with the players; the England team coach even gave me a lift to a party once because the venue was on the way back to their base at Burnham Beeches. It was slightly surreal to get off the bus outside a bar with the team waving goodbye as they drove off, but these guys were my mates as well as clients.

Graham was very supportive from the beginning. I was in the room when he gave his first team talk and, upon its conclusion, he turned his attention to the players' pool. 'The minute you tell me you don't want Jon, he's out. He's got to perform in the same way you have to in order to stick around,' he said. I couldn't argue with that. Sadly the results didn't come for him and as they got worse, we had to keep scaling back our plans.

It wasn't like the old days with Bobby. Towards the end of Bobby's reign, I was pushing things to the absolute limit. We organised a pre-match game called the 'Sonic Challenge'. I made a note in my diary at the time: 'Speak to Bobby - could we get Sonic on the bench?' It didn't happen but that's how far out there I was at the time.

We had a jobbing actor dressed as Sonic the Hedgehog on the pitch and I told him once the game ended to stay on the pitch a little too long as the serious stuff was about to start. That way, when Bobby and the team walked out, Sonic would be in the television shot. In my heart I knew it was a bit ridiculous to push it further and have a fake hedgehog on the England bench. Players and fans were acclimatising to the increasing commercial involvement in football but during one of our regular FA meetings, this was an occasion where I couldn't really negate the argument this was a step too far.

The first two years under Graham went well enough but, after England finished bottom of their Euro '92 group – drawing 0-0 with Denmark and France before losing 2-1 to Sweden – the sponsors distanced themselves from the team. Inevitably, as results suffered, the FA began to question whether our commercial endeavours were taking up too much time and proving a distraction from preparing for games. England then failed to qualify altogether for the 1994 World Cup, by which time the FA had appointed their own commercial director, Trevor Phillips.

Missing out on USA '94 took everyone by surprise, not least the host nation; I was friendly with the United States Soccer Federation prior to that World Cup and still possess a rare T-shirt emblazoned with all the teams set to participate in the finals. They went to print before the qualification campaign ended with England's name on them because the hosts thought it was a foregone conclusion.

It was reported at the time that England's absence from the World Cup cost ten million pounds, and the FA sought to offset that loss by agreeing a deal with Littlewoods to sponsor the FA Cup. Here was the first time in 123 years that the FA Cup had been branded but they received good money – fourteen million pounds over four years. Trevor came in initially to negotiate that deal and he brought me to the table near the end to help make it work for both parties as best as possible.

We used the same system in place for England sponsors with Littlewoods; selected photographers would take heavily branded shots of the FA Cup trophy before each round, which made it an easy sell. Nobody was allowed to touch the real trophy but I had a replica I was allowed to carry around and often called it the real thing for promotion purposes.

In hindsight, Trevor's decision to use First Artist in this way, as I would later find out, was nothing more than a sop to me because, plans were afoot to take my biggest client away. Perhaps I should have realised I was being marginalised but my confidence endured because the players remained wholly supportive of me regardless of performances on the pitch.

* * *

It was approaching midday on an unremarkable morning at our Wembley office late in 1994 when an assistant knocked on my door and gently laid down a fax on my desk.

I read it. And read it again. The words didn't change but I couldn't believe what they added up to – the England team had decided they were not going to renew our contract. This deal had been the foundation of my company since 1986 and now David

Platt and Stuart Pearce, the head of the players' management committee, were taking it away. They felt I was too close to the Football
Association to look after their interests sufficiently in the latest
contract negotiations. It was a hammer blow which hit me very
hard. I felt personally rejected, not least because I had spent the
previous nine months negotiating on their behalf with Trevor,
whose brief was to take control of, promote and maximise their
properties, which primarily meant the England team. Inherent in
all those discussions were the team's playing fees (minimal), their
charity donations (sizeable) and the new marketing partnerships
which by now stretched through all the FA's key properties (very
sizeable). It had been a difficult negotiation but we were closing in
on an agreement when this bombshell was dropped.

I always felt a key strength of mine was the closeness I eventually
engendered with the FA. Over time, I tried to break down the 'us
and them' mentality that existed at the outset, when certain board
members were sceptical of my involvement.

It doesn't have to be 'us and them' in a negotiation. You can be
civil yet tough; you can even remain mates. I have always reached
agreements far easier through compromise than confrontation. Of
course, there are times when you need to take a stand and, if it is
me or you in a fight, I will make sure I win. But seven times out of
ten, you can do it by conciliation.

I harboured a concern that because Tony Stevens represented
Platt and was very close to Pearce – who was in turn cosied up
with another rival agent Jon Holmes – there was a Machiavellian
coup in play but, to the best of my knowledge, that wasn't the
real motive. The players simply felt I couldn't negotiate them the
best deal any more. They thought the whole process was taking

too long to materialise and sensed a weakness on my part. I could probably have fought it but with no guarantee of success. I chose not to, partly out of pride but also because it became clear Trevor and the FA wanted to take the whole operation in-house. I was utterly heartbroken.

This decision cost me a lot of money and influence. The kudos had been huge, delivering me major corporate clients on a regular basis.

I was worried that losing England would come to define us. I felt like Brian Epstein losing the Beatles – yes, you have all these other acts but the star horse has left the stable. Looking after England created so many opportunities and there was no guarantee those chances would still come our way without our flagship client acting as a standard bearer.

We had to carry on somehow and continuing work in international football became a priority for us. I was very close to FIFA at the time and a small but interesting opportunity arose. Bolivia qualified for the 1994 World Cup and I was asked by Guido Tognoni – FIFA's chief marketing officer and later senior adviser to President Sepp Blatter – to organise friendly matches for them.

We set up a programme including games against the Republic of Ireland, two matches in Greece, one against Saudi Arabia in the south of France and another in Romania.

Everybody was seemingly always paid in cash because bank accounts didn't really exist over there. One of the senior Romanian FA officials came to meet Phil and me in Phil's hotel room to give us our match fee. We were in there talking with one of the Bolivians when this guy walked in, opened up what looked like a doctor's bag, turned it upside down and poured out 150,000 US dollars in cash on Phil's bed.

He looked at Phil and me and said, 'Do you want to count it?' It was all perfectly legal, this was just how they conducted business, but doing so would take a while and in any case, it seemed rude. We declined.

He added, 'OK, forget the game then. Let's go get some hookers and drugs!'

We looked at each other in bemusement and shook our heads.

I'm pretty sure he was joking. The Bolivians also gave me a llama as a thank-you gift. I had a private zoo at the time comprising various animals including a kangaroo, an emu and an aardvark but they kept escaping. Over the years, there were a few occasions when one creature would disappear, prompting an awkward phone call from the local police telling me which one had gone walkabout. So to make sure I kept the authorities onside, I arranged a seven-a-side game with the police on the football pitch at my house on Monday nights.

My two sons Ross and Scott and I always comprised part of one team, occasionally playing alongside professionals including Nwankwo Kanu, Bobby Zamora, Freddie Ljungberg and Geoff Hurst, whose credential of scoring a hat-trick in a World Cup Final did not prevent us putting him in goal during one such match to mark my fiftieth birthday.

Needless to say, the police team struggled. At about 6-1 ahead, I politely explained to Kanu's brother that we had to conspire to lose to keep the police happy. He looked at me with bemusement – that competitive instinct never dies – so I went in goal and started making a few 'mistakes'.

We had a few matches like that. Charlie Nicholas stayed over at my house after an Arsenal game once. I got up on the Sunday morning to find Charlie in the bathroom with the door open.

'All right, Jon? What are you up to today.'

'Er,' I said, slightly perturbed by the absence of conventional social boundaries. 'I'm off to play football at Edgwarebury Park.'

'Oh, I'll come along, too.'

Charlie did just that and played on our team, which was a huge thrill for me as a lifelong Gooner. And Andrey Arshavin once had a kickabout with us after he signed for Arsenal, but players simply can't do it now because of the insurance premiums built into their contracts.

We had friends in high places. I became a confidant of Kenny Dalglish after fostering a friendship during the Peter Beardsley deal and working with a few of his players. After completing a couple of commercial contracts for him, Janine and I went out with Kenny and his wife Marina one night. Kenny can often be reserved – and difficult to follow in conversation given that thick Scottish accent of his – but that night in particular he talked about Heysel and Hillsborough. He even hinted that his time in football management might be limited as he struggled to centre himself after the shockwaves of the Hillsborough tragedy, such was his affection for Liverpool fans and the region. There are very few people who I regard as highly as Kenny Dalglish, both as a human being and a football icon.

We helped advise Kenny during the 1994–95 season as his Blackburn Rovers side won the Premier League title – but there was a wobble in our friendship when we brought in Ruud Gullit to replace him as Newcastle manager.

I was in an invidious position because we were getting Ruud an excellent job opportunity as my client but at the expense of the employment of a close friend in Kenny. Before Kenny was sacked, Newcastle were talking to me about Ruud. I sat at the house agonising over what I should do. I wanted to phone Kenny and tell him but, if I did that, the deal for my client would have been scuppered. I chose to bite my tongue and Kenny was very unhappy when he found out. Unquestionably, it had an effect on our relationship going forward yet I was only doing my job. This is where the issue of only having a finite number of clients can cause the most acute problems for a football agent. Sometimes, you find yourself on the front foot with a player, manager or a club in one deal and then firmly on the back foot a few months later.

It is an emotional game and people can bear grudges. Walking the line between personal and professional relationships is difficult but also an unavoidable part of the job. Wherever possible, I tried to be personal but, ultimately, my client's best interests had to come first because that's what made me what I am.

Years later, I was on *Newsnight* with Jeremy Paxman and Kenny's daughter, Kelly. She took a very aggressive stance against me as I defended footballers' lifestyles. I was there to take blows like that on the chin, but we didn't speak much afterwards and I always wondered whether she positioned herself so robustly against me because of what happened with Ruud.

I found *Newsnight* petrifying the first time I went on it. People who coached me over the years advised always trying to go into make-up with your interviewer as it helps create a bond between you. I made a point of doing that with Jeremy and we even went to the toilet at the same time; standing next to your forthcoming inquisitor at a urinal just makes it more difficult for them to be aggressive later on. It is a moment of awkward intimacy that reduces the distance between you. He could have eaten me for breakfast but, as the opening credits were rolling, he leant across to me and said, 'Don't worry, this will be all right.'

After I went on with Kelly, Jeremy asked me up to his office for a chat over a glass of wine. Forty minutes or so later, we walked down a staircase to leave, at the bottom of which there was a runner organising cars for everyone. 'Car for Smith!' he shouted as I reached the lobby. Jeremy and I began to say our goodbyes as the Dalai Lama appeared, having filmed a programme elsewhere in the building. I was taken aback by the sudden presence of such an iconic figure but, before I could fully appreciate the gravitas of the moment, the runner shouted, 'Car for Lama!' Jeremy and I each let out a roar of laughter.

Losing our principal source of clients – the England team – was no laughing matter, however, so Phil began targeting a series of players to help First Artist expand its player-management portfolio. One of the first players he ever sat with was Steve Froggatt. He had asked Phil to go and negotiate his new contract at Aston Villa. Steve believed he was worth more than Villa were offering him but then manager Ron Atkinson said he if didn't agree the terms in front of him, he wouldn't play him in the 1994 League Cup Final against Manchester United at Wembley. Rather than fold, he stood defiant. 'That's fine, gaffer, don't play me,' he said, sitting back and folding his arms.

Ron turned to Phil and said, 'You're supposed to be advising him . . . sort it out.' Phil paused to find the right words – after all, Steve was showing courage in refusing to sign a substandard contract in the belief he was worth more – but before he spoke, Ron added, 'By the way, who the fuck are you?'

Steve just laughed. Phil couldn't see a reason to advise Steve to take the deal. In any case, it was Phil's job to back Steve's decision, especially given he was so adamant.

Steve stuck to his guns, missed the Cup Final and joined Wolves for more than the figure he was asking for at Villa. It was a shame he missed out on the Cup Final because he deserved to play, but everything worked out for the best in one sense – Villa won 3-1 and Steve got the contract he wanted.

We ended up looking after Ron as a broadcaster. Phil recited that story back to him years later. He just shrugged his shoulders and said, 'That's football.'

Phil may not have been able to do too much for Steve but he has since gone on to become one of the most respected agents in England. We are very different people but we operate with the same ethos – footballers are not purely dispensable commodities but human beings, sometimes vulnerable to the vagaries of a ruthless industry. Kevin Phillips is a case in point; Phil played a pivotal role in ensuring Kevin became a household name rather than a builder living with regret for the rest of his life.

Kevin was out of favour at Watford and coming to the end of his contract in 1997. Graham Taylor wanted to keep him but Kevin felt things had run their course at Vicarage Road and it was time to move on. His only previous club had been part-timers Baldock Town – having previously been rejected as an apprentice playing at right-back for Southampton – and no club was willing to take a punt on a twenty-three-year-old with such a modest pedigree. He was at a low ebb because his dad had recently passed away, and considered giving up the game to work on construction sites.

Phil phoned then Sunderland manager Peter Reid and asked

him to do us a favour. Peter was initially receptive but needed convincing that Kevin was worth a punt. After a couple of lengthy phone calls, Peter took him on trial for two weeks. Within two days, Peter was convinced of Kevin's ability. Kevin snapped at the chance to revive his career and never looked back.

Phil was leading the way for First Artist on football as the 1990s drew to a close but I still re-engaged whenever necessary. We had a good relationship with Sunderland, so much so that owner Bob Murray asked us to organise the opening of the club's new home, the Stadium of Light, also in 1997. Our events company was hired to plan the day and were charged with booking a world-famous band as the headline act. Bob was delighted when I pitched Status Quo.

Simultaneously, I was negotiating Jody Craddock's move from Cambridge United to Sunderland. Chelsea were also interested but kept dragging their heels, while talks moved forward with Sunderland. On the Stadium of Light launch day, Jody's deal also had to be finalised. I was in the boardroom working on Jody's contract when runners came in to tell me Status Quo were arriving and setting up. I had to dart around all over the place co-ordinating the stadium event while making sure Jody was looked after.

Peter Reid trusted our judgement; I recommended Stefan Schwarz to him in 1999. He knew of Stefan but I'd seen him play for Sweden against England and just thought he was exactly what Sunderland needed. I phoned Peter and made the case. He decided to look at some videos and Peter's backroom staff saw potential benefits in signing him. It was one of the easiest deals we ever did. Stefan had enjoyed his time at Arsenal five years earlier and wanted to come back to England – terms were a formality on all sides as Valencia were happy to sell.

In the same summer as Kevin's move to Sunderland, we also dealt with their fierce rivals Newcastle when facilitating Les Ferdinand's transfer to Tottenham. We'd known Les for years, not just through England, but also dating back to his days on loan at Besiktas from Queens Park Rangers in 1988.

A Turkish custom dictated that, upon signing for the club, he had to walk over a sheep with its throat slit as a mark of respect. Whenever we saw him for dinner out there afterwards, he never ordered lamb from the menu.

We also took him into Newcastle in 1995 when QPR were very reluctant sellers. Phil went on QPR's end-of season tour to Barbados, bizarrely, in very close proximity to where Aston Villa had taken their players.

Villa were keen on Les before Newcastle ever got serious. Then owner Doug Ellis caught Les and Phil having a drink one night and practically pinned them to the bar, demanding they came in for a meeting at Villa Park.

Les still had to negotiate his exit from QPR. Player-manager Ray Wilkins took full advantage of the salubrious environment and was never out of the sea. Les ended up having to go and meet him out in the water to discuss his future. Phil watched as they thrashed out Les's situation, half-submerged against a backdrop of clear blue sky. The players knew what was happening and as he began to walk back to shore, they all started that slow chant, gradually rising in pitch, of "whoa". As he walked past them, Les confirmed he would be allowed to leave and they all cheered.

Villa offered Les more money than Newcastle ever did but he didn't see himself going there. Doug locked Phil and Les in the Villa Park boardroom at one point insisting he signed a deal but eventually they made their excuses on the grounds that other clubs had also expressed an interest and needed to be heard.

We were eventually given permission to talk to Newcastle chairman Freddy Shepherd, who made a late decision to pitch up at my house a day later. Little did he know that, at that precise moment, Les was sitting in my lounge. Now, this is where the regulations made fools of us all because we could talk to Freddy and also to Les but they couldn't talk to each other until a bid had been accepted. Given QPR were searching for any excuse to pull out of a deal, we had an even greater incentive to do things by the book. Freddy arrived and I told Les we had to conduct ourselves completely correctly.

Les saw a go-kart I had sitting in the garage and took it out for a spin in one of the fields at the back of my house. There may have been a temptation for Freddy to talk to Les given his close proximity and sudden opportunity but Les kept driving in circles on the go-kart, revving the engine and shouting, 'Can't talk!' at the top of his voice. It was a ridiculous situation. But eventually all sides reached an agreement and Les had two great years at Newcastle before moving to Tottenham – another deal we played a role in – in 1997.

We went to then Tottenham chairman Alan Sugar's house. Les, Phil and I left at one point to go for a walk and discuss the terms on offer. 'We'll just walk to the end of the garden,' I told Alan. 'Won't be long.'

The three of us walked ... and walked ... and walked. We couldn't find the end of the garden because it went on for ever. He owned acres and acres of land. We gave up and sat under a tree instead while Les went through his dilemma; Newcastle had treated him well but Spurs were one of his boyhood clubs.

Newcastle were a great club to deal with. Kevin Keegan used to come and pick us up from the airport sometimes. There was the Newcastle manager stood at Arrivals alongside taxi and private hire drivers with a board which read 'Phil Smith'. Nobody cared – they loved him up there. Newcastle Falcons and England rugby player Rob Andrew came and met Phil when we took Darren Huckerby up there. That felt like a move to impress Darren as he wasn't convinced about moving to Newcastle at the time but Kevin genuinely made the effort out of the goodness of his heart.

That warmth endured after Kevin left. I went up to St James's Park to renegotiate Andy O'Brien's contract in the early 2000s. Freddy Shepherd disarmed me in the conversation before it began by giving my son Scott, then about ten years old, a Newcastle shirt signed by the whole team. It's difficult to beat someone up in a negotiation when they've just made a gesture like that!

Talks went smoothly and, afterwards, Freddy invited us to travel with him to watch the Sunderland versus Newcastle derby taking place on the same day. We agreed and the ride was pleasant enough until we got about 500 yards from the Stadium of Light and a Sunderland fan recognised Freddy in the car. Suddenly we were bombarded with abuse. I have no idea who brings a tomato to a football match but somebody threw one at us, people spat at the window and I did my best to shield Scott from the verbal onslaught as we left the car and entered the ground. I hid him inside my coat at one point.

We were greeted by Sunderland chairman Bob Murray – who didn't get on that well with Freddy – and he showed us into a lift up to the Directors' Box. Bob, Freddy, Scott, the Secretary of State for Health Alan Milburn, a big Newcastle fan, and I were crammed into this lift when it got stuck . . . for ten minutes. It could have been frightening but how could we be in danger with the Health Minister in there with us? Bob and Freddy did little more than exchange pleasantries. Eventually, they fixed the problem and we made it out for kick-off. The game was terrible – Newcastle won 1-0. I think I preferred it in the lift.

The rivalry up there is remorselessly intense: before one of the derbies in the 2015-16 season, the Sunderland players asked an agent to produce a T-shirt depicting a Black Cat savaging a Magpie. They were going to wear it under their kit during the game and at full-time, presuming they won, all take their tops off and run towards Newcastle supporters showing off these T-shirts. In the overall scheme of things, who cares? They aren't necessarily breaking the law. But in football, emotion runs so high it could create a disturbance or even a riot. And in that riot, if one child gets hurt, it is appalling. If one child dies, it is a tragedy. That's what we have to contend with.

But it took that agent six days to talk the Sunderland squad out of it. He told them they would be fined hundreds of thousands of pounds but they didn't care; there is at least something to be said for players being so impassioned by the cause that a financial punishment did not deter them, especially given the prevailing perception of footballers being driven solely by money. Here was the antithesis – they wanted to sacrifice money in a public show of hunger to avoid relegation.

While Vincenzo Morabitto continued to deliver talent from overseas, Phil and I expanded First Artist domestically. We represented nearly 500 players at our peak, all acquired through a mixture of reputation, hard work and a little luck.

Phil went after Leroy Lita during his time at Bristol City. Leroy was playing the field at the time in search of an agent. Phil attended a City game with an assistant and told him categorically that they couldn't afford to leave without speaking to Leroy. They missed him in the players' lounge but eventually caught up with him in the car park outside. Leroy refused to speak to them and got in a car with several of his mates but, out of an eagerness to impress, Phil's assistant took his instruction literally. Reaching in through an open window, he grabbed the steering wheel as they tried to drive away. Suddenly his feet were off the ground with the car picking up speed. Leroy said, 'Look, I've got to leave. I don't want to hurt you but let go of the wheel.'

'I'm under orders not to let you leave until we have a conversation,' said Phil's assistant. 'Please slow the car down.'

'Fair play,' said Leroy. 'If you are prepared to do that, I'll listen to what you have to say.' He signed for us shortly afterwards.

Sometimes you have to do almost anything it takes. There are occasions when you have to swallow your pride or endure experiences you would never otherwise put yourself through in the hope that at the end of it you win their trust. Players used to take us to lap-dancing clubs or casinos to make sure we were one of the boys. We had to make a judgement call as to whether they were taking us for a ride because they usually expected us to pick up the bill.

When Andy King was manager of Mansfield, he invited Phil to come in for a team meeting. Phil didn't think he should be there but Andy insisted and it is always useful to be taken into the inner sanctum like that, even at a modest club like Mansfield; and after all, the sanctity of their dressing room for Mansfield supporters is just the same as Old Trafford is to Manchester United fans.

The meeting began and Andy said, 'It is a big game tomorrow. If you play well, you might just find yourself at a bigger club. That bloke at the back, his agency has worked with some of the biggest names in the game. Don't impress me on the pitch. Impress him.'

He used Phil's presence as a motivational tool. They lost the game 1-0 and Andy was sent to the stands for abusing a linesman. In the dressing room afterwards, he walked over to Phil and said, 'What a fucking waste of time that was bringing you in.'

An agency's success in acquiring players is often determined by how far they are willing to kowtow to the player in question. Everton owner Bill Kenwright introduced us to Jose Baxter and his family. Bill thought he was going to be the next Wayne Rooney and the Baxters were seeking formal representation. Phil arranged to visit Jose at his family home in Toxteth. The Baxter house was the only one left standing in the surrounding area – all the others had been knocked down. His father, Andy, was a great bloke and a Liverpool fan. Talks were progressing well and we asked Phil Thompson to get tickets for a game from Steven Gerrard so they could sit alongside the players, not in the match-day squad. They were more interested in that than sitting in the boardroom. We got to Anfield and met Gerrard, who was always very friendly and gave us the passes. After the game, we tried to get into the players' lounge and the security guard told us we didn't have the right accreditation. A huge altercation ensued and Gerrard was summoned by security because we were all listed under his name. He approached Phil as the argument subsided and said, 'Thanks for that, mate.' Ironically enough, Jose didn't sign with us in the end because he held off agreeing terms and eventually went with Gerrard's agent, Struan Marshall.

Phil's initial remit was domestically focused but he inevitably branched out into overseas transfers, too. In 1997, he took Ian Crook from Norwich City to Sanfrecce Hiroshima in Japan. They weren't one of the fashionable teams but Hiroshima was a fascinating place given what happened there during World War Two. With the deal complete, they went to watch the team play in Osaka before flying home.

The Japanese decided to split our sixty-thousand-pound payment 50-50 between telegraphic transfer and cash, with the latter payment made in Osaka. Phil was on the pitch alongside Ian in front of twenty thousand people just before the game when a man came up to him and said, 'I have the book you want.'

'What book?' said Phil.

'No, you are expecting this book. Take it.'

'I don't want a book. I'm here for the game.'

'Please take this book.' And with that he thrust a large, heavy opus into Phil's hands. He opened the book to find it resembling a scene from *The Shawshank Redemption* – the pages had been cut out, leaving a hole in the middle stuffed full of Japanese yen banknotes. Phil immediately slammed the book shut and looked around at the crowd. 'Er, Ian, I think we'd better leave the pitch now,' he said.

As they took their seats for the game, the Japanese hosts asked Ian what he wanted to eat. 'McDonald's,' he said. They thought he was joking. 'No, I really want a McDonald's.' He couldn't stand sushi so they went shopping downtown and got him one.

Phil rushed to the airport after the game but had a problem in getting that amount of cash through Customs. Ian wanted nothing to do with it so Phil brought back as much as he could; in any event, of course we banked the cash with it noted in our accounts. That Christmas, it would have been easier to pay the First Artist bonuses in yen.

Later that year, we took Nigel Quashie from Southampton to West Brom. It was done late in the evening on deadline day. There was a full set of fixtures that night and West Brom were playing at Charlton. His medical had to be conducted by West Brom's staff and, because they were at the Valley, we had to take him there to undergo the requisite tests. We arrived at the stadium but a few Charlton fans misunderstood the situation and thought he was signing for them. Word spread fast inside the stadium and, as the game kicked off, the Charlton fans were chanting, 'There's only one Nigel Quashie!' Just after the final whistle, it was confirmed that Nigel had, in fact, signed for West Brom.

Misunderstandings happen more than you think, especially with the onset of 24-hour news and social media. Everyone is a journalist these days, yet fewer individuals actually fact-check with people in the know.

We were involved in moving Nolberto Solano from Newcastle to West Ham on deadline day. The paperwork was dragging late into the evening as we were waiting for the results of various scans which formed a key part of his medical. Phil was there with Scott Duxbury, the club doctor and a cleaner. Sky Sports had somehow found a vantage point to peer into the room, where they sat as the minutes ticked by. They had Sky Sports News on in the room as breaking news came in.

'We believe that Ronaldo is in the building at West Ham,' the reporter began, referencing the veteran Brazil striker, not Cristiano, although either way it was bonkers.

Scott and Phil looked at each other. 'Is he?' said Phil with complete bemusement.

'Not as far as I know.'

They both began frantically looking around the place and as Phil was about to start making calls, he clocked the cleaner. From a certain angle, he bore a passing resemblance to Ronaldo.

Phil told him: 'You are going to have to go outside and present yourself.' He did and Sky quickly moved on.

Phil did his coaching badges to UEFA 'B' level through Gordon Bartlett, who was – and still is - also manager of Wealdstone FC. They remained in touch afterwards and occasionally Gordon would phone Phil about a player. On one such occasion in 2006, he rang him about a striker named Jermaine Beckford, whose attitude wasn't great but Wealdstone let him get away with it because he scored so many goals for them.

Phil was asked to take a look at him when Wealdstone played at his local club, Edgware Town. Beckford stood out immediately. Wealdstone were looking for funds because they needed to move to another home ground and were keen on selling. Chelsea had asked to look at him because he used to be on their books but in reality he wasn't going to get in there. Phil rang Alan Curbishley at Charlton and also Watford, who agreed to take him on trial.

They were keen to do a deal but Beckford already lived in the area and wanted to experience somewhere else. It was also suggested that moving away from his present geography would help him mature, thereby completely ruling out the remote prospect of a move to Chelsea.

Phil and I used our relationship with Ken Bates. Phil rang Ken and he wanted him immediately. We did a deal with Leeds – to Watford's fury – and things took off for him.

He scored 71 league goals but his most famous came when Leeds dumped Manchester United out of the FA Cup at Old Trafford in January 2010. He went to Everton and Bill Kenwright phoned Phil up on the last day of the 2010–11 season and declared Beckford's goal against Chelsea – where he ran from inside his own half, through the Blues defence before chipping Petr Cech – as the greatest he'd ever seen at Goodison Park.

The shame was it never quite happened for him at Everton, he went to Leicester City and his career fell away. But it just goes to show that Jamie Vardy's dramatic rise at Leicester was not the first. There are very good players in the lower leagues – they just need to be given a chance.

Beckford was something of a shooting star passing through English football whereas Jesper Gronkjaer never burned as bright as so many clubs anticipated. He is the football manifestation of that Cliff Richard album 'I'm Nearly Famous'.

We brought him to Chelsea from Ajax in 2000 and he polarised fan opinion at Stamford Bridge – one week he was a worldbeater, the next very poor. It was reported he cost nearly £8m and Chelsea sold him to Birmingham for about £2.2m four years later. Five months later, he went for a bit less than that to Atletico Madrid and then the following summer to Stuttgart for around £5m.

We did all of those deals, too, and each one was a significant fee for a player who just perennially underachieved. He made it to the top of the game but sometimes when a player reaches a high rung on the ladder, it is so easy to fall off.

Football was the key component of our business but the events operation continued to throw up interesting propositions throughout the 1990s and 2000s. We organised Combat '95, a martial arts event in Birmingham and another NHL event in Houston, Texas, but in the middle of this, Jarvis introduced me to Lud Denny, a larger-than-life Texan who had a US company called Pro Set which produced collectable cards of American Football players and wanted to launch it in the UK. Merlin were the big player in that market at the time but Lud believed that, with my connections across football, I would be able to get the rights to challenge their supremacy.

And we did. Jarvis and I chucked some money into Lud's business and Pro Set took off in the UK in January 1991. It paid off admirably and three years later it was time to sell, at which point I tripled our investment.

* * *

First Artist's developing global profile allowed me to be creative. My work with Mikhail Gorbachev had left a positive mark in government circles and I was brought in to help co-ordinate the celebrations marking the fiftieth anniversary of Victory over Japan Day (VJ Day) in 1995. They put me in charge of a mile-and-a-half of the River Thames.

There are two offices at the top of Tower Bridge. I had the one on the left as you look at it from the Tower of London. I don't know anything about water – I get seasick in the bath – but I was given complete control with harbourmasters seeking instruction from me. It was great fun.

One more serious and significantly positive change I helped bring about was in being part of the group charged with repositioning and laater eliminating tobacco advertising in sport. Then

Minister of Sport Tony Banks invited me into the lobbying group just after Tony Blair's Labour Government took office in 1997. I abhorred smoking, having briefly taken it up for a few years before quitting after I met Janine. I knew all too well the influential power of sports advertising and hated the idea of young people being lured into smoking if brands were highly visible on sports stars and venues. It took a few years to implement but the British Grand Prix banned tobacco advertising in 2002 and, a year later, it ended across all sports. Embassy was allowed to continue its sponsorship of the World Snooker Championships until their agreement concluded in 2005 but, overall, it felt like a major victory in the fight to improve long-term health prospects.

The alchemy of sport, entertainment and political influence taking place at First Artist gave us the opportunity to explore different combinations within that vast scope. We branched out into television talent management. Ruud Gullit had planted a seed in my brain when wowing Phil and I at a dinner during which he spoke so elegantly about the game and I knew that kind of insight would resonate with a wider audience. We originally took Andy Townsend on from his playing days to ITV through the relationship Phil and I had with Brian Barwick, who was at the station at the time. Subsequently, we represented Clive Tyldesley and Ron Atkinson on our way to becoming one of the leading television talent agencies.

We decided to start our own production company. We were going to call it First Artist Television but the acronym spelled 'FAT' so we sought an alternative. We went with First Artist Radio and Television because we thought 'FART' was a lot better. We produced a coaching series for kids, a couple of programmes with Rangers and, through this vehicle, we filmed a Football League Awards night at Planet Hollywood called The Footies, which featured Ant and Dec in a presenting capacity for the first time. You could see the chemistry between them even back then and it was no surprise how big they went on to become – they were an absolute delight to work with, too. Our involvement in The Footies made us an early form of what would now be termed 'content provider'.

The growing power of Sky television was acutely identifiable in what happened to Andy Gray in 1997. Andy wanted to replace Joe Royle as Everton manager after his resignation in March that year. We represented Andy and worked hard with chairman Peter Johnson to take his candidacy seriously. Eventually, Peter offered him the job. I was excited because it felt like a hard-earned next step in Andy's career – and a validation of Sky's coverage into the bargain. But then Sam Chisholm called me.

'We're not losing him,' he said in no uncertain terms. 'I need to talk to him.' They swiftly made him the first million-pound pundit. He did a fantastic job for so many years and formed a great chemistry with Richard Keys. It was sad that it ended so acrimoniously. I remember going up to see Andy at his home after Sky had sacked him and he was a broken man. It was incredible to see someone so ebullient become utterly devoid of enthusiasm for anything. He deserves credit for rebuilding himself at beIN Sports, the great contribution he made to Sky and the development of Premier League football worldwide.

First Artist changed football and football changed First Artist; the two were inextricably linked. I was about to find out just how true that was.

13

From the Abyss to
the Top of the World

You might not be surprised to read that I believe cash is king in business. After all, that's all agents are interested in, right? Except that throughout the 2000s, I wasn't operating as a football agent but more as CEO of a company forced into radical alterations by the advent of transfer windows in 2003.

First Artist was a magic company to me; if you threw us in the Thames, we'd emerge bone-dry with raincoats on.

Acquiring the England football team so early in my career opened doors we strode through with conviction, filling each adjoining room as we went until we built a house really worth looking at. The corporation morphed into a multi-faceted entity over many years because we were proactive. First Artist ventured into unexplored territory and, although there were a few missteps along the way, the perpetual growth of our bottom line was proof positive we were doing plenty more right than wrong.

The boom years of Tony Blair's Labour Government encouraged entrepreneurship and we had forged our reputation on operating ahead of the curve, but you can only stay there for so long. Transfer windows meant the heart of the group – our football business – could only trade for four months in every year. We couldn't afford to hibernate so I embarked upon buying a series of businesses from 2003 onwards to help give First Artist an active portfolio all year round.

Business acquisition was a relatively unknown process to me so I sought the help of a corporate adviser. I met Greg Clarke when we were both part of a transaction involving a software company and, although that particular deal did not come to fruition, I made a point of getting close to him during and after the event.

Greg was immensely acerbic but that characteristic attracted me because I couldn't see how he was ostensibly a dreadful communicator yet so successful in his chosen career. I found that underneath the dour exterior was a supremely funny and intelligent guy who thought around corners and asked the questions everybody else was afraid to ask. I brought him on board in an official capacity and we began to identify businesses we could incorporate into First Artist. We bought Optimal, a financial services company; Sponsorship Consulting, which did what it said on the tin; an events company called Finishing Touch; and Nicola Ibison's talent agency – then Nicola Ibison Management, now Ibison Talent – which centred on developing entertainers and TV presenters. That agency helped fuel my thinking on how footballers were becoming entertainers and where the crossover opportunities were both during and after their playing days.

I had lunch one day with Bill Kenwright. Football fans will know Bill as the Everton chairman but he is also one of the most successful theatre producers around, responsible for a number of

West End hits including *Blood Brothers* and *Joseph and the Amazing Technicolor Dreamcoat*. We had gone some way to developing First Artist's revenue streams but I felt we needed a major acquisition to move forward. He told me to look at buying Dewynters. They were the definitive theatre business steeped in history – founded in 1876 – but the owners had been investing for many years and felt they were coming to the end of their run. The brand resonated with me as a logical progression in First Artist's evolution as a sport and entertainment company.

We were among a number of parties to circle it for a while without making a concrete offer. The acquisition was the biggest First Artist had undertaken to that point and sourcing the requisite funds took time. Through a combination of our own money and bank financing, we bought Dewynters for twelve million pounds in 2006. It was a big statement of intent and transformed our scope overnight. First Artist only had around thirty employees at the time, whereas Dewynters had in excess of a hundred.

Our turnover jumped from twenty to seventy million and there was now plenty of cash flowing through the business. Underneath this, the football was chugging along well enough. It had contributed about 99 per cent of First Artist's profits but, with Dewynters and the rest on board, that figure had dropped to around a third. 2006 and 2007 were fantastic years as a result, but I felt we could do even more. We were in a dominant position in the football world and I wanted to replicate that in theatre. I am normally a conservative player – if I win a few, I quit while I'm ahead – but on this occasion I wanted to gamble. We were on a roll. The banks loved me, the figures were good and the companies we bought were doing OK.

Football was still the headline-maker. If I really wanted access to anyone, I was 'Jon Smith – football agent'. The fact I had a successful public company did not open doors for me in the corporate world in the way I felt it should have done.

My PR advisers kept telling me not to appear on football programmes if I seriously wanted to change my image. They didn't like me going on *Newsnight* to defend footballers. They only wanted me on Bloomberg, BBC Breakfast and the like. I listened to them and just answered the call for wider sports stories. I would appear on the BBC to discuss what emerging sportsmen or women were worth and how they could be marketed going forward, but dismissed other opportunities related solely to football.

In hindsight that was a mistake; it is almost impossible to do too much media, no matter what the subject, unless you become repetitive or boring. But I wanted to make big waves in the theatre world and not just be known as a football agent. Perhaps I was trying to become a person that nobody wanted to see me as.

First Artist was at its zenith but I was now operating at a corporate level beyond my previous experience. I had a team of advisers around me all of whom agreed with the prevailing mood of the period – finance growth through debt, and not existing cash, because it is cheap money.

Against that backdrop, I was faced with a big decision in the early part of 2008: whether to buy Dewynters' American 'sister' company called Spot and Co. Having a strong theatre presence on both sides of the Atlantic opened up a plethora of possibilities. We could cross-promote any new show requiring marketing and advertising on Broadway and the West End.

I spoke to British Airways about flying theatregoers from London to New York. They had started a thirty-two-seater business flight from London City Airport and I thought that, during off-peak periods, we could find shows that weren't in London but on in New York – or vice versa – and charter jets to fly people across the Atlantic. We could move into the travel business that way, too. If we missed the opportunity, we would stay at the same level as a business. I had designs on building a little empire but I had to borrow a further seventeen million pounds to do it.

Debt felt like the new cash. It was by far the largest amount I'd ever sourced and it represented a huge gamble on Spot and Co delivering immediate growth. To offset the immediate liability, whenever we bought anything as a group, we arranged an initial down-payment with subsequent performance targets which, if met, triggered further cash payments at set intervals. We implemented this policy with Dewynters and planned to do the same with Spot and Co. We forecasted – building in sub-calculations guarding against other businesses within the group underperforming – that football would continue to earn us three to five million pounds in cash each year. With NBM, Finishing Touch, Optimal, the two theatre businesses, sponsorship and consulting, there would be enough cash coming in from those revenue streams to service the overall debt.

We gave ourselves a significant amount of blue sky between the numbers we required and those which would prove problematic to us – the other businesses could drop to 60 per cent of our anticipated revenue levels without it proving an insurmountable hurdle and we didn't strictly need the full seventeen-million-pound loan but that figure included a contingency fund as an additional insurance policy. We entered into negotiations with Allied Irish

Bank and the deal advanced to a place where we would proceed once they granted the loan. The wider economic picture made me decidedly sceptical it would be signed off.

Dark clouds had been gathering for some time and then, suddenly, the unthinkable happened – Lehman Brothers went to the wall. That was surely the end. It was a certainty to me that we would have to close the acquisition of Spot and Co down. Yet something remarkable happened – Lehman Brothers filed for bankruptcy on 15 September 2008 and the next day my seventeen-million-pound facility came through from Allied Irish. I still had the opportunity to pull the plug but I wasn't scared by the depression because I had a good team around me supplemented by forward-thinking advisers. We believed we had identified how the world was changing. Our track record proved as much.

People had far more electronic gadgets in their lives, not just with children playing video games but adults merging their television viewing with Internet surfing or online social interaction. They were on their devices all the time and that meant that when people finished work, they wanted to go out and physically re-engage with society. The bars were busy and live performances were hugely popular. I remember thinking at the time that, in previous recessions, people used to go to church and pray. The 2008 recession, although in its infancy, felt different. Everybody just seemed to say, 'Sod it. Let's have a party.'

Football and theatre attendances were high. Pubs, bars and clubs continued to do relatively well. It was my decision to make but everybody thought it was the right call to expand. Spot and Co were available and could we really lose this opportunity to have a twin theatre presence either side of the Atlantic?

We took the plunge. Spot and Co was irresistible because it was palpably on a growth path and it continued along that road after joining the First Artist Corporation. Their success was obviously a positive thing for the group but we made a down-payment of five million pounds and set earn-out figures triggering further instalments of one million if they hit certain targets.

Spot and Co did that and more. We were keen to see the selling party, fronted by Drew Hodges, take some equity also to become part of the overall management going forward. They were keener, understandably, to have the cash. We gave them cash on the first two earn-outs, some equity on the third and then more cash towards the end. Those last payments began to cause us problems because while they were performing superbly, the profits Spot and Co were throwing off only worked if the rest of the group performed to 60 per cent of its capacity.

The world was starting to change. What tends to happen is that, when theatre shows succeed, you reinvest profits back into the next show and grow in increments.

My view is that a glass ceiling exists in the theatre business – there are only so many theatres you can service in the West End, Broadway or anywhere else. We had a studio called Newman's which designed and manufactured all the theatre and movie signs. It was flying. Even our competitors used them. But they could only make half-a-million a year so I wanted to take them into the corporate world. I introduced them to Marks & Spencer's and other companies, but that was going to be two or three years away from being realised.

I also wanted to get into ticketing and the music business. Paul McCartney loved Dewynters. We did the design work for many of his albums. I thought if McCartney loved us, plenty of others in music would. I wanted to take western theatre to Asia, too. We opened *Mamma Mia* in Beijing, which was really successful, but that was a one-off and, with longer-term yields, you begin to chase your tail as you wait for that growth to materialise on the balance sheet.

The theatres were doing well but I still had to contain our borrowings and paybacks, which meant all our businesses had to be yielding a certain amount of profit to go towards managing those costs. Except the recession was really beginning to bite. The financial world was in a state of shock after an earthquake registering higher on the Richter scale than anything since World War Two. The world shifted and suddenly we were on the back foot, reacting and recalculating. It was an unfamiliar dynamic to me but just one aspect of a perfect storm that gradually threatened to destroy everything I had built over the previous twenty years. The clouds were starting to gather.

Our other businesses began to struggle. Finishing Touch had performed well initially but it fell away late in 2008 and then alarmingly so in 2009. It was heavily reliant on corporate business but companies were looking for cost-cutting measures after the financial crash and an obvious place to start was with Christmas parties and team-building excursions.

Sponsorship Consulting was a bad purchase. It never did very well but also suffered from the same corporate cutback mentality. Companies simply thought if they were faced with having to lay people off to balance the books, they would cut back on sponsorships where possible instead, and not put as much money into the marketplace. They needed top-line advertising, not below-the-line sponsorship. Nicola's talent business ticked along without being spectacular.

But what really destabilised First Artist was the drop in football business. All through the 1990s and the early part of the 2000s, it had been fantastic. But towards the end of the 2000s, we had become a trading entity rather than a player agency and the big deals began to dry up.

English football was insulated from the global crash but 2008 was still a bad year for us. Emmanuel Adebayor's twenty-five-million-pound move from Arsenal to Manchester City helped our football figures improve in 2009 – although not enough to offset the group's overall decline – but 2010 was another terrible year all round.

Football outside the UK was really struggling, and our Danish and Milan offices were no exception. Milan was my biggest worry because that serviced the southern European market, which had contracted hugely – Spain and Italy were bust. Hardly anyone was spending money. The Premier League was going from strength to strength but we were seventeen years into the adventure and English football was now a breeding ground. Every agent worth their salt was here and the deals that would have come our way as a matter of course no longer did. Overseas agents like, for example, Fulvio Maruko, who looked after Gianfranco Zola, didn't need us to make introductions any more – they would go to clubs directly.

We needed to try and sign more players ourselves because we could see that the other agents weren't doing it for us. So we set up offices in Scandinavia and expanded the office in Italy. We did a deal with a company in Barcelona to have a sub-office in Spain. We also had sub-offices in Australia, Qatar and another in South America: the latter we shut down when that market became flooded to the point of saturation. But it wasn't enough. The Premier League has been a non-stop financial success story but the plethora of agents and agencies – Wasserman Media Group (WMG), Base and Stellar had emerged as big domestic rivals to us by now – plus the lack of movement in Europe meant the football business simply couldn't generate the revenues we needed to offset what was going on elsewhere in the group. We didn't make the same money as before on auxiliary player services, as WMG and the like had followed our lead and become catch-all agencies looking after a client's every need, diluting our impact in the marketplace.

The football business was having to reconstitute itself, but we could only ever try to put things right twice a year because of the timing of trading windows. Big deals had to earn us seven figures now to counterbalance shortfalls in other areas of the group; commissions worth a hundred thousand pounds were nice but they weren't going to solve the issue.

Football was becoming so problematic that sometimes we weren't getting paid even when we completed a deal. In conjunction with a likeable and busy agent, we arranged a complicated deal to move a player to a foreign club. We worked hard to pull that deal off and it was lucrative on all sides – we were due to earn a seven-figure sum from it – except the club in question refused to pay us. The deal was done, the player travelled, the paperwork was signed but then no money arrived. Normally, the funds would arrive to the selling club on the day of the transfer. The English club got theirs but we didn't get ours.

We took the club to FIFA but FIFA claimed they couldn't adjudicate and suggested instead we go to the Court of Arbitration for Sport. We did and it took another year for the case to reach its conclusion; we lost. And the reason? The contract had been drawn up in the name of First Artist and FIFA's regulations only allowed for the use of individually licensed agents. On the most tenuous technicality, CAS declared they could not adjudicate and so the club remained adamant they would not pay up. It cost us fifty thousand in legal fees and the absence of that one-million-pound fee – which we had been counting on in good faith – only added to the growing list of setbacks First Artist was suffering virtually simultaneously.

In 2009, we owed the banks about twenty-three million pounds. We had started paying it off but, instead of doing so from profits of four or five million, we were having to do so out of barely one million pounds profit. As a stand-alone football agency, if you only make two million in a year instead of four million, it is a blow but hardly a disaster. But in our group, that two million was sorely needed because the other businesses were not performing.

The spend on Dewynters was changing to reflect the growth of digital platforms. Instead of opening a show with a full-page advert in the *Times* newspaper, now Facebook and Twitter were spaces that could not be ignored. Monetising them was challenging; the commission on a prominent advert in a reputable newspaper could be sizeable, but to work a show using electronic media was clever and effective yet not particularly profitable.

Several marketplaces were shifting simultaneously and, to make matters worse, my management team systematically disintegrated around me. Greg, my Chief Operating Officer, had suffered from skin cancer some years earlier but it returned aggressively and dramatically in the form of a brain tumour. I lost him as a support as he underwent a series of operations. William Fitzpatrick, my Financial Director, was trying to balance things because we didn't realise how badly affected by all this Allied Irish Bank would be. The recession was brutal for everyone and the guys at Allied I was dealing with were being attacked by their bosses urging them to make cutbacks. At around the same time in 2010, both William and my Company Director Julie Anne Coutts decided to resign. The dual loss left me very exposed.

I was in LA trying to get Spot and Co the rights to tour some of the shows on the west coast when my fabulous PA, Hayley Adkins, acquired a bizarre stress-related illness which left her intermittently paralysed. She received lengthy treatment and was incapacitated for long periods. Any company would struggle to cope in a turbulent period amid such a debilitating and widespread loss of expertise. I felt like the last green bottle hanging on the wall. And to add to the challenges, tragedy also struck the family when my stepbrother was killed with his wife in a road accident.

I was darting back and forth to America so often it felt like my head was spinning but at least physically I was holding up well enough. The group was now turning over £130m and I could no longer be a football agent also sitting on top of a PLC. I physically had to run it on a day-to-day basis.

I had become increasingly removed from football for some time because I had two theatre companies, one in London and the other in New York, turning over in excess of ninety million and I had to be supportive to the teams ensuring the new shows being delivered by promoters such as Cameron Mackintosh or Andrew Lloyd Webber went to one or other – or occasionally both – agencies.

I had to re-engage a new team to embrace the new digital theatre age. We were set up as an acquiring vehicle. Today, if I was going to set up a similar enterprise, I would ensure it was a medically qualified acquiring vehicle. In other words, I would only buy companies where I had the skillset already in place to make it better. At the time, I thought we would simply just own Dewynters, the football business would do what it does and the other companies would tick along adding small profits on the balance sheet. The football and theatre arms were supposed to be the big money earners but the former was underperforming and the latter was being attacked by my rival Adam Kenwright, who was trying to ramp up his operation, Adam Kenwright Associates (AKA).

In our inimitable way, we had made a lot of noise when buying both Dewynters and Spot and Co, and AKA were desperate to match our volume by undercutting us everywhere just to win our business. When we took over, we had about 80 per cent of the West End and 40 per cent of Broadway – AKA and a couple of others basically had the rest. Our share went down to 60 per cent, which was a blow only partially offset by an increase to about half of Broadway, largely explained by that being a growth market at the time which meant more room for everyone.

I had mates in the city Press who softened some of the edges but they couldn't disguise the worst of it. One *MailOnline* piece from 2010 described us as the 'Dog of the Day'. It read: 'First Artist Corporation crashed nine pence – 50 per cent of its value. Investors kicked the shares into touch after reporting an interim loss of £1.72m.'

We reported bad interims in 2010. Our interims came out in April but, because the football business only had one month of trading to report, we always had to caution the result. The market understood this but it still didn't help the general perception of our decline. We had paid down some money at that time because the net debt in that *MailOnline* report stood at £17.6m. We dug into resources to pay down the debt which was technically the right thing to do but perhaps that was another mistake. Maybe we should have kept the banks rolling. I was brought up as an old-fashioned businessman with a simple edict: don't have too much debt. In normal circumstances, seventeen million was a manageable debt for that business, but I was afraid that the bank could destroy us at the click of a button because the revenue from our businesses aside from Dewynters and Spot and Co had dropped to a staggering 40 per cent of anticipated levels.

Greg sadly lost his battle with cancer and died. I felt his passing deeply, both personally and professionally. There was no time to mourn corporately as things went from bad to worse, so I appointed Shirley Stapleton, a stoic Kiwi, as my right-hand woman and, thankfully, she was very strong. I could sit on top of things while Shirley implemented my decisions at management level.

However, I did have an external adviser named Peter Abbey, whom I brought on board because over the years I learned he had the innate ability to find solutions to obscure corporate questions. He proved invaluable to me during this period as we sought to find a way out.

I made what proved to be a shrewd move in appointing banker, Bob Baldock, to my board in his first non-executive chairmanship. I could see in 2009 that, whatever happened, we were going to have to bolster our ailing company for two or three years – nobody knew at the time how long the recession was going to last.

Bob was very useful because he could see it from the banker's point of view. Allied Irish Bank had needed to be bailed out with a sizeable investment from the Irish Government. His insight as to how we should present ourselves was very useful. I felt he could be seen as one of their own and therefore keep us off the immediate hit-list.

Thankfully, an extremely rare situation in British politics also influenced their thinking. The Irish had a budget deficit of 32 per cent of GDP in 2010 and that needed to be addressed but, at the time, RBS and Lloyds had outstanding loans to Irish banks of £50bn and £27bn. Mindful of the impact a repayment failure would have on Britain, then chancellor Alistair Darling committed the UK to a £50bn European Union bailout scheme after Labour had lost the 2010 General Election. The meeting came during the five-day period in which the coalition Government was formed but, because constitutional rules dictate that existing ministers remain in power in a hung Parliament until a new administration can command a majority in the House of Commons, incoming Chancellor George Osborne was powerless to stop it. Osborne was apparently vehemently opposed to the UK signing up. Timing is everything.

I sold the financial services business for a one-million-pound profit which helped ease cashflow concerns. It needed too much hands-on managing in a period when the financial services industry was becoming increasingly regulated and we felt we couldn't give it the attention required to succeed.

I needed the bank to reschedule our £17.3m debt. We owed it over ten years but I wanted to push it out to fifteen. The bank couldn't do it, not because they didn't want to, but they were in the hands of others who weren't about to make an exception for us when they were closing down businesses all over the place. In fact, had we owned property, they might have taken us out for our asset values. We've never been an asset-rich company because of the line of business we are in.

We looked at bringing in another funding partner to take Allied out of the equation. RBS were initially responsive but they later had their own financial issues. We tried a couple of venture capitalist houses but they would have taken all of us to the cleaners. I thought about going to some of my high-net-worth individual friends but that didn't feel right. I couldn't do it and I probably never will. My pride would prevent it. I have a lot of wealthy mates and they are friends in part because they know I'm not ever in the room with them for their cash.

Some people around me were losing faith. One of my biggest supporters was Tom Winnifrith, who at one point made an approach to buy Finishing Touch, but the offer was too low for us to consider as it wouldn't have made much of a dent in the bank facility that we were attempting to lower. Tom started offering jobs to our staff and setting up a rival agency whilst being a key shareholder in our PLC. We thought it was a bizarre position for him to take, to say the least.

Nevertheless, something had to give. In 2010, my managing director Richard Hughes told me he wanted to buy Dewynters. What a stroke of luck, I thought at the time. If I could sell Dewynters for fifteen million then I could redesign the business, remove us from the downward spiral that was so far proving inescapable and reboot.

A few weeks later, he told me he was struggling to come up with the money but I found it for him through a venture capitalist fund.

Everything was in place, the deal was edging to completion but it collapsed. To this day, I don't know how. The ball was a yard from the goal-line with the goalkeeper caught upfield and somehow no one scored.

He gave a presentation to Dewynters co-founder Anthony Pye-Jeary and his staff. Shortly afterwards, Anthony phoned and told me they couldn't work with Richard and his team. He had one final payment left as an earn-out on the 2006 deal and therefore had the power of veto over us until that was made. We couldn't pay him ahead of schedule and, equally, we couldn't wait for six months until it was due. The VC fund found out and pulled out of the deal because they had no interest in continuing with Dewynters and Richard at loggerheads. We were so close to solving all our problems only to suffer yet another setback. Had that deal come off, we could have had five million in the bank and sat around smoking cigars for a year figuring out what to do with it.

Instead, I had damaged goods because now Dewynters knew I was trying to sell them; the relationship was corrupted. Dewynters' main conduit to us was Greg but he had passed away and they hated Shirley because she was a numbers girl.

In 2010, by the time we accounted for rising interest and bank charges, First Artist was losing money for the first time in its history. The football business lost three million pounds alone that year. Psychologically, that was hard to take. And my worry was, as I looked to the horizon, not being able to see obvious areas for improvement. Dewynters wasn't winning every show like they used to.

My management team had planned for all sorts of consequences and I believed we had a good balance of corporate experience, enthusiasm and numerical management to handle most issues that came our away. But having them all served up at the same time with a diminishing management team was incredibly challenging.

I needed to sell and began actively courting possible buyers. One interested party, headed by Bob Benton, a theatrical and movie entrepreneur, wanted to junk the company. His plan was that we would go into voluntary liquidation. He would then pick First Artist up for a fraction of its market value – it was worth about fourteen million at the time. He wanted to buy it for one million, reschedule the debts and give me a million to walk away.

In one sense, it was tempting. I was coming up to fifty-nine years of age and had enjoyed a great run. It was nearing time for me to reacquaint myself with my family and sit looking at the ocean at my home in Spain without six phones ringing at the same time.

Part of me wanted to lie down and let them run me over. After all, I wasn't going to die. Financially, I had earned enough to lead a comfortable life but my days as a respected businessman would have been over. I didn't tell Janine how bad things were because I didn't want her to worry. But by cutting my losses in this way, my reputation would be destroyed and, significantly, I also had around 500 shareholders, many of whom would have been badly out of pocket.

The corporate world looks at your EBITDA – earnings before interest, taxes depreciation and amortisation. I was sitting there thinking only about cash but, as a public company, we have a duty to our shareholders and to continue trading in the interests of all participants. Obviously, without cash none of that matters but while we were trying to control that situation, we still had to manage the corporate side of our business – what the assets were and how we were depreciating or maximising them.

Was First Artist Football going to invest further into buying more player rights? Would we invest in a new digital team at Dewynters? What would happen in the longer term to sponsorship and corporate entertainment? Mr Winnifrith continued his competition with Finishing Touch but it was only producing a small amount of income so, in our overall priorities, his involvement with them was merely an irritant. My biggest concern was football being so haphazard. As a private company, we would have been fine because it was still producing seven-figure profits most years. But in this environment, with research teams around you appointed by brokers who analyse your stock for the marketplace, I had to give them a cogent view of where we were going. We were in danger of being completely swallowed up by the most basic ingredient – lack of cash.

The collapse of the financial world and lack of support staff fostered a siege mentality in me, Peter and Shirley, which centred on us trying to tell the marketplace that although we had seen better days, we still had good businesses and had reason to be confident they would produce sizeable profits in the coming years.

In the midst of all of this, I still had to act as a football agent from time to time. I was heavily involved in the Arshavin deal and, when you become embroiled in a football transfer, it consumes you. A big deal pulls at the emotional heartstrings of two clubs with a person's life trapped in between, all under the glare of the media spotlight. And against this backdrop, I had to manage a set of corporate circumstances around First Artist that were nearly beyond belief.

In the summer of 2011, I had one big earn-out to pay Spot and Co. It was a staged payment but we had rolled a couple of others into this one, deferring it on what proved the false assumption that the football business would generate the income we needed.

Finishing Touch had virtually collapsed. Dewynters' turnover had dropped from £101m down to £70m.

In advertising, if you book for, say, March, you have to pay by around 12 April. For the first time, I talked to the clearing house for advertising revenues - known then as the Newspaper Publishers' Association – about deferring. We went to present to this receptacle body which acts for the advertising industry and I had to admit we didn't have enough money. They were poker-faced and not particularly helpful. After years of feeling like Superman, I was now going cap in hand to a group of people with the power to kill us off. Had they said no, we would have had to close. I would have lost everything.

There was the odd media report but nobody really knew how close things were to collapsing completely. I would go home at night and feel sick to the pit of my stomach, lying awake not knowing what tomorrow would bring.

We put a payment plan in place. I hated doing that and it was the point at which I knew there was no going back. The group was potentially dying as I knew it; however, Peter, Shirley and I were still managing to focus on the positives, of which there were a few. The share price was holding and the Irish Government hadn't sailed across the river to pay us a visit, so we continued to pump out positive news wherever there was any.

Shirley and I knuckled down and stuck to the monthly advertising payment plan, paying them promptly every time. We had to visit them every month and give them cash forecasts in quarterly periods for the subsequent three months each time.

We managed to push the last bank quarter payments of 2010 into the following year as we hung on, hoping the football business would chuck out some cash. The summer window came and went and January wasn't going to be big enough. We tried to do deals early on but the numbers were so big, it couldn't have helped. I had to find about nine million pounds to get us through the next tranche of bank payments and Spot and Co's big earn-out.

The Irish Government had taken sizeable shareholdings in a number of their banks. The senior management at Allied Irish had just changed. The new CEO was a very hands-on ex-HSBC executive and I was seriously concerned that his team might not have thought twice about dissolving First Artist. Once again, I was delighted that Bob Baldock was my chairman.

We owed one final payment to Anthony Pye-Jeary at Dewynters. We had given him £12 million and I asked him to defer the last instalment of £1.3 million. Instead, he tried to implement a lawsuit against us. It was beyond belief.

Can you imagine how I felt having made a lot of people like Anthony very rich and now I could lose everything while he pulled up a chair to watch it happen? And he would make it even more painful for me if it meant getting the last few pennies in his pocket.

Thankfully, I had found another potential buyer – a theatre mogul based in New York named David Stoller. I was keen on him because he had no interest in football and therefore I could take that part of the business with me as I left. In a public company, I could make a very good case for it not being there as much as being there. He was desperately struggling to get the money together because he was funding the acquisition through a family trust which was sceptical about the investment.

Word got out that we were being looked at as a takeover target and the share price began to rise. It was the first piece of good news

I'd had in months. However, David still had to put the deal together. He was my very last port in a storm that threatened to wash my entire livelihood out to sea. Each morning I would slope down the stairs at home to check my emails in the hope that confirmation from David had arrived in my inbox overnight from New York.

David and I spoke daily as Shirley helped me work through the cashflows. Peter, Shirley and I ran through the various scenarios of his potential acquisition, finally concluding that the football company should leave the business model and so the group he was buying became the two theatre businesses and the rump of Finishing Touch. Tom Winnifrith had re-emerged as one of David's potential supporters by this point.

My brother Phil and I completed a deal to exit the football business and retain the First Artist name while they would trade under the banner of Pivot Entertainment. John Duff and Barry Hodges, two of the senior guys at Allied Irish Bank, who had become nearly as important to me as my mother and father, together with the new management team, were immensely supportive, for which I will always be grateful. But they kept cautioning me that the Irish shareholders and senior executives would not wait forever.

We desperately needed to bring down the bank facility. Was it just a matter of time? Or did they have more important matters to wrestle with at that moment? This was a gamble that could be a bluff too far for me if I got it wrong. One of the options would be to unfreeze my personal assets and transfer the cash into First Artist – but in my mind I had to be the lender of last resort. The problem was the last resort was just around the next corner. The pressure kept coming and potentially the hole could grow bigger. Time was undeniably running out. I remember looking out of my window at the office on Oxford Street in London one evening with everyone scurrying around doing their Christmas shopping and thinking, How can everyone else's life be carrying on regardless? I called David Stoller and Jeremy Barbera, his then partner, but again more obfuscation.

I was losing my baby – the Irish were just a phone call away. By early evening on 9 December, everyone had left the office, probably retreating to the nearest bar for alcoholic relief, but I needed to be clear-headed. I made myself a cup of green tea and ran some more calculations, and concluded we had thirteen days of cash left. At a push, Jesus's birthday would buy us some more time but, either way, it was going down to the wire.

* * *

And then the tide turned. We got to the afternoon of 10 December and Allied phoned me to say they'd had notice from a bank in New York that the monies from the Stoller foundation were coming across. That was the first indication I had that a sale was about to happen. Within an hour, a signed letter of intent arrived via my fax machine, but it didn't mean anything until the money came through. Two hours later, it did.

I ended up twelve days away from running out of cash. Everyone thought I did well. 'Hey, well done, son. You've sold out in the middle of a recession – what a big Christmas present for you all.' The Stoller transaction included him inheriting the seventeen-million-pound overdraft and valuing the company at fifteen million. That wasn't all mine, of course, but I was suddenly perceived as the saviour and someone who had pulled off a successful sale during the worst recession the country had experienced for sixty years.

I was delighted for David Stoller, who had worked so hard and very diligently to pull this off.

It was one hell of an emotional roller coaster because the bank could have pulled the plug at any time. Luck and judgement pulled us through. If we were guilty of anything, it was under-estimating the depth of the recession. A brilliant friend of mine named Alan Fernback advised me that the American sub-prime mortgage scenario was going to wreak havoc in the global econ-omy way back in 2006 when I was out in the marketplace putting in borrowings and earn-outs as part of an expansive acquisition programme. I should have listened to voices like his and acted with more caution but we had been walking on water for so long I felt I wouldn't get my feet wet, let alone drown. But at least that mentality helped steer me through and masked our problems to the wider world. Greg said to me once in a bank meeting as the group started to experience serious difficulties, 'Nobody can smell the fear on us yet.' Thankfully, nobody ever did.

That's how you have to be. I remember Rangers owner Sir David Murray, one of the true inspirations in my life, telling me a story about how he coped with an oil price crash in 1986 after his Murray International Metals company had enjoyed a positive start to the 1980s. He suddenly had thousands of tonnes of steel plates and pipes going nowhere and rusting. So David decided to develop a new office park at the Gyle near Edinburgh Airport with the architect under instruction to use his most overstocked item – 100 tonnes of 28-inch diameter pipe, the vast majority of which was part of a previously cancelled order. He then bought a new Bentley to send out a positive message; that show of strength helped him turn the corner, not just as a psychological boost, but as a public signal of his financial health. There are a few of us who have ridden that horse.

When a much-desired deal breaks down, it is sad but, five days later, you recover because the pace of business demands it. Here, I fell into the abyss yet defied the irresistible force of financial gravity contained within to drag myself back. It is an experience I wouldn't wish on anybody.

I guess the overriding lesson is, when it is really dark, always carry a torch in your heart. Never give up. It is a cliché, but it is always darkest before the dawn. You have to believe that nothing is for ever – there is always going to be another day and positivity must endure. I could have exited earlier and stuck two fingers up to my shareholders but I remained committed to them; it wasn't an entirely altruistic act because I wanted to salvage my reputation and, of course, I have benefited well from the sale, too. But if I'd acted solely for the money, I could have saved myself a few months of heartache and pain when the whole situation was biting hard.

Dewynters and Spot and Co were always going to be fine but the earn-outs were killing us, having been negotiated in 2006 when the financial climate was markedly different. When you run a company, you are only as good as your cash. If I buy and sell companies these days, I am completely cash-focused. All the credit in the world buys you things that you can acquire, be and run, but only on the proviso that the lender sees the cash is stable enough to support your borrowings.

The strange position we find ourselves in today is that as a nation, a business community and a society as a whole, we have reverted back to where we were. Money is so cheap now. You can get a mortgage for 4 per cent and lock it in. Everybody said after

2008 that you had to provide your own support through cash but it has changed because people are looking at using cheap money. History continually repeats itself, and the lesson is that debt won't be cheap for ever.

We managed to find a way out but, in the end, I got lucky. Luck is a good asset to have on the balance sheet and I have always courted it assiduously. Corporately swimming with the sharks without armbands was a whole new world for me. Trying to understand how the market needed to continue to focus on us in a positive way was as much a part of my everyday lifestyle as it was managing my staff, the businesses and the odd football deal. I used to write myself notes last thing at night and stick them on my computer insisting 'somehow everything will be OK' with a smiley face. In the morning, I would tear them off my computer because it wasn't. That went on for nearly eighteen months and, by the time we sold, I was mentally exhausted. I stayed on for a few months as non-executive vice-chairman to help with the transition but it quickly became clear they wanted to take things wholeheartedly along the theatre route.

While I retained an interest in that, I had more unfulfilled ambitions so they decided it might be best if I took a pay-off and left. I was quite happy to do it because I wanted to channel all my negative energies into one big blow-out. I googled 'toughest challenges on the planet' and a marathon at the North Pole came up. I had read a story about a child named Alex Field who had brain cancer – just like my mate Greg – and needed to raise money for an operation. It really resonated with me while also sating my desire for a new challenge. After a lengthy training period, we eventually went to the world's northernmost city, Longyearbyen in Svalbard, Norway.

The sun sets on 25 October each year and does not rise above the horizon again for four months. It also means in summer the days are continuous.

They created a course 1.9 miles long circumnavigating the North Pole that we had to negotiate fourteen times. With every completed circuit, you ran around the world. At the back end of lap eight, I found myself on my own. I stopped for a moment to appreciate my utter insignificance in the world. The visceral purity overwhelmed my senses – there was no pollution so I had crystal vision, and the pressure of running on the ice would send a sonar noise across the ice and ping off the snow that had mounted up beside the course. It was the only sound I could hear. There was not a breath of wind.

The sonar noise would also turn the ice a shade of lime green as it travelled. The sight was astonishing. During the race, my eyes closed up due to a leaky visor allowing moisture to build up and freeze on my eyelids. I did what my coach, the uniquely wonderful Professor Greg Whyte, told me not to do under any circumstances and took my gloves off to free my eye. In those few seconds, I got frostnip on the corner of my fingers. Luckily, I was close to the supply tent and we were told after every couple of laps to come in and make sure we were OK. I ran in and they put a blowtorch on my hand. I couldn't believe how quickly I could have been hurt by something so beautiful.

I was the oldest guy there and just wanted to get around while the youngsters and military guys were competing hard with each other. I did it in eight hours and thirty-four minutes. At the end, I stopped to conduct an obligatory television interview during which all the sweat on my body turned to ice due to the extreme temperature. I started shaking involuntarily and was moved quickly into the accommodation tent, where all those beefy military guys who'd been running past me for hours suddenly lay on me to give me their body heat. A strange moment!

We raised more than two hundred thousand pounds for Alex to have his operation. Sadly, he died a year or so later but, hopefully, his family at least took some joy from their extended time with him and science learned something from the groundbreaking operation.

For me, I think I physically had to go to the top of the world to confirm for myself that I could return there commercially one day. First Artist was now solely a football business which had to redefine itself. And while we'd also bought property to hedge us everywhere, I had absolutely no idea what to do next.

14

Back in the Room

I finally pushed the bar on the exit door. As it slammed shut behind me, I could feel the sun on my face and breathe in fresh air for what felt like the first time in years.

The sale had left me with a small football dealing agency which Phil could run successfully without my input. I was always available if he needed me – particularly towards the end of trading windows – but I felt able to stand up straight after years of heavy pressure on my shoulders.

I came back from the North Pole and spent a few weeks winding down with my family. I had to get to know them again; I had always tried to be around as much as I could but the pace of life had been so intense for years that I needed to discover them anew.

We went around the world taking in China, Indonesia, the Middle East, Spain and Israel to see my 94-year-old aunt Freda before moving on to visit my dad in Canada and venturing on to the States. Scott had been in America for a year while trying to become a professional footballer. I got him trials at Rangers and Dagenham & Redbridge, during which one of the coaches for LA

Galaxy asked him to play in their youth team. He performed well and the team won the youth championships that year but Scott decided that, although the adventure was great, he wanted to run his own business.

Ross had a health scare which turned out to be a false alarm but, at the hospital where he was given the all-clear, we saw a number of people who had not been so lucky. Ross and I decided to take part in a charity bike ride from Paris to London to raise money for people who needed treatment there.

During those months following the sale, I tried not to think too much and to enjoy the simple things again. I had a lot of people I wanted to thank so there were plenty of lunches and plenty of trips to the gym to work them off.

But, within a year, I began to notice my new, quieter place in the world. I used to get around a dozen invites every week to something – a reception, a party or the opening of an envelope. They gradually began to dry up and, within a year of selling the PLC, I realised my former close associates weren't in fact that close at all. The opening of an envelope began to look rather appealing. I had thought my importance would endure, but actually, in most cases, your importance in someone's life is almost exclusively determined by what you can do for them, close friends and family aside.

I had some wonderful friends around me; my dentist Peter Rabin, who is also Tottenham's official dentist, invited me for free dental checks because he just wanted to talk football. Thankfully, he resisted the temptation to subject an Arsenal fan to unnecessary pain.

I used to have long lunches with Stephen Purdew, who owns Champneys and is very involved with sports rehabilitation, where we talked about life and football. I had more time to engage with causes that meant something to me, working closely with Norbert Lieckfeldt's team at the British Stammering Association.

I became a part-time receptionist for Janine and her business partner Laura Langdon at Splash Events. Laura's partner Ian had previously been a good friend but the traumatic events of the last eighteen months had prompted us to drift apart so we made a point of reconnecting with him, as well as referee John Nitka. I have great sympathy for referees and, while I will always be supportive of players, officials deserve a greater level of respect on the pitch – more akin to the standard generally witnessed in rugby – at all levels of the sport. John was involved in an incident where the players got a taste of their own medicine. I can't condone it but I understand why it happened.

A few players got in his face during a game he was officiating and, in an attempt to protect himself, he struck out and hit one of them. I think it is probably the only recorded incident of this type and he was, of course, disciplined. Along with other referees, John has consistently lobbied for the football authorities to take a stronger line in response to aggressive behaviour from players and managers. Finally, they listened, and the 2016-17 season began with officials instructed to issue yellow and red cards with more frequency in such instances.

I invested in various companies including a content business aptly called Contented and later another by the name of Infinity Creative Media Ltd with Lord Michael Grade, Todd Ruppert, Russ Lyndsey, Neil Blackley and Johnny Hon – five really great guys. Infinity was responsible for *The Classic Car Show* on Channel 5 and also *The Wine Show* on ITV among a number of projects.

In addition to the small dealing agency, we retained the name

First Artist and our Wembley office. It was nothing like the dynamic enterprise of old but Phil, Ricki Cohen, Jon Greene and I retained the odd big client and sometimes reignited past relationships when the opportunity arose.

I had always enjoyed working with Freddie Ljungberg over the years and could not resist the chance to help facilitate his move to Japanese club Shimizu S-Pulse in September 2011. Freddie's soon to be father-in law, Daryl Foster, is one of my best mates and he called me in to help close the deal.

I arrived in Shizuoka to a visceral reminder of the Premier League's global reach. Freddie was treated as an idol from the minute he stepped off the Bullet Train. Our Japanese hosts were even keen to work with Freddie's then fiancée, Natalie, in the fashion business, while I felt like I had the freedom of the city just for accompanying such a superstar.

It was a culture shock for Freddie and Natalie and when I returned to Spain a few days later I felt like I had left them in a whole new world. I was primarily helping them as a friend but it only went to underscore how players of any age travelling around the world often need their agent's logistical support; the importance of this will only grow in intensity as the Asian market opens and players begin to move both ways between the dynamically different cultures.

I did a reasonable job in securing Freddie a good contract as although Shimizu S-Pulse were immensely accommodating and I only had to push gently for the doors to open, the odd shove gave Freddie the chance to expand his image rights into the Japanese fashion market had he wished.

It was a gentle reintroduction into football transactions, bereft of the complexities Phil and I encountered as we were thrust back into the spotlight while representing Harry Redknapp in 2012. I've personally known Harry for many years. He's always respected me as a straight-shooter and was fond of Phil because of his go-getter attitude. When Harry was manager at Portsmouth, Daniel Levy asked Phil to deliver him to Spurs.

Phil and I worked hard to create a pathway Harry could walk down; he was in demand after winning the 2008 FA Cup but Spurs were an obvious lure, even if it meant Harry leaving his beloved south coast. The deal was finally done but we were fifty thousand pounds apart on our commission for bringing Harry to the club. Eventually, Daniel agreed to give us the money but only if we bought a box at White Hart Lane – it cost us forty-eight thousand pounds!

It was classic Daniel but kind of cute at the same time. Once Harry took charge, we regularly offered seats in the box for his family and friends at matches and became very close to the Redknapps as a result. I've always liked Jamie – I tried to sign him on so many occasions but we've continued to be mates rather than adopt a professional relationship.

We were acting on behalf of Harry by the time his tax-evasion court case began. We wanted to go to Southwark Crown Court and show our support but Harry's legal counsel told me the jury might view his client negatively if he had a football agent in the room with him. 'If you are there, they will think about money and the ugly side of the game which could jeopardise Harry's chances,' he said.

He was staying at a London hotel the night before the verdict and we went to see him in his room. He was pacing around the bedroom working out how big his cell was going to be. Harry knew he was innocent but felt convinced he was going to be penalised for who he was more than anything else. There were people in court trying to read the jurors and one of them never looked up. They felt that whatever happened, Harry couldn't convince that person. The police tried to stare Harry out while he was giving evidence to make him feel uncomfortable. Those intimidation tactics took their toll.

The day of the verdict arrived – Wednesday 8 February, 2012. I was driving back to the First Artist office at Wembley when I heard it announced on the radio. On two counts of tax evasion, he was acquitted of one and found guilty of the other. I was devastated. I walked into the First Artist office and everyone was celebrating.

'Why are you all cheering?' I asked.

'He got off on both counts – the initial report was wrong.'

I puffed my cheeks out in relief. Harry's phone was off so I rang his son Jamie who was extremely ebullient but asked us to give them some space for a few hours. Then, suddenly, Fabio Capello resigned as England manager. Harry's Tottenham team had been flying up to that point and now, here he was, a free man and the people's choice to be Capello's successor.

We phoned Harry later that evening. He was celebrating in his own inimitable style – a cup of tea and biscuit with his wife Sandra. It was typical Harry but remarkable nevertheless given the situation; he'd gone from thinking he was going to jail at 9 a.m. to being widely considered England's manager for Euro 2012 barely twelve hours later.

As the dust settled on the court case, we began discussing England. He had an exit clause in his contract at Spurs and everybody knew it. We had to formulate a strategy which began with becoming masters of our own inactivity because the FA knew Harry was available so I didn't see the need to phone up chairman David

Bernstein – a good friend of mine to this day – and tell him the obvious. I left it for a couple of days but heard nothing so decided to pop a call through to David. The response didn't feel right. I got very short but polite answers acknowledging both Harry's interest and availability; in these situations, it is not a case of being able to phone a contact and ask their plans outright. There is a line thin between personal connections and professional etiquette. We always tried to stay on the right side of that line.

'Leave it with us ... we are well aware of Harry's position,' David said.

Phil and I met with Harry and Jamie shortly afterwards. Harry's view was that Daniel would make it too expensive for him to leave and, as a consequence, he wouldn't get the job. The FA had been castigated for throwing millions at Capello only for it to end acrimoniously and the prospect of paying a seven-figure compensation fee would be a hurdle they wouldn't be prepared to overcome.

The FA were eerily quiet in the weeks following Capello's departure. It reached the point where we had to start negotiating with Tottenham over a new contract because Harry only had just over a year left. Daniel presumed Harry wanted the England job and tried to make out he already saw his future beyond Spurs. That wasn't the case.

'If England comes up, then of course Harry would be interested,' I explained to Daniel. 'But we are here negotiating with you, which should indicate all you need to know about the FA's current position.'

As I understand it, Tottenham co-owner Joe Lewis wanted Harry out because he wasn't bringing through enough young players. Joe didn't want to buy a new team every year with a stadium redevelopment to finance. They were being very careful with the balance sheet – that January, Harry wanted a centre-back and a centre-forward. He asked for Gary Cahill and Carlos Tevez but got Ryan Nelsen and Louis Saha. Performances started to slide as well and, although they finished fourth, Chelsea's Champions League win denied Spurs a place in Europe's premier competition, which was as unlikely as it was unlucky.

Meanwhile, we had still heard nothing officially from the FA but my contacts within the organisation were informing me that Roy Hodgson was the frontrunner. Roy was represented by Leon Angel, who was originally my accountant for many years before I took him into football. Leon and I would skate the same ice without any problems but I couldn't exactly phone him and ask whether he'd heard anything. And then, on 1 May 2012, the silence was broken – Roy was unveiled as the England manager.

Harry has always blamed the compensation clause in his Tottenham contract but, months later, when I met David Bernstein for breakfast at his Finchley tennis club, he told me that that had had nothing to do with it. Roy was, in his words, 'always top of their wish-list'. The FA saw Roy as a top-to-tail England manager better suited to the new era of St George's Park and improving corporate relations with UEFA and FIFA in addition to his success as a coach around the world.

We still had to try and negotiate with Spurs at the end of the 2011–12 season but progress was non-existent so Harry felt he should change agents. Coincidentally, we were coming to the end of our contract with Harry and were planning to ask about an extension but he wanted a fresh approach. I understood his position because we didn't get him the England or Tottenham contracts, but neither were down to us. The FA and Spurs simply wanted other people.

So the story goes, Harry's subsequent representative allegedly went in to meet Daniel with a list of demands and the contract terms they wanted with a quasi-ultimatum – sign it or there is no deal. Daniel didn't want to sign it so there was no deal. Spurs sacked him in mid-June. Harry didn't bear a grudge towards us and neither did we; he went on to work with my son Scott so he's back in the family!

Phil ran this new streamlined version of First Artist on a day-to-day basis and, while I came in to help at the end of transfer windows or with the bigger situations such as Harry and England, I felt peripheral in the world. I missed the buzz of a deal, the excitement of being at the hub of something millions of people cared about. Ex-professionals often talk about missing the limelight of their playing days and some do anything to try and recreate it, ranging from management and coaching to alcohol, drugs or gambling. The problem with an emergency exit door is you can't open it from the outside. Someone from within needs to help you out and that's where Nick Bitel came in.

Nick, my lawyer and great friend, originally sat on my board at First Artist and later became chair of Sport England, CEO of the London Marathon and someone for whom I have great personal admiration and professional respect. I told him I wanted to get back into the room. I wanted to extend beyond football; I occasionally reviewed papers on Sky News and hosted a sports-related chat show on Sports Tonight TV and even gave speeches to universities, colleges and corporate conferences on business practices, but I missed the frontline activity.

Nick was kind and connected enough to introduce me to several investment funds looking to buy into sport and entertainment. Here was something I could do – sport and entertainment were in my DNA. There probably wasn't a player in the game I didn't know or couldn't reach. And there was a possibility I could bring even more money into the game by highlighting the springboard a Premier League or top Championship club could have in promoting an individual, brand or organisation. It was an easy sell.

Over the next few weeks, I met with a series of sports and investment groups of seriously high net worth. The world being what it is now, money was leaving difficult places like the Middle East or Russia and looking for safe homes. People like placing their money in England because it is politically stable. London is a potential target for terrorism but so is almost every major city in the world. I'm not saying multiculturalism works everywhere, but I believe it does in London. The pace of life dictates that everybody has to get on with it and so London has become the perfect place for the world to meet. Being outside the euro made London insulated from the uncertainty over whether that currency could co-habit in so many different countries, yet there was still the benefit of EU membership.

That dynamic made England the target for a lot of inbound funds. The knock-on effect has been to ramp up property prices to a level most Londoners cannot afford. It has also brought us a lot of fascinating wealth creators and I believe our sporting institutions – particularly football clubs – have benefited from multicultural ownership.

Of course, supporters of clubs that have suffered downturns under foreign ownership would disagree and their passport is often used as evidence that they don't understand the region or even the sport. There is an apocryphal story about the Venky family when they bought Blackburn Rovers in 2010. During final-stage negotiations over the sale of the club, they were told, 'Don't worry, if you are relegated from the Premier League, you'll be in the Champions League then. You must have heard of it.'

They believed it, so the story goes. They seemed quite sanguine about being in the Championship for a while. That only made people joke that perhaps they didn't realise it wasn't the Champions League!

The level of investment required to own a football club has escalated to the extent that the only people who can afford to get involved are those who operate on a different planet from the rest of us. It used to be the case that if you had ten million in the bank – a large sum by anyone's estimation – you could become a serious player. Robert Maxwell nearly bought Manchester United for that amount in 1984. At most Premier League clubs today, ten million won't even buy you pitch-surround advertising. At the top end, you need hundreds of millions or potentially billions; it is the domain of the super-rich or the super-supportive – a wealthy eccentric who has been a fan of one club all their lives.

David Sullivan and David Gold's ownership of West Ham is an excellent example of the latter. They bought and financed the club they supported as children with their own money and actually made it work. The Hammers were in dire straits when they took over in 2009. The deal valued West Ham at £105m and they had to put up guarantees to the bank because the balance sheet was such a mess. In tandem with Karren Brady, they turned things around, made an excellent appointment in Angus Kinnear – a managing director destined for very big things – and within six years West Ham was worth four hundred million pounds.

Football clubs used to operate independently of conventional economics because historically the banks would never close down a club due to fears they would lose the custom of people in that particular area, probably for ever. However, RBS came very close to shutting down Liverpool under the George Gillett/Tom Hicks regime. They didn't ideally want to because of the abuse they'd receive, but it was a reality they were prepared to face.

Clubs now have a sense of their own mortality, meaning potential owners have to be sizeable movers and shakers in society, sufficiently insulated from the vagaries of a fluctuating economy. If you want to buy Stoke – something of a journeyman club but an established top-flight side nevertheless – it will cost about a hundred-and-fifty million. You'll then have to throw another fifty to eighty million at it to make anything approaching a success. To do that, you have to be seriously wealthy, even with the money coming in from television. This year the team finishing bottom of the league will still receive 'prize money' of £94 million pounds. That will contribute but it can't be your entire war chest.

The emotion that runs alongside the ownership of a sporting franchise is very often to the detriment of its success. Decisions are made in everyday business with your head but, too often, they are influenced by the heart. For example, if you go into any football club and ask them to look at an investment programme in social media to engage with supporters, there will be some interest because engagement is obviously important and the club can make some money out of it. But the level of resource made available will pale into insignificance compared to me walking into their boardroom and saying, 'I've got this amazing player from Lithuania who you must see but the problem is the authorities who own him want ten million.' They would find that ten million in a heartbeat if they thought the player was right for them. I'd struggle to find ten thousand pounds for a marketing project even if it was sexy, fun and potentially very lucrative. That disproportionate interpretation of opportunity creates problems.

Sometimes the ownership of football clubs can be a useful adjunct to any global businessman's group of assets. A football club's finances are truly international therefore giving rise to global economies of scale.

Motivations vary and it is not always clear which candidates will turn out to be credible owners. I cut my teeth on selling Leyton Orient to Francesco Becchetti in 2014. Talks had ground to a halt with buyer Becchetti and seller Barry Hearn a million pounds apart in their valuations of the club. There were just three of us standing at the bar in the boardroom at Brisbane Road looking out towards the Olympic Stadium. In his inimitable way, Barry said to Francesco, 'Go on then, I'll toss you for it.'

I rushed to provide the coin. The only denominations I had were £2, 2p and 5p. I thought it best to use the £2 considering what was at stake.

'Who's calling?' I said, as Francesco became noticeably frosty. 'Come on, Francesco, we are only having a bit of fun,' I said.

'This is stupid, childish,' he responded.

Barry continued to wind Francesco up, putting his arm around him. 'Let's do it and get this sorted.'

I didn't think Francesco would pay the extra million. Barry deserved it because he had dropped his price so I was trying to negotiate an agreement where he would earn it through other means based on Orient's future progress. But Francesco was not for turning. He threatened to leave the room. I held him by his forearm and said, 'I'm going to put the coin back in my pocket.' He shook off my hand and headed for the door. Was this the stereotypical 'staged' walkout, I wondered. I let him almost reach out for the handle, Barry and I looked at each other, we both smiled and Barry said, 'OK, Francesco, let's talk about this extra million.'

Francesco came back, he calmed a little and eventually agreed to two £500,000 top-ups if Orient were promoted, firstly to the Championship and then the Premier League. Throughout the whole episode, we had one piece of paper on which they kept writing numbers and scribbling them out. Lower down, I kept writing other numbers outlining where we were at various points and, at the end of it all, when everyone shook hands, I put it in my pocket. I've since framed it alongside a press release with a note that says: 'This is Leyton Orient.'

That deal had some interesting moments along the way but it satisfied all parties and did not in itself lead to the downturn that followed. That failure should be levelled at the management.

As Becchetti's life begins to settle down, there is a reasonable chance of him turning Orient's fortunes around. Or perhaps he will sell it. Maybe that's a phone call I should make.

The future ownership in the Premier League is going to look a lot like the American franchises – the super-rich and conglomerates. The model could be Liverpool – Fenway Sports Group – or a senior version of what Steve Parish has done at Crystal Palace, where he connected a number of wealthy people together as a conglomerate. But either way, the entry level prices are only going to rise. That will force interested parties to gamble on top-end clubs in the Championship and it was precisely that thinking which put me at the centre of a Chinese consortium's bid to buy Hull City in 2015.

The fascinating aspect of that proposal was that the Chinese didn't look to the UK to make their money. The key was Hull achieving promotion because the Premier League is huge in China and, as a consequence, they would generate revenue there from merchandising – visual, audio or physical – and the UK income would be used just to run the club.

In fact, I have since spent time in Beijing with the Chinese FA and the intense support for the President's vision of football as a future frontier for the country is in one sense a huge compliment to English football but, in another, a significant future threat to the dominance of the Premier League. Aston Villa and West Brom have already succumbed to this trend.

I looked at getting a very long lease on the KCOM stadium and a proposal to build hotel and leisure facilities to boost local revenues. Football stadia will follow a more European model in the coming years with the arena encased in shopping, dining, enter-tainment and accommodation facilities but, for the most part in the case of English clubs, they will be owned by wealthy consortia rather than local authorities. Chelsea operate like this to a degree already although it is harder to expand this way in the middle of a major city, but there will be all kinds of bolt-ons. Bolton, in fact, did something similar with the Reebok Stadium, which made them an intriguing proposition to foreign investors. I first met this particular Chinese group when they looked into buying Bolton earlier in 2015.

Bolton's finances were an absolute mess. In various forms, the management lost all the money that Eddie Davies put in – more than two hundred million of his own cash. The club's hierarchy dragged their feet for weeks and, eventually, the Chinese walked away but wanted to consider other options in the UK.

They looked at Gillingham, who were flying in League One at the time, but the area didn't have enough of a profile. I suggested Hull because more work had been done in developing the club, Steve Bruce was there at the time and it was possible the Chinese could pick up a Premier League club-in-waiting. Hull valued themselves at about a hundred-and-fifty million, which was a little higher than the going rate for a lower Premier League club in 2015, but owner Assem Allam felt they had invested enormously in the local community and were a Championship side going places.

Assem and his son, Ehab, have helped bring a vast array of entertainment to the KCOM Stadium including Twenty20 cricket, England Under-21 football internationals and concerts featuring Sir Elton John, Bryan Adams, Bon Jovi and The Who. Assem had a self-appointed mission to pay the city back for the hospitality it gave him upon arriving in the area. He came from a wealthy Egyptian family but when Gamal Abdel Nasser was in power, they were exiled to the UK. The story goes that he arrived with only a solitary £5 note to his name, and even that was a forgery. He had to start again and built up his wealth with the help of a leg-up from his new neighbours.

Assem said he wanted eighty million with two further bonus payments bringing the overall package to a hundred-and-fifty million, the first triggered by promotion to the Premier League and the second for avoiding relegation in their first year back in the top flight. However, if they were relegated from the Premier League in that first year, a smaller bonus payment would still be due but only on achieving promotion the following year.

The initial offer from the Chinese was fifty million pounds. Assem rejected that but indicated he would drop from eighty to seventy million. The problem was seventy million became his backstop – if nothing else, he wanted that guaranteed. That would have been the highest price ever paid for a Championship club.

We hinted quite strongly that we could go to sixty million. There was never an official bid at that level because the Chinese have a respect agenda which must be adhered to – they didn't want to be rejected twice. So it was my job to feel out where the common ground would be. These deals are complex; it is not a case of making a bid, having it rejected and making another. There are a series of contingency clauses and detailed reports to consider, often produced by senior accountants and advisers such as Deloitte or KPMG, but the only two numbers which ultimately matter are the top-line income – TV, gate receipts and sponsorship, because the rest is ancillary – and the player wage bill. In some cases, ridiculously, clubs spent 90 per cent or more of their gross profit on their playing staff. If you and I had a business and ran it that way, people would say we were barking mad.

Despite those skewed finances, the brand value of leading clubs is always going to be a huge number because of their cultural resonance worldwide. Assem was proud of his achievements at Hull – and rightly so – but the rest of the world did not identify with the club as strongly as he did, which made seventy million an unrealistic valuation.

The Chinese were prepared – verbally – to go to sixty million if they knew that Assem would drop into that ballpark. The last thing I wanted to do was encourage a formal bid at sixty million because they would walk away from us and any future dealings because of what they would have perceived as a lack of corporate respect. So I said to Assam, 'It is not going to be what you ideally want but I can get you sixty million. That's not to say it might not end up being circa sixty-two million. But it won't be seventy.'

Nothing moved. Days turned into weeks and the Chinese withdrew their interest – Hull's subsequent promotion in 2016 displayed their conservatism in a negative light. The seventy million rising to a hundred-and-twenty million looks cheap six months later because now the going rate is a hundred-and-fifty million. How astonishing it is that these prices are real.

The particular deal was about the two parties involved and the possible benefits for the local community, but I also received nothing for all the time I invested in trying to bring everyone together. People often reference the big paydays agents receive but the flipside of working in sport is that, unless you complete a deal, you don't get paid. There is almost never a consultancy fee in this context.

We weren't directly involved in the Jermain Defoe deal taking him from FC Toronto to Sunderland in January 2015 but we helped advise on the positioning of the player and the monies because it was a difficult situation – the numbers didn't really work and the exchange rates complicated things further. Eventually, the deal was completed and Toronto gave us a small five-figure sum as a thank you. That is exceptionally rare. Most clubs would see it as money for nothing given we weren't the central agent involved. Some might put you on a retainer to help them in those situations but, essentially, you eat what you kill as a football agent.

There have been a number of different approaches for clubs and a variety of people queuing to come into English football. At the time of writing, I am aware of further Chinese investors who are interested in acquiring English football clubs. There is considerable interest from high-net-worth individuals from the south-east Asian community who are continuing to express an appetite to enter this market. There is also, of course, some interest already registered by two or three leading American purchasers who have, among others, Citibank as their representatives.

The problem is getting proof of funds at the level now required to invest. Very often you meet interested parties and soon realise they don't have the money. The high-net-worths behind them are really the puppet-masters and you only meet them close to the end of the initial discussions once a deal has been potentially mooted. You end up kissing a lot of frogs, which is why there is such scepticism among the élite ownership in England towards unseen potential purchasers. Today, it is not unlikely that you will be asked to place funds on deposit before you enter initial discussions, which narrows the field down somewhat, as having cash to the tune of eight or in some cases nine figures is still the bastion of the few.

Fenway Sports Group have a great heritage and know how to run successful franchises. Liverpool is in safe hands. Manchester City was bought as a sporting project with sister companies in Melbourne, Japan and New York. It is a good, solid operation which is very professionally run.

The thing that went wrong at Manchester United was Sir Alex Ferguson and David Gill leaving at the same time. It was like the pilot and the co-pilot walking out of the cockpit simultane-ously. There are some good people in senior positions at United, including Ed Woodward, but it was almost inevitable that the plane would steer off course under those circumstances; appointing José Mourinho gives them every chance of getting back on track.

Newcastle thought they had a plan. By importing a phalanx of players from one region – predominantly France – they aimed to create a community within the club, but the mistake they made was in failing to connect with the fan base or Newcastle as a region. Relegation in 2016 may force a return to grass roots which could benefit them in the long run.

I think Daniel Levy has done a fantastic job at Tottenham. He didn't have the expertise when he came in but owner Joe Lewis gave him financial support in addition to his own – Daniel isn't poor. He has walked that difficult line between maintaining a strong balance sheet and a strong team. He learned on the job and has finally got what he believes is the right man in Mauricio Pochettino. Daniel tells me he has never had a happier dressing room and I think that shows.

Talking of happy dressing rooms, that is what took Leicester to the Premier League title in 2016 more than anything else; they played with unswerving faith and are surely the most powerful sporting example of how far complete conviction in your ability can take you.

Arsenal are a difficult case. I am a huge supporter of both Arsène Wenger and Ivan Gazidis, having been close to them for many years. Arsène has done a remarkable job despite the latter-day criticism from prominent Arsenal supporters, such as Piers Morgan, and will leave an indelible mark not just on the club but indeed the global game when he departs; they will need every ounce of Ivan's intelligent stewardship to avoid the problems Manchester United had when Sir Alex Ferguson retired in 2013. But he fitted into a model which is led by the ownership whose mantra is 'steady as she goes'. There is no great dynamism among the ownership to win something every year and nobody pushing to gamble, spend big and roll the dice. Success is defined on the balance sheet as a top-four finish and qualification for the Champions League group stages each year – Arsène has achieved this every time and therefore Stan Kroenke is content, although I am sure he would be happier still if and when they win a major competition.

They have a contingency plan built into their finances which requires Champions League football to be secured in three out of every four seasons. That is why they keep a healthy cash balance – to guard against the shockwaves created by a sudden loss of income from Europe's premier competition. It would, of course, be great if they won the FA Cup or even the Premier League but fourth place is fine by this logic. Stability is the key factor for Stan, and Ivan Gazidis, a very solid and professional chief executive, has given him that in tandem with Arsène.

In my opinion, one change they need to make regardless is an adjustment to their transfer policy. Since Stan Kroenke took a majority shareholding in the club, they have created matrices for players, a bit like *Moneyball*. And if a player doesn't quite meet all the criteria, the matrix tells them not to offer more than a certain amount. That is what Arsène means when he talks about value.

Since 2012, Arsenal have used a performance comparison system to help identify and assess players. Chief Financial Officer Stuart Wisely's role is to model the financial impacts of the various decisions Arsenal have to make. Four years ago they bought a company called StatDNA in Chicago, which owns an operation in Cambodia where they crunch every conceivable number relating to a footballer. They will take a player and collate data based on every pass, sprint, shot, assist, goal – you name it – he has ever made. These stats are fed into a computer that assesses strengths and weaknesses against every professional in the game before producing an overall value of that player. That data is analysed, collated and compared in various ways. Two such examples are Hot Streak Bias versus Confirmation Bias; for example, a left-back attacks and creates chances listed as positive stats, but how many chances does he allow for the opposition by being caught out of position?

This particular comparison is used by a number of clubs although Arsenal are not among them. Arsenal tend to use statistics to raise questions or confirm observations on possible targets and sometimes to unearth new players for scouting.

There are occasions where it will cause them to re-examine a candidate who has been scouted but senior figures at the club believe the data can remove doubts that they might otherwise have had or encourage them to sign a player under-scouted by their rivals. Stats speak for themselves but if you look at Leicester, their players' numbers would not have been that good in 2014–15. Computers cannot legislate for the human spirit. That dramatic, unquantifiable improvement can never be a permutation within a rigid algorithm. A combination of both is required – you have to watch a player, you cannot just look at his stats.

Some clubs place a high degree of stock in this approach but Arsenal insist they take decisions primarily driven by scouting, and the human rather than numerical characteristics of a potential target. Ultimately all decisions are made by Arsène.

Perhaps it has led to a degree of inertia in Arsenal's transfer dealings. It is like being an investment fund manager: you find it easier
to say no when somebody presents you with a bunch of figures.
If you go to a VC house, they will have a matrix that calculates an
exceptionally complicated formula which concludes what figure
represents value. But that doesn't legislate for a CEO being so
enigmatic that he can give his company a market edge. Very often,
banks don't lend money because the figure doesn't match the one
they have determined as your reasonable market share.

Football is an industry. The matrix works to a point but it is
also the business of human flesh. For me, clubs should calculate
their decisions based on 70 per cent of the human element and
the rest on what a matrix defines as acceptable. Relying on the
matrix alone makes it easier for people to say 'no', and some argue
it therefore contributes to transfer market inertia.

Many Arsenal fans certainly wish the club had conducted more
business in recent years. Some of the major signings they have made
since using StatDNA – Mesut Ozil, Alexis Sanchez, Petr Cech and
Danny Welbeck to name four – were virtual no-brainers at the
prices involved. They have unearthed some gems in Santi Cazorla
and, to a lesser extent Nacho Monreal and Mohamed Elneny, but
Calum Chambers, Mathieu Debuchy, Gabriel, David Ospina, Lukas
Podolski and Olivier Giroud have ranged from merely a pass mark
to downright disappointing. However, overall, Arsene's ability to
spot a player is still outstanding and Arsenal supporters should be
intensely grateful for 20 years of remarkable football. His kind may
never emerge again.

Buying and selling football clubs isn't exactly stable employment
in isolation. After all, there are only ninety-two professional clubs

in England and sales don't occur all year round. I have only seen a few through to completion – these deals are capricious by their very nature. But there is a rarity of expertise in this field and so, over time, I have become a lightning rod for foreign investors looking to ground themselves in the UK, especially as I retain strong relationships with most of Britain's leading clubs.

It gave me a real relevance at the sharp end of football again. Dealing with club ownership catapulted me into the stratosphere of the football's administrators, powerbrokers and leading financiers, many of whom transcend into other sports, entertainment and politics. I was back in the room.

15

The Next Step

English football is an export of excellence and we should all be proud of it. All I ever wanted was to be a little bit special and looking at the modern game I helped create fills me with pride and only a modicum of regret. The steps we took in the 1980s and 1990s created a rock-solid foundation upon which football has flourished. In retrospect, I would have preferred to help create this unique product with a little more sharing down the food chain but I suppose human nature will always endure.

I made many mistakes – some of which I have admitted to in these pages – but the rest will remain between myself and my conscience. As time passed, I helped change football and football changed me.

After breaking the British transfer record three times in as many years, I remember doing a photo shoot with the *Sun* and the photographer told me to put on more gold rings. I had a Bentley at the time and they wanted me to lean out of it, flashing the rings and a gold chain. That was the wider perception of agents back then and I was asked to conform to that stereotype. Harry Enfield's 'Loadsamoney' character was the image I fought against.

OK, I had gold rings and a very nice car but they occupied a more subtle place in my life. I positioned myself differently, not through doing anything radically alternative or even original. I wore a suit and worked especially hard to make sure the deals I was involved in worked for everyone.

Ironically, it has gone full circle now. There are kids coming along with street cred representing players because they think they are cool. But, in fact, Wasserman Media Group, Base, Stellar, James Grant, Impact Sports Management, Unique, Key Sports and World in Motion perform 80 per cent of the deals. Others just make up the numbers, so how cool can they really be? These kids might get one or two players but professionalism is hugely important. I wanted to be the first widely respected agent. I wanted to be the Mark McCormack of football, which I pretty much achieved. I couldn't own the events like he did but, for a few years, I controlled most things around it.

Now I am at a stage in life where I can take a prominent position on major sporting boards – at the 2016 Rio Olympic Games, I was chair of the national governing body of British Taekwondo – and invest in companies helping to shape the future of key elements within sport and entertainment. I bought into a company called Storelli which occupies a space where health and safety meets sport. In America, safety and sport go hand in glove, hence the uniforms, the helmets and the prominent health-conscious rhetoric. It has only flickering resonance in the UK whenever an incident triggers a debate – i.e. the change in cricket helmets after the tragic death of Australia batsman Phillip Hughes. There is a movement now towards protecting footballers. They notoriously hate wearing shin pads because it can inhibit their movement so Storelli make shin pads which wrap around the calf to feel more like a second skin.

The debate over treatment of head injuries in football has only just begun; health and safety will become a big issue in the coming years in football, as will cyber security, particularly in ticketing.

During the 1990s and 2000s, I felt like the most popular man in London during May every year. Cup finals, internationals, play-offs – everybody wanted tickets. People would phone up after years without any contact and meander through two minutes of chit-chat, which I would interrupt with, 'Yeah, yeah. What event do you want?'

'Oh . . . yeah. Do you have any spare for the Cup Final?'

The cheek. But the demand made me curious so I delved deeper into the ticketing market and met some interesting people. These were the days before secondary ticketing became official so either you bought first-hand or you went to a tout – there was nothing in between.

I never understood how touts got their tickets. I was told that in certain parts of the world, the tickets come direct from the players. Some sporting organisations try to stop it by giving players their tickets as late as possible but teams often find a way around it. Their biggest challenge is physically handing the tickets over to touts – who, of course, pay a little more than face value for them and then sell on at an inflated fee. I heard one story involving a rugby team; they split open a rugby ball and stuffed all the tickets they were selling inside it before stitching it back up again. They went out to train and, at some point, the players would gravitate towards the end of the field where they trained and 'accidentally' throw said ball too far so it disappeared over the fence.

'Don't worry, lads,' one of the players would say. 'I'll get it.' He would scamper over the fence to retrieve the ball in the woods, where a tout was waiting at a pre-arranged point to take the ball in exchange for two wads of cash. The player would stuff the cash into his socks, jump back over the fence and say, 'Sorry, guys . . . lost ball.' This type of thing went on for years.

Players sometimes sell spare tickets if their families don't want them or give them away to their favourite charity. Nobody regulates this secondary distribution of tickets. Even now, about eight thousand tickets for the FA Cup Final are allocated nationwide through the County FA structure. Would all of them bother to come to London for a day out or, instead, prefer to make some quick money by selling them? Ticketing agencies will phone them up and offer several times the face value. If they have five tickets at a hundred pounds each and an agency offers them ten times face value, that's five thousand pounds, which represents a significant sum to a small club. There's no tax on it either.

People want more fans from the competing clubs to attend – they currently receive 80 per cent of Wembley's capacity between them – but that figure will not rise significantly because privately some of those receiving tickets want to keep doing so in order to make extra money and/or keep their privilege.

Some of the secondary ticketing agencies today do legitimate deals with players because they have paid the club to be their ancillary ticketing service. StubHub have a partnership with Tottenham; Ticketmaster with Coventry. Seatwave and Get Me In are the other major players – they have serious budgets behind them.

Theatre proprietors do the same. They will take out three prominent rows for a show and sell them to a secondary agency which pays several times the face value. These tickets are then marketed as 'VIP' and are accompanied by an interval drink or sometimes nothing at all beyond a premium seat.

I steered clear of it before because I thought it was a bear trap. It really is the soft underbelly of sport and entertainment. Instead I'm a shareholder in a cyber-protection company called WISeKey, who boast the United Nations and various governments around the world among their clients. Founder and chairman Carlos Moreira is very friendly with the hierarchy at Real Madrid and Barcelona and both have signed up to a three-year trial programme with WISeKey aiming to improve ticketing security for fans. Supporters must join WISeKey before they can buy tickets or any official merchandise by providing details to create your own sporting passport. The system is encrypted – unbreakable, so they say – but electronically monitored and accessible everywhere, like Apple's iCloud. If you bought a hot dog at a ground, it would be logged. And each fan will receive tailored marketing according to the activity on their card. You'll be able to access any sporting environment logged on the system and WISeKey's task now is to get major sporting clubs and events around the world to join their network. That would eliminate the tout outside the ground on the day by creating a secure environment for your ticket purchase away from the stadium itself. Ticketing is an issue the industry has to combat and security for match-day-going fans is vital to ensure stadiums remain full.

After the Paris attacks of late 2015 which involved an incident outside a football match at the Stade de France, the drive behind such an initiative palpably grew for obvious reasons. Ticket touts are a major security risk in this day and age. A terrorist with a strap-on bomb just needs to buy off a tout and, presuming there is no pat-down security – which isn't always the case at sporting events – he's in the stadium.

Technology will change the game in other ways. There is a

big evolution afoot in transmission and broadcasting. Richard Scudamore was no doubt rubbing his hands together after the deal Amazon struck with Jeremy Clarkson, Richard Hammond and James May. That move is a game-changer in terms of habit of consumption. I'd be concerned if I was Sky because BT's involvement has driven the price up to a place which hurts them. If the tech companies really want to be in this space with a desire to take football on to another platform – be it mobile phones or internet-encoded viewing – then the next broadcast deal could jump from eight billion to ten billion or even higher. Football has never been more popular all over the world. NBC have good viewing figures in the United States for the round ball, not just the oblong one. China and India are two of the biggest consumer markets in the world and both are now fertile territories for expansion.

During 2014, I was brought in to look at the possibilities for growth in Australian football by a contact I had at A-League side Central Coast Mariners. The club's majority owner Mike Charlesworth was familiar with the work I had done in the Premier League and asked for my take on the available options. The A-League only spans Australia and the problem with that country in this context is the lack of major cities. They have ten franchises including one in New Zealand and there is simply nowhere else to go; the next franchise would have to be near an existing one or you go somewhere like Ayers Rock, which doesn't exactly work!

We came up with an idea to take the A-League and its excellent organisation into south-east Asia. It was a no-brainer. The Australian Sports Ministry loved it because that region boasts some of their strongest trading partners. The logistics worked in terms of road trips through Malaysia, even as far north as Hong Kong.

In the end, having shown all the research to Football Federation Australia (FFA) and the ways it could work, they decided instead to consolidate at home first. Chief Executive David Gallop was instructed to proceed on that path. We disagreed over that course of action but nevertheless David has great insight into the game and is undoubtedly a name for the future in that corner of the world. And it is still a conversation waiting to happen because neither FIFA nor the Asian Football Confederation were saying no. Small leagues in that region – Hong Kong, the Philippines and Singapore – will probably join up and form a south-east Asian Superleague to then attract big money. Broadcasters like beIN Sports would get involved. The same conversations are happening in the Caribbean, joining national leagues together for a regional division.

The English Premier League will continue to go from strength to strength and the Championship should be pulled along with it. I fear somewhat for Leagues One and Two in terms of their long-term growth, especially given the Football League lacked the bravery to make a forward-thinking appointment in deciding its new chairman in 2016. Ian Lenagan is a lovely man I'm sure but, as chairman of Oxford United, does he really have the expertise to grow the Football League or will he merely keep it ticking over at a lower level? It is one thing to protect interests, but how will it ever be more than the sum of its parts with that attitude?

Tech companies will dictate to a degree what it costs and the platforms on which we view football in the future. I'm sorry to say, it is never going to get cheaper. The danger is in multiple choices fragmenting the audience – that will depend on broadcasting authorities and governments deciding to intervene. Will they decide that a terrestrial broadcaster should still be relevant or will the inexorable shift towards Internet viewing simply facilitate the sale of all rights to the highest bidder?

There may be certain regulatory issues and how do they come to the correct appropriation of rights? It has to be for the benefit of the viewers and ensure the price for consumers doesn't rise too high but, at the same time, the tech companies have to be allowed to invest in the sport at a level that is meaningful to them. That will drive further investment and keep the Premier League juggernaut powering forward.

The Premier League is one of England's most prestigious exports of all time, and I am very proud to have played a small role in making that happen. China is the latest country to really go for it now. The Chinese president believes football is their next frontier and they are sucking in Premier League technology, coaches and players. More than a fifth of the world's population watches the English Premier League every week. We spend a lot of time knocking the organisation and the players but they are the ones that made it happen. It is an astonishing achievement.

There is a growing subsector of industries that feed off the success of football and footballers. Estate agents are one obvious area. When very wealthy players move into certain areas, the local economy is positively impacted. Hull owner Assem Allam insisted he would only agree contracts with players if they moved into a house with a Hull postcode to ensure a large percentage of the money they spent went into the local community. Football is funding sub-industries all over the place whether it is in housing, car dealerships or restaurants. People often talk about the money flowing into the Premier League but a significant chunk of that money is reinvested through auxiliary services, many of which didn't exist before.

A lovely lady called Rebecca Peterman brought me a great idea that I am going to do something with one day soon – football nurseries. It harnesses all the great things that football clubs can do for the community. We went to see Watford just before the Pozzo takeover and they were very keen but it got lost in the change of ownership. If you are a Watford fan, wouldn't it be great to send your child to 'Watford Nursery'? So the child is immersed in the club from the get-go of his education. By the time they are five or six years old, kids are aware of what is around them and footballers could drop in and engage with them. That gives clubs the chance to interact with their future fans in an educational environment. I had a chat about it with Arsenal because they have a nursery run by a private company housed within their stadium complex but is entirely outsourced. I thought they had missed a trick. Somebody will do it because Rebecca's plan is out there now and it is eminently workable.

A company called The Wood Works has become the go-to company for players wanting kitchens and bathrooms. David Beckham used them and many players have since followed his lead; one car dealer, for example, could win the confidence of a couple of players in a dressing room. Word spreads fast and therefore the power of that dressing room for driving further corporate referral sales is huge. And when Ross worked at First Artist for a short while before branching out on his own, he spoke to Harrods and Selfridges to set up pop-up shops at training grounds. We didn't get that project off the ground at the time but it has since happened.

A welcome by-product of the Premier League success has been the millions of pounds given back by footballers in charitable donations each year. And players can now set themselves up for life even if they last just a few years at the top level. I helped make that a reality, something I passionately wanted to achieve from the moment I heard Alan Skirton was delivering milk to the doorstep of the ground where he once stood so tall. I tracked Alan down many years later and can happily report he enjoyed a better life than the one I was told befell him after football. He never delivered milk; that story turned out to be apocryphal, which is the best of both worlds for me because Alan did not suffer a fall from grace and yet that prospect still drove me on to ensure few top footballers ever will.

The world has evolved since I started watching football. My parents were old at sixty. I am sixty-four and think I have got a good ten years of high energy left in me yet. I see myself being able to continue assisting the evolution of sport and entertainment out of the greatest capital in the world over the next decade.

I've been a successful football agent, but many more people in the sports and entertainment world have benefited from everything that First Artist had to offer as it became a classroom for many movers and shakers in those realms. That is something I am very proud of. The University of East London, an institution I have admired for years, asked me to join the Board of Governors and that enables me to feel I am giving something back. My biggest legacy is my children, but I like to think I helped change the face of sport, less so entertainment, but certainly football on a global scale.

I brought many of the other big agents operating today into the game. Leon Angel was my accountant; Jerome Anderson was my original partner; and Mel Stein acted as a lawyer of mine. I helped Jonathan Barnett to get started and we remain very good friends to this day – we even talked at length about the social media element of Gareth Bale's world-record move to Real Madrid. We pick each other's brains regularly.

Recently, I have joined the smaller First Artist Agency with Adam Wheatley and Kevin Pietersen's Mission Sports Management so that First Artist Mission can deliver a more rounded service, better suited to the current football and sporting markets. I think the market will be increasingly dominated by bigger agents as we move forward.

We also worry about the future. The Association of Football Agents has grown to become a sizeable operation, more important than ever now FIFA have deregulated the agent industry. Now no qualifications are required to register – just five hundred pounds and a clean criminal record.

There are some key parts of the football agency world that FIFA didn't want to be a part of or even try to understand. They deregulated the industry and threw it at the associations, many of whom have set up their own individual licensing arrangements, meaning if an agent is transferring a player from one country to another, he may have to be registered in both by separate criteria. It is said that to register in all the territories where you might want to do business, the administrative fees will cost seventy-two thousand pounds.

But regardless of whether an agent is registered or not, the individual FAs are incapable of regulating the infrastructure efficiently because they simply don't understand what goes on in a deal. They don't know that sometimes managers and coaches around the world favour agents who put money in certain places in a deal. And sometimes they overpay to release cash from their home country so they aren't paying tax in that territory. They could pay their preferred agent five times what he should receive and take cash out of the country as his commission, and park it in another country where they will help themselves next time they go there. FIFA and the governing bodies don't investigate this. In one sense, I understand why. It is dangerous in certain parts of the world, with levels of corruption that render them almost lawless where big money is concerned.

When people say 'agents are taking money out of the game', this is, in fact, the genuine reality: some clubs bring in two or three agents, overpay them considerably, overpay for the price of a player coming out of a certain country and then the spoils are shared in another country where the tax regimes are more favourable. Or it is simply all paid in cash. It can happen in two or three different ways. Representatives can help football clubs fund their squads, in which case they may own a piece of that player and, when he is sold, the money goes back to wherever that ownership resides. So, if the ownership is in Bulgaria, even if they have an office in London, the money will go back to Bulgaria.

Then there are situations where players come from sub-Saharan African countries and are owned by tribal elders or syndicates from around the world. That money will go to the club where that player has been parked. For supposition's sake, they take a player from Sierra Leone to a club in Greece and the money would go back to Greece or wherever the Greek club sends it on to. So the money for a player who is now moving north through Europe will go back to the licensed club, who will have an agreement with the third party.

Alternatively, a club might employ an agent to sell a player abroad. That club might only want three million for him but the buyers agree to pay five million; that means two million comes out of the system for themselves. The agent will then park the money wherever he can across Europe or further afield. His commission may be charged as two million – obviously disproportionate on a three-million transfer – but everyone seems to be happy. It is interesting to watch some of the foreign agents turning up in a deal between two English clubs, charging exorbitant agency fees and taking that money out of the country. That happens. These are the areas where we need to shine a light; essentially, the English game is a clean enterprise but there are dark corners that the game's authorities refuse to visit, which is exasperating to us all.

There are some who choose not to be regulated and therefore are not subject to governance. Why? Technically, they are not allowed to operate and if a club is found to be dealing with them, they are supposed to be punished . . . but it almost never happens. Authorities turn a blind eye because it is too difficult to go after them – these are often individuals with big reputations, even occasionally backed by unsavoury organisations. The authorities don't look there because they lack the know-how and the hunger to pursue it. It is complicated to prove and, in any case, it will be impossible to find the money. This is why agents need to be included in regulatory discussions, not treated as outlaws.

We constituted the AFA and it now represents most of the football agents in England. In Europe, they have done something similar so we are starting to bring a sense of management and self-regulation to our industry, possibly in conjunction with the PFA. We can't have a judiciary of our own but we can have some of our own sitting on it because we know what to look for. We know what works. Between the top agents, we can run the regulatory side of our business. We will instigate and enforce rules we know will work.

We won't skew the system in favour of the big boys. It is about making such an influential sphere within football a more level playing field. As you've hopefully seen in these pages, so much goes through our domain. We should not only be treated as part of the football family but those among us who are trying to operate in the right way should be supported by financing from the authorities. We should also have a seat on the FA Council. It is madness that its 120-odd members – which is far too many anyway – include archaic representatives from lower-league clubs. Do they really know how the game works better than the leading agents? Is there really not at least a conversation to be had?

Tony Kleanthous owns Barnet Football Club and has sat on some of the most senior committees governing football in the UK. Several times I've thought, You are a nice guy, Tony, but what are you doing up there? Especially when the leading agents who created modern-day football are not considered a stakeholder in it.

We represent the heartbeat of the game – the players. Football should not have to endure a lawless world of secret agents. You may have bought this book in the belief that that is exactly what has been going on, and FIFA's deregulation would somehow expose nefarious practice. It is quite the opposite; the intermediary system now in place is not working. There is more money disappearing out of the game through agents operating with impunity, but the authorities do not want the fight. It is much simpler for them to create complicated regulations that trip people up and then penal- ise those individuals based on spurious technicalities to claim they are governing the sport.

Take this example: third-party ownership is banned. But say, for example, an agent negotiates the sale of a player and, within that deal, he agrees a lump-sum sell-on fee should that player move on again, FIFA say that is fine. However, if the sell-on fee is agreed as a percentage of a future transfer fee and not a fixed sum, that is deemed third-party ownership and therefore punishable by individual associations. What an utterly arbitrary line to draw in the sand.

All the good guys want to clean up a world that is getting dirtier and dirtier by the month. The FA are beginning to listen; the game's major stakeholders are talking to us and progress is a genuine possibility if the moment is seized. Because, despite whatever preconceptions you may have, there is nobody who would rather bring the agent world out into the open than the leading agents themselves.

I hope that what I have tried to achieve in football, music, entertainment and media has helped bring about positive advances in those fields. Sometimes I got it wrong, sometimes I scored a vital penalty, but I always tried to push the boundaries with the intention of furthering the success of those who are most deserving.

It has been great fun . . . and I haven't finished yet!

16

Brexit

BREXIT has created an uncertain future in many walks of life including football. We are in uncharted territory – nobody truly believed it would become a reality, especially those in the Remain campaign who I advised in the run-up to the referendum on Britain's membership of the EU on 23 June 2016.

My involvement began in April following a conversation with my friend and former leader of the Scottish Labour Party, Jim Murphy. We were debating the merits of the forthcoming vote and I made my position clear: if this was 1975, I wouldn't vote to enter the Common Market in the form it is today because I believe it is undemocratic with an insufficiently accountable financial structure. However, we are where we are and it is probably a good place to be. Certainly in football it plays a significantly positive role.

Jim suggested I speak to an adviser at Number Ten named Ameet Pal to offer my services. I did so over tea at Downing Street two weeks later and during the following eight weeks, I was charged with the responsibility of garnering the support of the sports industry in voting Remain.

The mood in the camp was cautious optimism. None of us

really felt that Brexit would happen, although a few weeks in, they received some alarming private polling figures from the north east and I remember at the time considering asking my son Scott to lean on his clients Andros Townsend and Fabio Borini – then of Newcastle and Sunderland respectively – to get them pictured with Prime Minister David Cameron to support the campaign. Fabio was receptive but Andros stated he was apolitical and in any case Cameron's proposed trip to the north-east was later cancelled.

Instead, we suggested staging a fans' game between Europe and the rest of the world in France on the night before the vote. We tried to secure the support of Leicester City because I could say to them: "You are actually in Europe now – why not stay there!"

Remarkably, most people in football wouldn't pop their head over the parapet and be supportive, largely because they felt the campaign had become so onerous that they didn't want to offend potentially half of their club's fanbase.

I did convince Sky Sports News to put out a number of features in support of the campaign to encourage people to vote and helped bring the Premier League out, backing them as a collective along with select individuals including David Beckham and John Barnes among others.

I saw no indication of the subsequent leadership machinations within the Conservative party existing as a subtext to the referendum vote but most people I spoke to accepted that if the country voted to Leave, it would cause pandemonium within the party and more importantly the nation as a whole. At the very top, there must have been some kind of plan but down the pecking order where I was, there wasn't a great level of concern as to 'what happens if?' because nobody seriously thought the 'if' was going to happen.

They still felt Cameron had no choice but to offer a referendum as a soft option against UKIP taking away a chunk of their vote which could have been large enough to hand the 2015 election to Labour.

The decision was understandable in that political context but the campaign they fought could only be considered a catastrophe.

I used to put my head in my hands when I sat in meetings and someone would say: 'OK, the Chancellor is going public to state that taxes will increase substantially if we leave Europe.' I would say to people I was working with in the committee rooms: 'Are we really threatening the electorate now? Is that the best we can do?'

I argued the only time many sportspeople felt truly European was during the Ryder Cup because we are too small to beat America on our own. But we love beating America and joining up with Europe brought us together. That's a great feeling – and it would be a powerful message if we could transplant that feeling from the Ryder Cup into lifestyle. It didn't help my cause, however, when they phoned a few members of the previous European team and they were all for Brexit!

I argued it would have been wise to get Jean-Claude Juncker over to the north-east where the Remain campaign clearly had a problem, have him photographed meeting the local people and listening to their concerns.

But what did he do on the night before the vote? He threatened Britain again saying, 'There will be no renegotiation'. I honestly think that lost Remain about 500,000 votes.

The political establishment fell like dominos thereafter and it is going to take years before a settled picture emerges. Football will have to adapt just like every other industry and Brexit raises a series of questions, the most important of which cuts to the heart of the deep-rooted structural issues in our game.

The obvious initial concern during the last trading window (summer 2016) was our currency. First Artist had a deal collapse on those terms about a fortnight after the Brexit vote. Reading were close to agreeing a deal with an Italian player whose terms were originally agreed at £11,000 a week. However, he had worked out that after the value of the pound plummeted, he had to be paid £15,000 a week to make up the loss he had on his final salary. Reading refused and the player stayed put.

A few of the top Premier League clubs would have hedged against currency, especially those playing in European competitions because they receive their prize money in euros; more than £1billion was spent in the summer window of 2015 and a lot of that would have been inbound from Europe so it would have been lucrative to do so.

Those top clubs that held sufficient cash balances in euros and sterling probably didn't need to hedge just before the Brexit vote but some of them may have done so previously.

It will be a matter of good business practice for the big clubs to keep cash in different currencies but the lower Premier League and Championship clubs bereft of good governance or the resources to ring-fence money in that way will be harder hit.

There could be issues over recruiting younger players with the EU rules currently in place allowing 16-18-year-olds to join youth academies in Britain. Cesc Fabregas is a prime example, joining Arsenal from Barcelona as a 16-year-old in 2003.

The work permit rules that define which players can come to England were tightened up by the English FA in consultation with the PFA, the Premier League, the League Managers' Association, other national associations in Britain and the Home Office in 2015.

The FA claimed that had the rules been implemented between 2009 and 2013, 87 of 129 non-European Economic Area players would still have been granted a work visa but it would have led to a 33 per cent reduction overall. Greg Dyke's 'England Commission' believed this would help deepen the future pool of talent eligible for the national team.

What happens now we no longer have to comply with EU law? Are we going to be able to lower the threshold so anybody around the world who's once owned an English sheepdog can now get a visa? Or will UEFA argue against it?

Given that Brexit was essentially framed as an immigration debate in the minds of many voters, it is unlikely the Home Office would afford football special dispensation to allow visa requirements to drop below present standards, even if it would enhance the commercial viability of the Premier League.

But that is not to say the Premier League can't make a very strong case for softening the rules and having a spat with the PFA, who will probably want to keep them as tight as they can to protect local talent.

Which brings us onto the crux of the future direction of English football: should it be the procreation of local talent thereby facilitating a greater pool of talent from which to grow a successful national team or is to have the best league in the world on your doorstep?

Brexit asks this seminal question of football's governing bodies. Are we prepared to sacrifice the pre-eminence of our Premier League for the sake of the England national team? The country felt miserable after our ignominious exit to Iceland at Euro 2016 but how committed are we to instigating the long-term change necessary for England to succeed at major tournaments?

Implicitly or otherwise, we have reached a place where the Premier League is our football. The England team is a biennial distraction – a roller coaster we have all ridden too many times before, offering hope in the build-up to the free-fall of disappointment that inevitably follows.

We support our national heroes. Andy Murray's 2016 Wimbledon final win over Milos Raonic drew in a peak television audience of 13.3 million. That is a huge audience in this day and age so national sport still has an emotional pull over us but most football fans get far greater – and more frequent – satisfaction from domestic football.

Some would argue the Premier League is more fascinating because of its entertainment value – the mid-table teams are stronger and the élite sides have dropped in level, as evidenced by their poor performance in the Champions League across recent years – but I think it is the cosmopolitan construction which makes it the product it is.

The blend works. The Premier League in its current form is a mixture of design, investment and luck. If you start gerrymandering it, everything could change. The 225 territories in which it is sold around the world then become 200, and then 150. The price drops accordingly and suddenly we aren't where we were. That could play as early as the next TV round or it could be as described previously with Amazon, Comcast and others, perhaps taking the numbers to a level that knock Sky out. Although I'm sure Rupert Murdoch has some kind of backup plan!

English football's governing bodies could either make it more difficult to play here, reflecting the will of the people, or they try to become more inclusive and allow people to come from all over the world because we have nobody to tell us what to do.

So let me leave you with this question: what future do you want to see? Now we have voted to leave the European Union, do you want your Premier League to become more local?

Are you prepared to sacrifice the instant gratification of the Premier League for the long-term goal of a successful England team?

In these pages I have tried to show you how and why English football has grown into the goliath it is today by drawing its commercial influence from the United States and many of the game's leading players from Europe and the rest of the world. The country has become isolationist. Football has to decide if it will follow suit.

Afterword

The transfer market moved to another level in the summer of 2017. If there was one early domestic deal which crystallised the step-change in player valuations it was Everton's £30m acquisition of Jordan Pickford from Sunderland. Pickford is a hugely promising talent and, aged just 23, he could develop into a top-class goalkeeper. But he had made just 31 Premier League appearances by the time he moved to Goodison Park and was not even a senior England International.

To pay £30m is a huge leap of faith – one made even greater by suggestions that just £5m of that figure was agreed in performance-related add-ons – but also symptomatic of a redefined marketplace. The Premier League's television deal is partly responsible for this, which raises questions as to how sustainable the growth is. The next television contract could easily be worth £10bn and that would guarantee football's robustness until 2022; there isn't a business anywhere in the world which can be confident in its projections beyond that given the volatility of global economics these days. Didn't we do well?

But the funding of transfers is already changing; Sunderland received £93,471,118 in broadcast and central commercial income from the Premier League during the 2016–17 season. Not bad for finishing bottom of the table. Yet, because the cash call on managing squads is so high now, clubs that don't have the global income of a top-four side don't want to use all that cash straight away to fund their transfer business. Some would rather borrow the money against future television income so they are factoring their own purchases.

Many wealthier organisations, such as Ecotonian and Elliott Associates, are charging to provide that service. The marginal rates can vary from 4 per cent to an average of 8 per cent and then a high of 12 per cent.

A few of the purchases of European clubs, including some Chinese takeovers, have been funded by finance houses based in Europe. They use some of their own money and then borrow funds leveraged against future television income and, in some cases, ticketing revenue too. However, what's particularly interesting is that we are now seeing major hedge funds moving into the football sector for the first time, not particularly as purchasers but as backers standing behind a purchasing entity and leveraging an interest rate.

So it won't be long before the player market is further ensconced with hedge funds and corporate lenders. If not commonplace, they are certainly appearing in the market with increasing regularity. That tells us the football market has now matured into a global business where major funds feel safe enough to invest seven- to nine-figure sums and my educated guess is that, in the near future, there will be a £1bn sale of one of the major clubs which will involve hedge fund partners.

I don't see anything wrong with that as long as there is responsible management of the process. It is much better than criminal money reaching the sector, although, as we've alluded to else-where in these pages, that exists at a lower level. FIFA and many national associations, including the Premier League, led by Peter McCormick, Chairman of their Legal Advisory Group, are now attempting to put together a charter for how best to supervise inbound funds into football.

This type of acquisition means, for example, that if Crystal Palace is worth £130m, you actually only have to put down around £40m to launch a takeover and borrow the rest. As long as the next Premier League television deal is strong, there will be a lot more of these constructs, financing both takeovers and big-money transfers.

In response, the Premier League have said they will sanction on a deal by deal basis someone who is lending to a club but they have to be licensed to take deposits from people in the United Kingdom. In other words, a bank. They are less certain about funding houses because it is harder to know where the money is actually coming from. Funding houses can cloud the picture by putting a bank in front of themselves which the cash flows through. The Premier League are now trying to identify which are the real ones and which are merely fronts. It is an exceptionally difficult task.

Clubs are also not allowed to take money from people already involved in football because that is potentially viewed as third-party ownership. But what if there is a big Japanese bank and their fund includes people who own assets all over the world, with one guy maybe owning part of an Australian football club? You can't examine every single investor and their influence within that fund.

There has to be some fluidity of movement but this area needs more regulation. I have been critical of the previous FIFA admin-istration elsewhere in these pages for an apparent unwillingness to address such complexities but there is a drive within the organisation to instigate tangible change in the form of a new FIFA committe chaired by president Victor Montagliani and comprising stakeholders including Richard Scudamore, the presidents of Real Madrid, River Plate, Ajax and the J-League, among others. It is due to meet later in 2017 in an attempt to make major revisions to the world game for the 2018–19 season.

One area of focus, in response to a series of complaints, might be the existing summer/winter transfer window structure. I don't think there should be windows at all, given the advantage they give better-resourced clubs in stockpiling players. But FIFA may take the view to change the way the window system operates – the matter will be addressed in a wide-ranging review.

A charter to address the funding of transfers as outlined above will be a high priority but a more conservative aim is to deal with overdue payments based on a complaint by FIFPro (International Federation of Professional Footballers) that the existing system is in breach of European Union competition laws. The issue centres on players and clubs who don't get paid, with the problems most prevalent in south-east Asia and eastern Europe. Currently, there is a three-month window to complete each tranche of those payments but often they overrun and nobody takes any action. The intention is to shorten the timeframe while also setting up a fund to help those players who suffer a lag in receipt of funds or who are somehow left out of pocket altogether.

Squad sizes are also likely to come under scrutiny with a particular emphasis on nationalities; the continuing Brexit negotiations would add a particularly intriguing dimension to any debate within English football over home-grown quotas.

Player salaries have taken another jump in 2017 with £300,000-a-week a much more attainable target for many of Europe's top players. FIFA are planning to look into this. But of course cannot regulate against the boundaries of European law. One idea could be to cap wage bills of clubs rather than any individual player. If every Premier League club, for example, could spend, say, £180m in wages – the year-end accounts for 2015–16 show only five clubs that were in excess of that figure, with Manchester United the highest on £232m – tough decisions would have to be taken to revise the hierarchal financial structure within their squad.

What is becoming evident is that Financial Fair Play, implemented for all the right reasons, has now become the driver of a major wedge between the biggest clubs and those immediately below them. For example, Manchester United can secure a deal with a local business that may potentially be larger than West Bromwich Albion can agree with a shirt sponsor, thereby increasing their turnover at a faster rate which further enables them to pay higher wages to players. Manchester City could put in place a contract with an associate of the United Arab Emirates government, which owns the club, for a sponsorship that transforms the income on their balance sheet to take their transfer spending power to another level, all within current FFP rules. These sort of deals are beyond the reach of all but the top six clubs and only serve to price out West Brom, Crystal Palace and others of their ilk in the transfer market. As a result, they in turn then have to look down the pecking order for players where wages aren't so high. Surely, for the greatest league in the world, that cannot be right. It is becoming too elitist.

The financial commentators in the sector are speculating that the level of transfer activity witnessed in 2017 is unsustainable. As previously suggested, the introduction of a tech company or social media behemoth such as Facebook could prolong this halcyon period but the informed view is that it is unlikely to last beyond the next television deal. Whispers are now taking place between some of the major top European clubs to potentially create what was originally considered a pipe dream fifteen years ago: a European Super League. This could replace the Champions League and allow the top European clubs to exploit the immense value in the market place that the Premier League currently has under its 'control' . . . and for which Europe has never quite forgiven us! But the Premier League model is predicated upon sharing, meaning the division's lesser lights receive an equal share of a huge pot disproportionate to the rest of Europe. That throws up financial anomalies that look faintly ridiculous in the cold light of day: for instance, Bayern Munich received less television income in the 2016/17 season than Sunderland who were relegated from the Premier League. It is fair to say that the biggest club in Germany isn't best pleased. It might be a few years away but a big change is coming because conversations at the highest levels of the game are beginning to focus on what happens beyond the Premier League's zenith and a redefinition of revenue distribution.

The complexities of third-party ownership have been outlined already in these pages and there is a desire at FIFA now to harden their stance in the coming years. It is commonplace still in Spain and South America, while Mino Raiola's £41m commission in Paul Pogba's £89m deal to join Manchester United from Juventus has sharpened minds among football's governors. I have defended Raiola in various interviews since that figure was made public, not least because it is a proportionate reward for the years he has spent helping to advise a prodigious talent on his journey to becoming one of the best in the world, but also because there is transparency in his methods.

The allegation was that Raiola negotiated to receive a percentage of Pogba's transfer fee over a certain figure in the tens of millions which, at the time, no doubt felt improbable and perhaps even fanciful given that he cost less than £1m – Juventus would probably have not agreed to it otherwise. Yet Pogba exceeded all expectations and cost a world-record fee. Top clubs will surely think twice before agreeing to such a clause in future.

However, consider this: if I find a player in Togo but his club are bust because they don't own their ground and have no asset value, I could put money into that club by buying the economic rights to that player. I then sell him to an English team and the money is going through me back to the club. That surely is an enhancement of the situation for all concerned.

I can't charge a commission because I am engaged in a shared ownership of that player but is it not better to have it as a matter of record that an agent is profiting from enhancing his player's career in this way, rather than more secretive figures – or even criminal gangs – operating in darker parts of the world with far greater sinister intent, hiding themselves away?

The new FIFA administration is increasingly receptive to these concerns, recognising the importance of reassessing the transfer system and the way the flow of money and funding of assets are policed. Although I have no desire to immerse myself fully in the football agent world again, any opportunity to play a part in shaping its future would be an exciting challenge.

A prominent theme in these pages has been the absence of engagement with agents from football's authorities. It would make me extremely proud if I could help bridge that gap.

To be potentially involved with this FIFA administration going forward is a genuine thrill and, I have to say, people like Zvonimir Boban and his associates are visionaries. They are surrounded by political bureaucracy but their hearts are in the right place and I have friends at the organisation who may afford me the chance to assist in helping to achieve a framework that is robust and fit for purpose moving forward into 2018.

The new committee will also analyse how and where agents operate, but they need someone who has been there and done it to talk to them. Nobody is going to be brave enough to chase the money in the darkest corners, but I can point to parts of the pipeline of cash and how better we can police the physical transaction before monies are taken from the game. I anticipate real change in this area in the coming 36 months.

It is possible there will be some sort of formal agent involvement in the governance of the game once this review is completed. That would, in turn, leave the FA with little choice but to invite us in 'for the good of the game', to coin FIFA's phrase. Perhaps we can give that slogan a positive meaning under FIFA president Gianni Infantino after the past controversies of Sepp Blatter's era.

Football has now become a very difficult environment thanks to the money involved. The mindset between the lower divisions and the top of the tree is so vastly different that it feels like travelling between planets. The conversations you have with chairmen, agents and players at the top of La Liga or Serie A are totally different because the game's upper echelons have gone on an interstellar journey. Many players who were worth between £8m–£12m are now worth £30m. That multiple is out there now. This summer has seen another jump in people's perception of market value. Who would have thought in 2016 that Romelu Lukaku would be worth up to £90m to Manchester United a year later? And in terms of salary, the £500,000-a-week player in a major European league will become a reality before too long.

Nothing goes up for ever, so there will be a levelling off in some way – and fans need some recompense in the next television deal – but while the deals continue to rise, those who make them happen will get richer. It attracts some questionable characters but that isn't the only reason why I won't go back towards the front line of transfers. The money involved means those agents like Raiola have to work for it and be on call 24/7 for the player and his family. I don't need that. Otherwise, players move around at the end of their two-year contracts. Some of them switch between big agencies because they don't feel they are always receiving due care and attention. I don't need all that in my life yet again. I've done it, made that money and now want to help shape the future – except perhaps when there is a big deal in my back garden!

Young players are being offered cash up front to help a family support their progeny, but also as an effective advancement against future income. Therefore, it is very difficult to enter the football agent arena and operate effectively without a cash fund. I'm fortunate to have one at my disposal but I don't want to plough cash in when I don't have to; I can make money by being involved in deals elsewhere, including helping my brother Phil with First Artist Mission or more entrepreneurial endeavours.

I am enjoying some quality time with the new FIFA administration, talking to them about the future of the game, the new Awards Ceremony (potentially back to the future for me!) as well as having interesting discussions about regulations . . . and of course agents.

Growth is inherently finite but 2017 is firmly housed inside football's steep upward curve. With the power of some of the biggest banks and funds in the sporting world behind me, I hope that I might just continue to make a difference.

Acknowledgements

S uccess is not always defined by material ownership. I have been
fortunate; I have earned well in my life but, moreover, I have
been blessed to travel with many uniquely wonderful people on
my journey.

I have worked with some of the greatest sporting and entertainment talent on this planet who, in many cases, have allowed
me to represent them professionally, accept my advice (sometimes)
and allowed me to share in their reflected glory (often). To all of
you – thank you. I have been fortunate to know you and privileged
to work with you.

Thank you to my publisher Little, Brown and my wonderful
editor Andreas Campomar for all your faith, support and guidance.
Thank you too to my own 'super agent' Neil Blair for your belief
in me.

To my colleagues across the world, there are a few I wish I had
never met, but many of you I am so grateful I did.

To my dear family and friends who have always stood by me
through the good, bad and astonishingly unique moments, I will
never be able to thank you enough.

A word or two from me to James Olley – indebted thanks for not only capturing my voice but also transposing my heartbeat. You have an astonishing ability to jump from being one of the world's best sports writers to being able to take lifestyle moments and turn them into meaningful words.

Allow me to borrow a comment from a cherished friend who wrote this while at Her Majesty's pleasure: 'They won't build statues or name streets after me, but please remember I sparkled and shone brightly for a while!'

Index